COSMOS

The Yearbook of the Traditional Cosmology Society

Volume 5
1989

POLYTHEISTIC SYSTEMS

edited by
GLENYS DAVIES

General Editor of Cosmos: Emily Lyle

EDINBURGH UNIVERSITY PRESS

Advisory Board

A grant from the Spalding Trust is gratefully acknowledged

© Edinburgh University Press 1989
22 George Square, Edinburgh
Set in Linotron Times Roman
and printed in Great Britain by
Redwood Press Limited
Trowbridge, Wilts

ISBN 0 7486 0135 X (paper)

Contents

GLENYS DAVIES

Introduction. Polytheistic Systems:
The Conference and the Book

The Traditional Cosmology Society's annual summer conference in 1988 was on Polytheistic Systems. The participants came from a wide range of disciplines and spoke on cultures and religions just as varied – Indian, Central American, Classical, Celtic, Near Eastern. A selection of the papers is published here, with one concerning the Far East written by contributors who were unable to be present at the conference.

It might be thought that with such heterogeneous interests the speakers would not find common ground for discussion or mutual questions. But in fact the discussions revealed that in all areas 'polytheism' tends to be a concept much used but little explored. The dictionary definition is sufficiently bland to suffice for all, without being satisfactory for any. (The *Concise Oxford Dictionary* defines polytheism as 'belief in, or worship of, many gods or more than one god'.) Yet polytheism – like 'paganism' – seems often to be defined by its opposite, being seen in negative terms as a contrast to what it is not, rather than in positive terms. Thus several papers and much of the discussion at the conference centred on the relationship of polytheism to monotheism and other non-polytheistic systems (see the papers by Deirdre Green, Karel Werner, Gavin Flood and John Gibson in this volume). In particular, we noted the modern Western tendency to see polytheism as more primitive, more 'popular', and less intellectual than monotheism – as a religious system that has not yet grown to maturity.

Such judgements aside, various cultures have worshipped many gods, and as a result have developed systems to explain the relationships between deities, and between deity and function. The best-known system is the Classical one: the family relationships of the gods in Classical Greek literature, as explored in Gordon Howie's paper. Such family relationships are also the subject of two papers on Celtic mythology, by Emily Lyle and Alan Bruford. However, this familial structure is less prominent in the Etruscan pantheon (see van der Meer), and the Indian and Central American religions indicate a rather different way of ordering things (see especially Flood, Shelton and Baquedano). At the conference we could only begin to explore the correlations between such different systems: an aspect of personal interest to me (since my own paper, not published here, was on the creation of new gods in the context of Roman Imperial polytheism) is how new gods arise and are incorporated into an existing system. And if new gods can be accommodated, does multiplication of deities inevitably lead to a tendency to see all manifestations of divine power as aspects of one Power? (A question that brings us back once again to the issue of polytheism vs. monotheism.)

Several of the papers published here (along with others delivered at the conference) present a detailed analysis of a particular manifestation of polytheism. Hilda Davidson's search for hooded men traces them from Romano-British *genii cucullati* to modern garden gnomes: persistent deities who never quite disappear and will pop up to help or cause mischief as appropriate. Glenys Lloyd-Morgan looks at the mirrors considered suitable offerings for Classical goddesses, and Caroline Karslake at the images and ceremonies associated with Otomi deities. Andrew Duff-Cooper and Teigo Yoshida complete the picture with a view of polytheism in practice in everyday life in Japan and Balinese Lombok.

From such papers we get an insight into how polytheism works, and what it means to its practitioners, past and present. By looking at various non-monotheistic religious systems we gain an over-view that enriches our understanding of polytheistic structures: I hope, therefore, that readers of this volume will find its entire contents rewarding and eye-opening, and will not just turn to papers they consider to be 'their' area, ignoring the rest.

DEIRDRE GREEN

Towards a Reappraisal of Polytheism

This brief paper is intended to raise some questions regarding our evaluation of polytheistic systems. I will be using material drawn from the Hindu tradition to illustrate my points, but I hope that this material will pose questions which are applicable to the study of polytheistic systems in general.

It is not difficult to find disparaging and condemnatory comments on polytheism as a religious system in many of the works on Hinduism written earlier this century, and indeed this same sentiment is by no means absent even from some books of more recent date. Theological bias, ethnocentric assumptions, and a quasi-evolutionist theory of truth all play a part in shaping these sentiments. Hand in hand with the pejorative attitude towards polytheism is often found an assumption that 'ethical monotheism' must be the only true form of religion, or the highest form of religion. A clear statement of this position is made by Farquhar in 1913:

> Though the Aryans of the time of the *Ṛik* [*Ṛg Veda*] were polytheists, yet they were far enough advanced in thought and religious feeling to be frequently led by their higher instincts to ideas and expressions which are scarcely consistent with a belief in many gods ... The worshipper is frequently carried forward, in the fervour of his feeling for the god who is the object of his adoration at the moment, to think of him as supreme, as the only possible object of adoration. The right way to interpret these facts is to say that the only really rational form of religion is the worship of one God, sole and supreme; that early man very seldom, if ever, reached the full perception of that truth ... (Farquhar 1913: 72)

Griswold, writing in 1923, likewise assumes that ' ... a true and consistent theism ever presents itself as an ethical monotheism', and holds that there is no true spirituality outside such a conception of Deity. He condescends to add that 'Some fundamental elements of

true religion may, indeed, be taught by the coarsest polytheism . . .
Thus even in connection with a polytheistic and not fully ethicised
conception of Deity, it is clear that the Vedic Indians had some
light, the Eternal God not having left Himself without witness
among them' (Griswold 1923: 347, 351, 352, 367).

More recently, Mehta, in 1956, distinguishing between inner
religious experience, and the outward expression and interpretation of that experience, claims that the essential religious *experience* is always monotheistic or else monistic in nature, that is, it is
always an experience of the unity of Godhead; in early times,
however, Hindus incorrectly *interpreted* their experiences within a
polytheistic framework. In the course of history, 'Objective, intellectual abstraction of truths, laws and principles quite displaces
animism and polytheism. The "poly" becomes "mono" when conceptions and interpretations and forms of expression have developed far enough, through man's own development as a thinking
human being, to coincide with his inner God-realization, which is
always, and necessarily, of a "mono" quality' (Mehta 1956: 350).

Common to such approaches to polytheism are ethnocentric and
evolutionist assumptions regarding the relationship between different forms of religious belief, shown in the assertions that monotheism is self-evidently the only 'rational' or 'objective' form of
religion and obviously the most 'advanced' or 'developed'. The
writers in question do, of course, attempt to defend these assertions
by theological argument. Thus, for example, a frequently encountered argument is that a satisfactory conception of Deity presupposes that the Godhead is One, epitomising Unity, and that only
monotheism fulfils this ideal. But this contention does not stand up
to closer examination, for the belief that religious and spiritual
Unity is the ultimate goal of humanity and the highest conception of
the Divine, is found not only in monotheistic systems but also in
monistic schools of thought such as Advaita Vedānta, which does
not grant ultimate reality to the personal God who is of such central
importance to polytheism's opponents. In Advaita, *nirguṇa Brahman,* the spiritual Absolute, is certainly one, eternal and unchanging, but is in no sense a personal God. Furthermore, it may be that
polytheism itself, *per se*, does not require us to deny the unity of
religious reality, a point to which I shall return.

Again, critics of polytheism may argue that the true God must be
unchangeable, whereas (as Griswold puts it) 'Polytheism inevitably
means the waxing and waning of gods, a concept so detrimental to
the idea of an Eternal God' (Griswold 1923: 343). But all this
assertion really means is that the various gods of a polytheistic
pantheon are seen to become more or less popular in the course of

that pantheon's historical development. Today, following the 'death of God' theology, in an environment that is both largely secular and multi-faith, we can see the One God of monotheism 'waxing and waning' too in terms of social adherence and belief. Griswold tries another argument: '. . . only the God of an ethical and exclusive monotheism possesses personality in the fullest sense, that is a personality worthy of the infinite and eternal God' (Griswold 1923: 352); but this assumption that the infinite and eternal must have personality would be the height of folly, again, to an Advaitin, even if we leave the polytheistic response aside for the moment.

Griswold further assumes that it is in the ethical element that 'the real worth of a religion lies' (Griswold 1923: 353). Now while I do not wish to deny that ethical values are *among* our most important values, nor that they play an important part in religious systems, the exclusive preoccupation with ethics shown by so many recent Christian writers does not do justice to the multifaceted whole that is religion. I personally would argue that it is living religious experience, rather than ethics, that forms or should form the 'core' of a religion. This, of course, is a matter for debate, but we must, I think, grant that there are other facets of religion which are equally as important as the ethical. Griswold and others have thought to find in Varuna, in his capacity as a god who is the guardian of moral law and to whom one prays for deliverance from sin, a candidate for the 'one true God' of ethical monotheism which failed to develop in the Vedas. (Griswold refers to this as a 'spiritual tragedy': Griswold 1923: 348.) Bowes sees this as '. . . a complete failure to comprehend how the idea of divinity functions in the Vedas'; morality is but one of many divine functions and does not, in polytheism, have the exclusive or overwhelming importance that it has in monotheistic religions (Bowes 1977: 121). Finally, Griswold desperately suggests that 'Another defect connected with polytheism is the opportunity it offers for the squabbling of the gods . . . Such squabbling is inevitable in every promiscuous polytheism . . . ' (Griswold 1923: 344).

Within the Hindu context, it is often suggested that all the different deities are ultimately one; an attitude that is found both among Hindus themselves and in the works of Western commentators. Thus, for example, Stutley says: ' . . . speculative monism has existed alongside ritualistic polytheism from Vedic times to the present day, thereby emphasizing that Reality is inexhaustible, beyond name and form, pervading and transcending all existence and earthly knowledge . . . all the gods . . . are regarded as one or other of the countless aspects of Ultimate Reality (*brahman*) . . . ' (Stutley

1985: 40). Even in the period of Vedic polytheism, it is generally agreed, some sort of unity underlying the plethora of names and forms was conceived, whether through the conception of *ṛta* (cosmic order) or through the more explicit search in the later Vedic period for a unifying god-principle, shown in the figures of Prajāpati, Viśvakarman, Puruṣa, etc., and in the 'One' of *Ṛg Veda* 10.129.[1] This notion of a unity underlying diversity, the belief that the different deities are all so many manifestations of one Absolute, has persisted throughout the history of Hinduism, though not unchallenged. All in all, the situation may be said to be rather ambivalent, particularly when one takes into consideration the popular Hinduism of the villages, which is unashamedly polytheistic (though the polytheism is different from that of the Vedas). Sometimes one may find that villagers will claim that all the *devatās* (local gods) can be subsumed under the figure of a supreme God or spiritual Absolute, or that all the *mātās* ('mothers', local female deities) are one *śakti* (goddess personifying the dynamic energy of a male deity). But in the village context such assertions are the exception rather than the rule.

When we turn to the writings of modern Hindu reformers, we find that some espouse the tradition that all the gods are actually one and the same, while others speak out against polytheism and so-called 'idolatry'. For example, Rāmakrishna asserts that ' . . . it is the same God towards whom all are directing their steps, though along different paths . . . He whom the Jñānis call Brahman is addressed by the Yogis as Ātman and by the devotees as Bhagavān . . . Some call Him Allah, some God, and others designate Him as Brahmā, Kālī, Rāma, Hari, Jesus or Durgā . . . ' (Nirvedananda 1969: 662; *Life* 1928: 353). Rāmakrishna's disciple Vivekānanda asserts: 'At the very outset, I may tell you there is no *polytheism* in India' and interprets images of different deities as 'simply so many symbols – so many pegs to hang the spiritual ideas on' (Richards 1985: 89). Rāmmohan Roy, greatly influenced by Unitarian Christianity, expresses the opposing viewpoint:

> I have observed that, both in their writings and conversation, many Europeans feel a wish to palliate and soften the features of Hindoo idolatry; and are inclined to inculcate, that all objects of worship are considered by their votaries as emblematical representations of the Supreme Divinity! . . . but the truth is, the Hindoos of the present day have no such views of the subject, but firmly believe in the real existence of innumerable gods and goddesses . . . and to propitiate them, and not the true God, are temples erected and ceremonies performed. (Richards 1985: 4)

We do not have time here to penetrate further into this ambivalence at the root of Hinduism; but we may add that the interplay between monotheism and polytheism has been an essential aspect of the religion throughout its history; and we may ask whether and to what extent the polytheistic pantheons of other cultures show a unity underlying diversity.

A crucial question, however, is why we feel that we want to reduce the many gods to one God in order to make them acceptable. In the Hindu context, some scholars feel that this is a form of apologetics for Hinduism which has been overstated in an attempt to make Hinduism acceptable to the West on the West's terms. It is interesting, then, to compare the viewpoints put forward by Miller in 1974 and by Bowes in 1977, in two works which may at last allow us to approach and evaluate polytheism on its own terms.

Miller, calling for a deepened view of polytheism, argues that the 'death of God' theology, as it has become known, is giving rise to the rebirth of the gods in the plural. The loss of a fixed centre holding everything together (as exemplified in monotheism) is the discovery of multiple centres (polytheism); polytheism best articulates our sense of diversity in modern culture, our sense of living in a pluralistic society. We as a culture no longer believe in one morality, adhere to one ideal or goal – our beliefs, values and lifestyles are many-sided and are no longer governed by 'a single principle of being and by a univocal logic that will lead to Truth in the singular' (Miller 1974: 40). 'Polytheism is . . . that reality experienced by men and women when Truth with a capital "T" cannot be articulated reflectively according to a single grammar, a single logic, or a single symbol-system . . . [it] allow[s] for multiple meanings to exist simultaneously . . .' (Miller 1974: 4–5). Our feeling that we have lost our one fixed centre can give rise to ontological insecurity, until we realise that it is not that there is no centre, but that there are many centres, and that through this new awareness of many centres we can find a sense of liberation from previously constricting boundaries. By contrast with this new way of seeing things, Miller argues, monotheism appears one-dimensional; it suppresses certain of our feelings and perceptions and does not express the richness, depth and diversity of life, for monotheism is controlled by a logic that demands '. . . a rigorous and decisive either/or: either true or false, either this or that, either beautiful or ugly, either good or evil. It is this monotheistic thinking that fails people in a time when experience becomes self-consciously pluralistic, radically both/and' (Miller 1974: 7). When we symbolize reality in a plural way (polytheism) all our experience can be expressed.

Miller further argues that the gods and goddesses of polytheism live on in us, representing powers fundamental to our beings, and the stories of gods and goddesses, told in concrete imagery, can infuse new life into our currently rather abstract and rationalistic religious thinking. The gods and goddesses are worlds of being and meaning in which we participate; it is our task to incarnate them. For Miller, the new polytheism is not exhausted merely by saying that our contemporary society is pluralistic, nor that our values are relativistic; these things are themselves manifestations of something deeper and more fundamental, that is that the gods and goddesses are re-emerging in our lives. Miller illustrates his argument with reference to the Greek gods, but it could equally well be applied to what has become known as Neo-Paganism, popular in Britain in the last few decades. But could it be applied to Hinduism? In spite of the undoubted insights provided by Miller's book, in a sense he is still reinterpreting polytheism for the West – but for contemporary Western pluralistic society, rather than for the relatively uniform, largely monotheistic Britain of the first decades of this century. Does the Indian villager really consider his or her polytheism as a means of articulating a sense of diversity and multiple meanings?

Miller's book is a courageous attempt to persuade us to look the fact of polytheism in the face and accept its diversity for what it is. Bowes's work however, is probably more applicable to the Hindu tradition. Bowes argues that whereas Western commentators have tended to see polytheism and monotheism as logically incompatible, for Hindus this is not the case: '. . . they embody two different outlooks on the divine, one sees the many in the One, while the other sees the One in the many . . . both are equally legitimate ways of searching for the divine, which it will be inadequate to finally characterise as one or the many, since in the Hindu tradition it is "the all". Being "all" the divine can be seen in either of these ways, depending on the vantage point from which one starts one's looking and searching' (Bowes 1977: 103–4). If our purpose is to adore the many as manifold expressions of the splendour of the divine – particularly as these impinge on what we value in life as matters of immediate concern – we use the 'language' of polytheism. If we wish, on the other hand, to seek the one principle that permeates all, we use the 'language' of either monotheism or monism. According to the Hindu tradition, one way of seeing the divine need not exclude the other; rather each 'language' can be appropriate in different contexts. Instead of prejudging that it is the language of monotheism that accurately reflects the way the universe is, we need to enquire into both languages to see the vision of the divine that they embody. 'The divine or religious reality . . . is strictly speaking neither one nor many, it is the inexhaustible source of all possibilities . . .' (Bowes 1977: 105). We can see it as one, as many, or as both.[2]

Bowes sees the language of polytheism as specifically concerned with our involvement with life in its everyday setting and the objects of our immediate concern and value, such as our physical environment and social relations; and with such things as health, wealth, power, glory, which Bowes argues are in effect still being worshipped by many today, only without being symbolized as deities. The gods, then, are embodiments of our values; and yet this does not mean that they are purely imaginary, for the Hindu teaching of the correspondences between microcosm and macrocosm means that the forces which generate gods in our minds also represent powers and potencies that regulate the exterior world. Miller touches on a similar point in a section of his book which I have not had time to discuss, in which he argues that the gods and goddesses are not simply aspects of our psyche, subjective dimensions of our being projected outward: they are worlds of meaning in which we participate and once we realise this, the dichotomy between the inner, subjective experience and the divine object becomes meaningless. Bowes continues:

> A suitable description for [polytheism] is not deification of a lot of ordinary things of this world mistakenly believed to be divinities by the primitive mind, it is seeing that divine essence – that which is the source of all value and existence – is manifested in things that men are immediately concerned with and which they value as fulfilling the possibilities of life on earth. So god-language can be a shorthand expression for this perception which is given concrete embodiment in the personalities of gods. It need not be thought to be a product of exaggerated fancy coupled with lack of 'information' about the one true God. (Bowes 1977: 109)

Vedic polytheism, which makes up the bulk of Bowes's illustrative material, shows an expression of joy and delight in the beauty of life, which is seen as a wondrous gift from the gods, and an organic vision of living as part of a cosmic whole. There is the suggestion that this entails an appreciation of life in all its diversity as a manifestation of divine powers and potencies, so to this extent, perhaps, Miller's theories are echoed. Bowes concludes:

> It is usual for people who hold an evolutionary theory of truth to believe that polytheism constitutes a primitive stage in the development of religious consciousness and that it is ultimately rejected in favour of monotheism, which represents the highest religious truth. I have tried to say that polytheism and monotheism (or monism) represent two entirely different kinds of

impulses in man's approach to the divine and that they should not be viewed as alternatives competing for man's exclusive acceptance. Polytheism is a religious outlook that sees the one as reflected in the many interests that belong to life on earth, and it cannot be outgrown as long as man retains any sense of value as regards his immediate concerns . . . gods were symbols through which man's perception of the values of this life and his adoration and admiration of these as divine gifts were being expressed . . . polytheism . . . can, so it seems to me, supply a religious world-view to man's pursuit of life and happiness – and not just of virtue and salvation after death – here on earth and make it integrative and wholesome. (Bowes 1977: 132–4)
Interestingly, much of Bowes's – and of Miller's – interpretations of polytheism would find favour with Neo-Pagans and with members of other modern esoteric movements, many of whom make creative use of polytheistic pantheons in ritual and meditation in order to symbolize awareness of the diverse aspects of the material world, of cosmic forces, and of life as a whole, as expressions of or gifts from the divine.

In conclusion, we need to reflect on whether we do indeed need a reappraisal of polytheism, and what guidelines might be helpful in our attempts at reappraisal; whether the models outlined in this paper can be applied to the different polytheistic systems of the various religious cultures of the world; and in what ways polytheism might best articulate our religious experience.

NOTES

1. Even Griswold grants as much (1923: 107, 108). See also, for example, Bowes 1977: 20, 28.
2. Bowes perceptively suggests that henotheism, as found in the Vedas, is not (as early Western writers assumed) 'a confused half-way house between polytheism and monotheism proper' but rather 'an expression of the attitude of mind which is prepared to use either of these languages and switch from one to the other according to need' (1977: 105). Unfortunately, I do not have time to discuss this fruitful idea in the present paper.

REFERENCES

Bowes, Pratima (1977). *The Hindu Religious Tradition: A Philosophical Approach*. London: Routledge and Kegan Paul.

Farquhar, J. N. (1913). *The Crown of Hinduism*. References are to the 1971 reprint, New Delhi: Oriental Books.

Griswold, H. D. (1923). *The Religion of the Rigveda*. London: Oxford University Press.

Life = (Anon.) (1928). *Life of Śrī Rāmakrishna*. Mayavati: Advaita Ashrama.

Mehta, P. D. (1956). *Early Indian Religious Thought*. London: Luzac.

Miller, David L. (1974). *The New Polytheism: Rebirth of the Gods and Goddesses*. New York: Harper and Row.

Nirvedananda, Swami (1969). Śrī Rāmakrishna and Spiritual Renaissance. *The Cultural Heritage of India*. IV, ed. Bhattacharya. Calcutta: Ramakrishna Mission.

Richards, Glyn, ed. (1985). *A Source-Book of Modern Hinduism*. London: Curzon Press

Stutley, Margaret (1985). *Hinduism*. Wellingborough: Aquarian Press.

KAREL WERNER

From Polytheism to Monism – a Multidimensional view of the Vedic Religion

The first part of the title of this paper should not be understood as implying an historical or evolutionary sequence, or a succession of stages in the Vedic religion during which it would have 'progressed' from some primitive form of polytheistic worship of anthropomorphic deities to an 'advanced' or 'developed' form of a philosophical understanding of the world or the whole of reality as identical with some divine essence or as sprung from and rooted in an underlying oneness. The evolutionary view of religion does not correspond to any known high religious tradition or to the nature of the changes taking place within it which can be studied over a period of time of its history. The pattern of changes within a high religious tradition as it emerges from objective study of its career, without imposing any preconceived theory onto it, is not one of evolutionary progress from a supposed lower, primitive form to a higher, spiritual or rational stage, but rather one of gradual, progressive deterioration of its original spiritual values, externalization and excessive ritualization of most of its practices and increasing institutionalization of its vocational functions.

If the tradition in question survives its low ebb long enough without being replaced by a new movement imported from elsewhere, and if it still has enough inner vitality left, it may undergo a rejuvenation, a renewal or a revival of its old values – no doubt with some necessary modifications – only to repeat the familiar pattern of its gradual deterioration again.

This is to say that historical evidence from religious traditions whose beginnings are not shrouded in the mist of prehistory testifies to the fact that at the outset there was in each new religious movement a profound grasp of some higher spiritual truth, some kind of deep insight or a visionary or mystical experience which gave the new movement its powerful momentum. This original insight or experience may have been vested in one person, later regarded by that particular tradition as a spiritually enlightened personality, as in the case of Buddhism, or even as an incarnation of God, as in the case of Christianity. But it could also have been transmitted by a succession of prophetic figures who were in the grip of a deep personal experience of a transcendent nature, and were recognized within the particular tradition as messengers of God or chosen spokesmen of God through whom he has made known his will to his people, as in the case of Judaism. I think that the history of all the three high religions just named clearly illustrates my contention about the nature of the changes within high religious traditions as proceeding from an initial spiritually inspired message to its externalization and more or less rigid institutionalization. And I do not see any reason to look at the Vedic religion in a different way.

The Vedic religion was, quite clearly, a product of a succession of prophetic figures, messengers of the divine or enlightened teachers, who had their own personal experience of the transcendent reality and who transmitted it to their fellow men in poetic creations known as Vedic hymns. They were referred to as *ṛṣis* (seers) and were regarded by the Vedic tradition as those who had seen the highest truth and found the path to immortality (RV 1,71,1; 1,105,15; 10,15,8.10; 10,14,2.7.15; 10,56,4; AV 6,41,3). Whatever view is adopted by modern academic research about such a claim, or indeed about the claims of all other religious traditions concerning the status of their founders and the nature and origin of their experience and message, such claims have to be interpreted rather than rejected – or brushed aside in favour of a theory which would conform to the prevailing intellectual climate of the time, as did the evolutionary theory of religions in the last century and the early decades of this one.

From this point of view, we must accept the claims of the Vedic religious sources that the founders of their tradition were, within its parameters, spiritual giants with the deepest insights and highest knowledge accessible to man as the Vedic sources understood it, and were thereby on a par with the prophets of God, human incarnations of God or fully enlightened beings of other traditions, if looked at from the vantage point of impartial research in religious studies. By accepting this one premise we shall gain the necessary theoretical framework for the understanding of the multidimensionality of the Vedic religion indicated by the second part of the title of this paper. In place of a linear notion of evolution of the Vedic religion from lower to higher stages we shall then have a structural notion of synchronicity, of simultaneous coexistence of multiple stages and layers of the Vedic religion. The first part of the title, 'From Polytheism to Monism', will then be understood as applying 'horizontally', so to speak, across the multi-faceted structure of the Vedic tradition. All the facets of this structure will then be seen as existing and fulfilling their functions side by side and in mutual interdependence, although their interrelatedness, as is inevitable in any structure, will be found to be hierarchical.

What does this amount to? There are many elements, trends, streaks of belief, partial practices and varied explanations of apparently differing value and sophistication in the Vedic religion. Scholarship in previous decades tended to regard some of them as survivals from more primitive times, others as newly evolved notions, still others as products of poetic creativity of successive generations of priests and others still as anticipations of rational understanding of natural phenomena, a kind of early process of abstraction. Now, however, we have to understand all these facets as parallel expressions of a complex, spiritually advanced and socially relevant view of reality, developed and maintained by an élite of seers as a result of their talent, effort and also, possibly, purposeful training, who were concerned with transmitting their insights to other sections of the Vedic people on different levels on which their recipients of different maturity could to some extent participate in them and incorporate them into their lives.

This brings us to the notion of the 'multivalency' of the Vedic message, which has been recognized by some religious scholars in recent years, but was known in ancient India at least as early as around 500 BC. Mircea Eliade, when referring to the myth about the Indra-Vṛtra combat, with which we shall deal later on, says that it 'is multivalent; side by side with its cosmogonic meaning there are naturalistic and historical valences' (Eliade 1979: 207; cf 1959: 19ff).

This principle of multi-level interpretation of the Vedas was for the first time expressly recorded in India by Yāska (Nirukta 7, 1–2; c. 5th century BC). Three levels of interpretation of Vedic texts can be adduced from Yāska's account: (1) *ādhyātmika* or the level relating to *ātman*, i.e. to the essential part or the inner core of man, all things, and reality as a whole: this level conveys the spiritual meaning of the texts often shrouded in symbolism; the term points to the propensity of the human mind to try to develop insights into the metaphysical realm through philosophical speculation and to penetrate to the 'numinous' through intuition or mystical experience; (2) *ādhibhautika* or the level of reality relating to beings and elements (*bhūtas*) as encountered in the manifested world, i.e. to the cosmological and existential sphere of reality; and finally (3) *ādhidaivika* or the level concerning the gods (*devas*), i.e. the theological-liturgical context in which the Vedas have been used for the purpose of worship and traditional religious observance.

If we apply this principle of more levels of meaning simultaneously vested in the Vedic texts as a hermeneutical device for interpreting them, and find it workable and justified, we shall also understand that the Vedic people themselves would also have had differing degrees of understanding or awareness of the multiple meaning of the message of their sacred texts. In the case of their originators, the *ṛṣis*, this knowledge would perhaps have been full and it may be assumed that they incorporated much of the multiple meaning into their hymnic creations on purpose.

A comparatively high, if not perhaps quite full, understanding of these messages would have been acquired also by pupils and successors of the ancient seers who functioned, over many generations, as the guardians of the sacred heritage of the scriptures, later to become known as *brāhmaṇas* or 'brahmins', i.e. priests. And that is where, inevitably, the gradual deterioration in the quality of knowledge and understanding would have set in. But at no time, in antiquity, was the knowledge of the multiple meaning of the Vedas entirely lost before it was recorded by Yāska. Yet it did suffer gradually from neglect and was virtually forgotten as a purposeful device later on, although it was even then reflected, or at least was present by implication, in the different types of post-Vedic literature, such as the Brāhmaṇas or priestly books, Upaniṣads or mystical and philosophical writings, Kalpa Sūtras or treatises on rituals which include legal codes, social organisation, customs and rules of conduct, as well as in the later vast literature of Hinduism. All those writings were at least partly based on, drew their inspiration from, and used quotations from, the Vedic hymns, interpreting them on their own particular level, without necessarily contradicting and ruling out interpretations on other levels conveyed in the other types of writings.

In this way various interpretations of the Vedas have coexisted throughout the centuries, and this has given the Indian tradition in general, and later Hinduism in particular, its peculiar feature of internal tolerance and absence of any centralized and binding set of dogmas.

We have to accept, further, that many people in Vedic times would have had at least a vague idea of this multi-faceted nature of their religious tradition, and while on the surface adhering to and experiencing fully only their own particular level of communicating with the higher reality, they would have unconsciously absorbed much of what was being conveyed to them by the texts and their ritual enactment on other levels. Some of this can be observed even nowadays in the context of Hindu religious practices, both communal and individual.

A conscious revival of the principle of interpreting the Vedic texts on several levels was attempted in the last century by Svami Dayananda, the founder of Ārya Samāj, who used it in his own commentary on the Vedas, but it went almost unnoticed for a long time until it resurfaced in the context of modern comparative studies of religion.[1]

I hope that we can now regard the principle of coexistence of several levels of meaning of the Vedic texts as fully valid for the purposes of understanding and interpreting them. Further, we can safely assume that the Vedic people's understanding of themselves, the world and, indeed, of reality as a whole differed from group to group or even from one individual to another, according to the level of their interest in, and their grasp of, the related questions, and that the perceptive minds at the top, the seers and the most gifted composers of the hymns, were consciously encoding into their hymns messages on several levels of meaning. If this is so, what consequences does this have for the theme of Vedic polytheism?

In the first place, it rules out the possibility of polytheism as such ever having been a sole, universally held or even prevalent view of the higher reality in the Vedas, if by polytheism we mean the view that the higher, transcendental reality which is believed to rule our world is fully and solely represented by a Pantheon, i.e. a community of divine personages which would be presided over, permanently or temporarily, by one of them as a kind of absolute divine ruler. At the same time, it is clear that some kind of polytheism is in evidence in the Vedas throughout (and has continued to play a substantial role in subsequent phases of Indian religion, including Buddhism, and is an important feature of contemporary Hinduism). I say 'some *kind* of polytheism' advisedly, since one part of the theme under discussion must also be an answer to the question concerning the *nature* of polytheism in the Vedas. For the moment it is enough to say that polytheism fits into the picture only as a part of a wider structural view of reality in the Vedas and that it appears to have a subordinate position in it, even though it plays the most prominent part in the Vedic ritual and in popular religious observances.

I maintain that the aspect of polytheism in the Vedas, however powerfully represented both in the hymnic creations and the liturgical procedures, represents a lower stratum of the Vedic view of reality, the higher or highest one being expressed by what we may call the vision of oneness, in other words by a monistic philosophy underlying the Vedic view of the world, later to become the most influential consciously adopted and conceptually articulated school of thought to emerge from India. This underlying philosophy of oneness is best spelled out in the well known Creation hymn, Nāsadīya Sūkta (rv 10, 129), which maintains that prior to the world there was neither being nor non-being, no death nor life immortal, no day or night, but only 'that one' which breathed windless. In other words, prior to manifestation and empirical existence and before time began, there was the mysterious and hidden dynamism of oneness. It was enveloped in voidness and, like undifferentiated water, harboured its potential manifoldness within. It then emerged into existence by its own inherent flame of creativity (*tapas*) and mental drive (*kāmas – manaso retaḥ*), which led to polarity and through it to manifoldness. Gods did not witness this process, because they themselves emerged from it and it is uncertain whether or not he who oversees the world in the highest heaven knows whence it all emerged.

Besides proclaiming a dynamic, transcendental and intelligent oneness as the primordial reality or the absolute, this hymn also clearly states the subordinate role of the gods as agents within the manifested world, ignorant of their own origin, a notion often found also in later writings, including the Brāhmaṇas and Upaniṣads, and even the Purāṇas, and thereby confirms the secondary place polytheism occupies in the Vedic view of reality.

Since this hymn belongs to the later strata of the Vedic texts, as is obvious, among other reasons, from the relatively developed conceptual idiom in which it is composed and which is reminiscent of the later Upaniṣadic language, the question arises: how is the notion of oneness and its primacy expressed in the earliest hymns of the Vedic collections, where the language operates mainly with symbols, metaphors and mythological imagery?

One of the oldest deities of the Vedic sources is the goddess Aditi, who does not appear later as a companion of the other Vedic gods, but has always remained aloof and mysterious, with descriptions of her appearance or her features as a person conspicuous by their absence. Her name, which means 'infinity' and 'boundlessness', has further been interpreted as 'freedom from bondage', and she is said to be the mother of gods and kings. In one of the oldest hymns of the rv (1,89,10) she is identified virtually with the whole reality. She is said to be heaven, the inner dimension, mother, father and son, all gods, all human races and all that has been and still is to be born.

There can be little doubt that the mythological idiom of earlier times expresses here the same basic insight which is spelled out in the later Creation hymn in more easily understood conceptual terms. Only the imagery of motherhood and the all-encompassing nature of Aditi would have had a more direct and powerful impact on the imagination and emotions of the early Vedic folks than the more sober speculations of the later philosopher-seer. In addition, what comes across more clearly from the imagery and epithets heaped on Aditi is the aspect of continuous support and sustenance she provides for the world, and all that is and ever will be. This expresses well the basic relationship between the divine or the transcendent and the manifested or created world in the Vedic and the whole of Hindu religious tradition. Manifestation or creation is not a one-off event, but a continuous process, constantly re-enacted in the cyclic movement of time from moment to moment, day in day out, year after year, and magically participated in by everybody in recurring rituals, the most conspicuous and telling of which was the New Year renewal rite.

Another aspect of the relation of the transcendent to the manifest which comes across from the Aditi myth, and which re-emerges later in the well-known formulations of the Upaniṣads, is the immanence of the transcendent in the manifest expressed in Aditi's being not only father and mother but also son. A later hymn even elaborates this by saying that Aditi gave birth to the god Dakṣa and became, in turn, his daughter (RV 10,72, 4–5). This may also be the first known allusion to the much later developed doctrine of divine incarnation, but in the Vedas it clearly has a more general meaning of divine immanence in the creation.[2]

There are several other instances in the Vedic mythology which show the secondary nature of the polytheistic picture of the higher reality in the Vedas, all of them connected with cosmogony. The best known among them is undoubtedly the mythological story about Indra, the king of gods, slaying (or defeating) the serpent-demon or dragon Vṛtra.[3] Although in later understanding Vṛtra stands for the forces of obstruction, darkness and inertia, in the cosmogonic myth he in fact represents the original, pre-creational, unmanifest dimension of reality which corresponds to the goddess Aditi (before she gave birth to the world, gods and other beings), and it also clearly corresponds to the transcendent dimension of 'neither being nor non-being' of the Creation hymn. Just as Aditi harbours the unborn world, so Vṛtra is hiding cosmic waters/cows/maidens, the creative energies of cosmos. Indra, in the cosmogonic context the active principle who creates and gives life to everything and who 'impregnates all female beings' (Gonda 1960: 57), who is born as a son of Dyaus (heaven) and the cosmic cow (probably Aditi – at least in Sāyana's view), for the specific purpose of slaying Vṛtra, pierces him with his spear, releases the waters and the world process begins. This combat, and therefore the renewal of the creative process of cosmic manifestation, is going on all the time and used to be the main theme of the New Year renewal rites.

One version of the cosmogonic myth represents the premanifest cosmic latency in the form of the giant 'cosmic person' (*puruṣa*, RV 10,90). It was utilized on the *ādhibhautika* level by the priesthood to give revelational sanction to the origin of castes, but its *ādhyātmika* message of its cosmogony is clear: in the process of manifestation or creation of the world, the *puruṣa* 'ascended high', i.e. withdrew into transcendence, with three quarters of himself, while 'one quarter came into existence down here again' to be transformed into the manifested universe by the performance of a cosmic sacrificial ritual.

Another version of the Vedic cosmogonic myth, not yet fully explored, presents the dimension of the unmanifest as the original unity of heaven and earth, the deity called Dyāvāpṛthivī (Gonda 1974: 98). When separated they become Dyaus Pitar (father heaven, heavenly father) and Pṛthivī Mātar (mother earth) and produce the creation which they then constantly sustain. Gods are named as their offspring.

When gods were born, they were not immortal, and an ancient myth about the churning of the cosmic ocean describes how gods and titans (*asuras*) joined forces to separate from it the drink of immortality in order to escape repeated death. In another context (RV 4,54,2) it is stated that the gods received immortality as a gift from Savitar, who represents here the life force symbolized by the sun, while men were given successive lives by him.[4]

Higher than immortality gained within the manifested cosmos was the status of reality 'then': namely, the status of *tad ekam*, that one, in *illo tempore*: 'non-being *then* existed not, nor being' and 'death *then* existed not, nor life immortal', only 'that one breathed windless' (RV 10, 129,1–2). This timeless reality beyond creation has another important designation in the Vedas, namely *aja*, the unborn. The unborn supports the heaven (RV 8,41,10) and the earth (RV 1,67,5)[5] and has established the six regions of the manifested world (RV 1,164,6); and there is an unborn part in man (RV 10,16,4). The fact that *aja* also means 'goat' fitted well into the metaphorical imagery of Vedic mythology; the cosmic 'one-legged goat' (*aja ekapād*) could then be interpreted as a symbol of the 'one quarter', i.e. the manifested part, of reality as distinct from its three transcendent parts. Later Yājñavalkya (BU 4,1,2–7) replaced *aja* with *brahman*, and used the expression *ekapād brahman* whenever he wished to refute an inadequate definition of *brahman* which would have explained its phenomenal aspect, but did not refer to its transcendent dimension (see Werner 1978).

The designation *aja*, however, continues to be used for the ultimate in the Upaniṣads as well (e.g. BU 4,4,22), alongside *brahman* or *ātman*. There is also a link to the early Buddhist terminology concerning the ultimate: *nibbāna* is frequently described as the unborn *ajāta* (Ud 8,2); there is, of course, no clear suggestion in the early Buddhist sources that the world and its beings might have been born out of the unborn and carry a portion of it within themselves or are linked to it, although in the late Mahāyāna context there is a development in that direction. In any event, as far as the Vedic sources are concerned, gods are manifestations of the one unborn element: whether it is Indra, Mitra, Varuṇa, Agni or lower deities like Garutmat, Yama or Mātariśvan, it is only that 'the seers call in many ways that which is one' (RV 1,164,46).

Perhaps the quoted examples of the origin and status of the gods in the Vedic view of reality suffice to demonstrate that my initial thesis about the role of gods being subordinate within the Vedic view of reality is justified. What, then, is the nature of Vedic polytheism and what function does it have in the global Vedic outlook?

The scholars of the last century and of the early decades of this century regarded the Vedic Pantheon as the classic illustration of the theory that the gods of primitive and archaic religions were products of the process of personification of natural phenomena. Their main problem was to find for each god his supposed nature *substratum*, and their main preoccupation then was to determine the stage of anthropomorphism which each particular deity reached and the degree of independence a deity acquired from its original nature basis. This was still the concern, for example, of Oldenberg (Oldenberg 1970/1917: 44ff).

Some Indologists were appreciative of the fact that the Vedic gods did not suffer at the hands of authors of artful literature as did the gods of the Greek Pantheon, where Homer, Hesiod and later dramatic authors endowed them with highly elaborated anthropomorphic features so that their supposed nature *substratum* was hardly or no longer detectable. MacDonnell regarded what he called the 'indefiniteness of outline and lack of individuality' in the Vedic gods as an indication that they were 'nearer to the physical phenomena which they represented than the gods of any other Indo-European people' (MacDonnell 1974/1897: 15). Keith also still thought that 'unlike the Greek deities it is seldom difficult to doubt that the anthropomorphic forms but faintly veil phenomena of nature' (Keith 1970/1925: 58).

And yet even these early authors run into difficulties when they cannot find nature *substrata* for a large number of Vedic gods, such as Dhātar ('establisher') and Tvaṣṭar ('fashioner'), the Vedic equivalents of Plato's *demiourgos*; Viśvakarman ('all-doer'), the skilful divine craftsman and artificer; or Prajāpati ('lord of progeny'), praised as the supreme lord of all that is alive, giver of offspring and life. Then there is a whole category of deities of whom we could say that they refer to the 'inner' nature of man rather than the 'external' nature, although this was not the way the protagonists of the theory of personification of natural phenomena looked at it; the gods of the 'inner' nature are, for example, Kāma (desire, love), Śraddhā (faith), Manyu (wrath), Nirṛti (destruction) or Vāc (speech). In order to explain the origin of these uncomfortable deities which obstinately refused to be derived from phenomena of nature both Oldenberg and MacDonnell took refuge in a rather artificial concept of deification of 'abstractions' of action (hence the term 'agent' gods) and of deification of 'abstract nouns' denoting mental forces which could dominate the mind. And they would have us believe that this deification process of abstracts was a result of the growth of speculative elaboration going on in the minds of priests (Mac-Donnell 1974/1897: 115–23; Oldenberg 1970/1917: 60–67).

Keith more or less followed suit, but felt somewhat uneasy about the theory of the origin of these gods in the process of speculative abstraction, especially because some of them can be traced back into the Indo-Iranian period. He says: '. . . to call them abstract is perhaps misleading; it is not to be supposed that in the period of their creation they were felt to be other than real powers' (Keith 1970: 65).

The word 'power' is important. Keith used here a concept whose potential he did not utilize, but which was more profitably pursued at that time by Rudolf Otto, who had criticized the naturalistic theories of the origin of religions long before (Otto 1907) and now argued that religious experience is the result of the impact of the power of the 'numinous', which is not mediated by sensory impressions but issues directly from the *fundus animae*, i.e. from the depths of the human psyche, and that the sensory impressions derived from the natural world are merely stimuli which provide the occasion for the numinous experience 'to become astir' (Otto 1923/1917). Arguing directly against the protagonists of the nature theory in the Vedic religion, Otto rejected the idea that the Vedic gods could be products of the impact which mere natural phenomena made on human minds, and maintained that natural phenomena *and mental forces* only provided the opportunity for man to apprehend the presence of the hidden power, the numinous, which then might be personalized into a divine figure (Otto 1932).

So we have here a suggestion of a mysterious, hidden power of the numinous and the acceptance of the impact of natural and mental forces as pointing to and mediating the encounter with the

one hidden power. But why personalize that dynamic and transcendent one power and the forces of nature and mind issuing from
it?

Nobody seems to have the answer. Gonda, for example, while
wrestling with this problem, complained that when it came to the
relation between the personal and the impersonal element in the
representation of a power, Indians 'easily shift their ground, drawing no hard and fast line between both these aspects of the unseen'
(Gonda 1957: 6). But he sees in the Vedic gods and demons (meaning titans, *asuras*) 'archetypes or prototypes, hypostases or representations of forces, phenomena and influences with which man is
confronted on different levels of his experience; they are numinous
feelings and life experiences which took on the shape of figures'.
They are to him also potencies which are either active or latently
present in the universe and in man, in the macro- and microcosmos.
They are further manifestations of universal forces which form
themselves into ideas in the human mind (Gonda 1960: 42).

Although they sound interesting and promising, Gonda's
remarks remain inconclusive. The reason may lie in the fact that
even he, as many others before him, looked at the Vedas as representing a lower stage in the evolution of Indian thought, to be
superseded by the development of conceptual categories of rational
thought and formal logic, as transpires from his observation that
'. . . the ancient Indian did *not yet* sharply distinguish between the
mental and the material (*Geist und Stoff*), the living and the lifeless,
person and non-person, abstracts and concretes, substances and
qualities attached to these, processes and states' (Gonda 1960: 29).

I think that this sounds rather patronizing. We are now, perhaps,
a little more modest in ascribing categories such as substance and
qualities, once introduced by Aristotle's physics, to objective reality since they have been dismissed by physicists of this century,
and we can hardly claim that we understand what is life and person-
hood, mentality and materiality better than did 'the ancient Indian'
of Gonda. As to processes and states, modern thinking is now
inclined to accept the former as the more likely approximation to
the nature of reality, while the latter tend to be regarded as convenient abstractions, which is a vindication of the ancient insight,
well known in ancient India and proclaimed in the West by Heracli-
tus, that everything is 'in flux'.

I do not think that I can offer here a satisfactory explanation of
what is the nature, position and function of polytheism in the Vedic
outlook, but I can visualize a certain broad outline of the Vedic view
of reality into which polytheism would fit as one of its aspects, levels
of understanding or structural constituents.

It appears that from the earliest time there was in the Vedas a dynamic notion of reality as pulsating between the dimensions of the unmanifest and the manifest, the numinous and the phenomenal. This process of pulsation was itself understood as going on on different levels and time scales: on the scale of cosmogonic cycles of creation and destruction or manifestation and reabsorption of the universe; on the scale of periodic ritual renewals of the existing cosmos and the social order in the New Year rites; and on the scale of constant momentary flow of support and sustenance to the phenomenal from the depth of the numinous, both on the general and individual level.

This global notion of reality was comprehensive and all-embracing, so that it was felt to comprise within itself characteristics or features which normally appear as mutually exclusive: that of a person (*puruṣa*); of a dual person (*dyāvāprithivī*); of two opposing dimensions, forces or persons (Indra-Vṛtra); of a dynamic force beyond being and non-being (*tad ekam*), which has a higher as well as a lower role, because it is also the power that came into being first when manifestation got going; and of an unborn base (*aja*) which is the support or axis (*ekapād*) of the born world and sustains everything in it.

Although some notion of this all-embracing oneness must have been present in various degrees in the minds of virtually all Vedic people, the concern for it in the sense of aiming at the full personal vision of this ultimate reality – in other words, the drive towards the *ādhyātmika* understanding and apprehension of reality – was then, as in all other times, limited to a minority. Far more interest was directed towards the diverse lower forces of manifestation issuing from the one power behind the scene. But the characteristics of this one power, however vaguely known or understood, were important, because they were more or less also the characteristics of the lower, manifested forces. The one hidden reality was, of course, conceived as a power which had divine nature. It cannot, therefore, be regarded as a mechanical, blind drive in the way the forces of nature such as gravitation or electricity or even the instinct to survive are regarded by modern science. This transcendent power can be described only in terms derived from the notion of mentality or mental existence; it must be understood as possessing intrinsic intelligence and inner structural unity, such as we know, on a much lower level, only from the study of human mind and personality.

All this follows from the various designations for this pre-creational source of creation, such as the Mother Goddess, the Cosmic Person or *puruṣa*, or even the *tad ekam*, seen in the first stage of manifestation to have a mind whose first seed was desire or love. So perhaps we can, with full justification, use for this transcendent power the term 'infinite divine personality', or simply God.

Consequently, the lower or minor cosmic powers issuing from the one transcendent power in the process of manifestation must participate in the qualities of the higher power which is their source. They are cosmic intelligences and agents of the transcendent on different levels. And that brings us down to the composition of the cosmos and the nature of the beings in it. This is the layer of reality known as *ādhibhautika*. On this level of understanding reality, one encounters a whole array of cosmic elements/forces/intelligences (called *devatās*) which combine in different configurations to produce the world, things and individual beings. The knowledge that universal elements and forces constitute individual things and beings, including their mental faculties, reflects the *ādhyātmika* unity of cosmos with its parts and inhabitants also on this phenomenal level. It was common knowledge and belief in ancient India that on the death of a man all the deities participating in and enabling his existence, i.e. the elements forming his body, his sensory and mental capacities and all other constituents of his personality, returned to their respective cosmic abodes, only to be reconstituted in a new and appropriate configuration when he was reborn back in this or in any other world. This unusual kind of what we could describe as 'immanent' polytheism, i.e. immanent to human personality and other individual things in the world, may be a phenomenon peculiar to the Vedas. It has not yet received much attention.

But even the *ādhibhautika* understanding of reality, though not entirely alien to ordinary men, was nevertheless rather remote from their everyday concerns. The imagination and the emotional needs of multitudes were better nourished by the poetic use of metaphors: by allegories disguising cosmic relationships and mystical insights as mythological events. In such narratives the cosmic powers or intelligences, which constituted at the same time psychic forces in man, acted as fully fledged personal gods.

This is the *ādhidaivika* level of apprehending reality and its function can be explained as having been eminently practical. What the seer perceived as essential unity radiating harmony into its peripheral, manifested regions, and the philosopher understood as oneness proceeding according to its own eternal law to produce and govern manifestation, the multitudes accepted as the expression of the struggle of the gods for power, happiness, world preservation and even immortality in competition or combat with their adversaries (the titans and demons). They learned about it all from mythological stories describing legendary actions and deeds of

heroism on a cosmic scale which were also reflected in the phenomena of nature. People participated in these events through their
periodic re-enactment in the drama of ritual, which thus constantly
renewed the impact of these events and their message on the minds
of all members of the community, which was thereby globally
influenced and shaped in the image of the cosmic order. This was
the way in which was achieved the integration of Vedic man into a
balanced social order which offered to him relative security in this
life and also a prospect for the hereafter with a virtually infinite
outlook limited only by the individual capacity to grasp it.

The polytheistic dimension of the Vedic religion is no doubt the
most conspicuous part of it. Its hold on the mind of Vedic man was
truly overwhelming and it shaped his life and outlook most effec-
tively by means of ritual observances and worship from womb to
tomb, and beyond. Despite that, the mystical and philosophical
message behind it was never entirely blocked. It kept alive at all
times a promise of release from the ritualistic and social cage into
which the system gradually developed and ossified in the hands of
generations of priests and from the limited forms of existence in the
manifested cosmos whenever anyone began to feel that it was
unsatisfactory. Thus from the global point of view, polytheism in
the Vedas, and of course in all the other subsequent phases of
Indian religion, represents, basically, only a provisional, tran-
sitional system. It can satisfy the needs of the masses for a long time,
but its true function is to be a stepping stone to a higher and
eventually to the ultimate goal of a consciously realized oneness.

One weighty reason why Vedic polytheism could never become a
self-sufficient view of the world, and as such eventually outgrow its
usefulness and be replaced by another religion as happened to
classical polytheism, is the earlier mentioned fluidity of the Vedic
deities which was so irritating to the early Indologists. It always
provided the opportunity to brighter minds to see through the
limitations of the system and to anticipate some higher reality
beyond it.

NOTES

1. One reason for it may have been the fact that Dayanada
   wrote in Sanskrit. In this century some of his writings have
   been translated: *Light of Truth*, Allahabad 1906 and 2nd
   ed. 1915; *Introduction to the Commentary on the Vedas*,
   Meerut 1925.
2. For further details on Aditi and her comparison to 'that
   one' of the Creation hymn, see Werner 1977 and 1990.

3. For the treatment of the Indra-Vṛtra combat as a cosmogonic myth see Brown 1942 and also briefly 1941; Gonda
1960: 55–58; Kuiper 1983; and Miller 1974: 27–41.
4. For the problem of the post-mortem destiny of man and the
ideas of rebirth, return and successive lives in the Vedas,
see Werner 1978.
5. This hymn appears somewhat truncated in Griffith's translation in which verse 5 of Aufrecht's edition of the RV
appears as verse 3 (Aufrecht 1877: 57–58; Griffith 1971:
91).

REFERENCES

Primary Sources

AV = *Atharva Veda.*
BU = *Br*hadâraṇyaka Upaniṣad
RV = *R*g Veda.

Secondary Sources

Aufrecht, Theodor, ed. (1877). *Die Hymnen des Rigveda* I
(2nd edn). Bonn: Adolph Marcus.
Brown, Norman W. (1941). The Rigvedic Equivalent for Hell.
Journal of the American Oriental Society 61, 76–80.
— (1942). The Creation Myth of the Rig Veda. *Journal of the
American Oriental Society* 62, 85–98.
Eliade, Mircea (1959). *Cosmos and History.* New York.
— (1979). *History of Religious Ideas* I. London: Collins.
Gonda, Jan (1957). *Some Observations on the Relations be-
tween 'Gods' and 'Powers' in the Veda.* 's-Gravenhage:
Mouton and Co.
— (1960). *Religionen Indiens* I. Stuttgart: Kohlhammer.
— (1974). *The Dual Deities in the Religion of the Veda.* Am-
sterdam: Verhandelingen der Kon. Nederlandse Akad.
van Wet., Afd. Letterkunde, Nieuwe Reeks D1.81.
Griffith, Ralph T. H. (1971/1896). *The Hymns of the Rgveda* I.
Varanasi: P. O. Chowkhamba. (2nd edn Benares 1896.)
Keith, A. B. (1970/1925). *The Religion and Philosophy of the
Veda and the Upanishads* Delhi: Banarsidass. (1st edn
Cambridge, Mass., 1925: Harvard Oriental Studies, 31–2;
Harvard University Press.)
Kuiper, F. B. J. (1983). *Ancient Indian Cosmogony*, ed. John
Irwin. Delhi: Vikas Publishing House.
MacDonnell, A. A. (1974/1897). *Vedic Mythology.* Delhi:
Banarsidass. (1st edn Strassburg 1897: Tübner.)

Miller, Jeanine (1974). *The Vedas.* London: Rider.
Oldenberg, Hermann (1970/1917). *Die Religion des Veda* 5th edn Darmstadt: Wissenschaftliche Buchgesellschaft. (1st edn. *c.* 1917; 2nd rev. edn 1923.)
Otto, Rudolph (1907). *Naturalism and Religion.* London: William and Northgate (Crown Theological Library vol. 17).
— (1923/1917). *The Idea of the Holy.* Oxford: Oxford University Press (= *Das Heilige*, 1917).
— (1932). *Gottheit und Gottheiten der Arier.* Giessen: Alfred Töppelmann.
Werner, Karel (1977). Symbolism in the Vedas and its Conceptualisation. *Numen, International Review for the History of Religions* XXIV, 3: 223–40.
— (1978). The Vedic Concept of Human Personality and its Destiny. *Journal of Indian Philosophy* 5, 275–89.
— (1990). *Symbols in Art and Religion.* London: Curzon.

GAVIN FLOOD

Waves on Siva's ocean: Polytheism and Cosmology in Monistic Saivism

A broad distinction can be made within Hinduism between the orthodox Vedic tradition, which reveres the Vedas as its authoritative source, and the heterodox Tantric tradition which reveres the Tantras or Āgamas.[1] The monistic Śaivism which developed in Kashmir between the 9th and 11th centuries CE revered the monistic Tantras as its scriptural authority. By 'monistic' I mean the Śaiva traditions which maintained that in reality there is only pure, dynamic consciousness (saṃvit, caitanya) of which the cosmos is a projection or a coagulation. I refer to three traditions with their own texts and lineages of teachers, namely the Trika, Spanda and Pratyabhijñā, which came to regard themselves as propounding the same 'truth' of Śaiva monism.[2] These traditions come together in Abhinavagupta (c.975–1025 CE) and his student Kṣemarāja (c.1000–1050 CE) who wrote commentaries on texts in all three.

Within monistic Śaivism there are a number of explanations for how human experience, which is inherently unsatisfactory, comes about and what forces are limiting it. These explanations can be seen to form a two-tiered hierarchy. At the highest level, human embodiment and experience are due to the contraction of supreme consciousness (saṃvit, caitanya), or Paramaśiva, into particular experients; that is, Paramaśiva manifests the cosmos and the beings within it due to the power of his will or freedom (svacchanda, svātantrya). The second level of explanation is cosmological: embodied experience is due to the action of cosmic powers, the tattva-s, which are also conceived as deities who participate in and share the qualities of Paramaśiva. Thus the higher level explanation is monistic, while the structurally lower one is polytheistic. These two levels are related in the sense that the lower explanation is ultimately reducible to the higher.

I will here examine certain features of this second level, cosmological explanation. I intend to show firstly that in monistic Śaivism (and indeed in Tantra generally) polytheism can only be understood in the context of cosmology – that the Śaiva concept of a deity entails the idea of a hierarchical cosmos; secondly how the monistic Śaivas incorporated Tantric polytheistic systems and viewed them through the lens of a monistic metaphysics; and thirdly how in the system of the twelve Kālīs deities and cosmology are 'psychologized'.

DEITY AND COSMOS

The Śaiva cosmos is filled with living entities occupying various worlds (*bhuvana*-s) which are ranged in a hierarchical sequence from the gross (*sthūla*) physical world to the more subtle (*sūksma*) worlds existing at a higher level of resonance. All beings exist within their own world or within their own range or sphere (*visaya*) of experience and perception. For example, a taxonomy of worlds in the MVT places the worlds of plants (*sthāvara*), insects (*sarpajāti*), birds (*paksajāti*), wild (*mrga*) and domestic (*paśu*) animals and the human world (*manusabhuvana*) all within the larger category of the 'earth' (*prthivītattva*; MVT 5.5). Similarly, above this level are more subtle and more powerful, though not necessarily more wise, beings such as the Gandharvas, the heavenly musicians, and the Piśācas, demonic beings. As a general principle, within the cosmic hierarchy the higher the being, the more subtle and powerful he or she is. So what are referred to as gods (*devatā*) are higher beings within the community of beings (*bhūtagrāma*) in the cosmic spectrum. Thus in contrast to the bound human experient fixed in the human world, the *devatā* is located at a higher, more subtle level of resonance.

In order to understand the Śaiva concept of a deity, we must understand the Śaiva concept of cosmology. The first important point concerning this is that in the hierarchical cosmos, lower levels emerge from and are coagulations of higher levels. For the non-dual Śaivas the lower levels are manifestations or appearances (*āb-hāsa*-s), which are concentrations of the subtlety and all-pervasiveness of the higher levels, though ultimately all manifestation is an appearance of Śiva. A thickening (*ghānata*), coagulation (*syānata*) and hardening (*styānabhāva*) occurs. Kṣemarāja, a renowned Śaiva theologian and student of Abhinavagupta, writes in his commentary on the *Spanda Kārikās*: 'The Lord whose nature is consciousness (*cidātma*) causes the universe (*jagat*) to emerge as a congealed form (*syānatarūpa*) of his innate essence (*nijarasa*).'[3] This coagulation of forms is likened to the coagulation of sweets. Maheśvarānanda, an 11th century Trika theologian in South India, writes: 'Sweets produced from the gradual coagulation of sugar cane juice are like the five elements produced from the light of Śiva; they do not lose their sweetness.'[4]

The cosmos is an expression or manifestation of the absolute Śiva who is pure consciousness which is ultimately the substance of all manifestation. In so far as it detracts from the light (prakāśa) of Śiva's consciousness, this thickening is a limitation which binds beings, keeping them in the cycle of repeated births throughout the different worlds and keeping them from the recognition (pratyab-hijñā) of their identity with Śiva.

The cosmos, and therefore the beings within it, is a coagulation of supreme consciousness which occurs through various stages of de-velopment. At each stage the distinctions between subject, object and means of experience become progressively greater. These cos-mogonic stages are expressed in a number of different schemes, particularly in the system known as the six-fold way (ṣaḍadhvan). This itself is probably an amalgamation of older distinct cosmol-ogies (SP 3: 48), the most important being the thirty-six tattva-s which I shall presently refer to in more detail. Although each of the six is a distinct cosmology in itself, this six-fold way is also divided into the ways of sound (vācaka), namely varṇa, mantra and pada, and the ways of objects (vācya), namely kalā, tattva and bhuvana (TA 6.34–37). These are also called by Abhinavagupta the ways of time (kālādhvan) and of space (deśādhvan) respectively (TS: 47), thereby making a direct correspondence between sound (vācaka) and time (kāla) and between objects (vācya) and space (deśa). But the main point I wish to make which has direct bearing on the Śaiva understanding of polytheism is that there is a homology in these systems of classification between sound and world or level of reality. Indeed, higher understanding is regarded as apprehension of such esoteric interpenetration.[5] This idea of correspondence is import-ant. Not only are the layers of the universe which are a manifes-tation of the consciousness of Paramaśiva regarded as worlds or places, they are also manifestations of sound. Indeed Kṣemarāja even says that the cosmos is an expression of the supreme power of speech (vākśakti) which is non-distinct from the light of conscious-ness (cidprakāśa), which he calls the eternally arisen mantra identi-cal with pure I-ness (ahantā), the pure subjectivity of Śiva (PH: 27).

Thus all manifestation can be regarded as an expression of sound, and there is a direct equation in the Śaiva cosmologies between levels of sound and worlds of experience. This is important to the Śaiva understanding of polytheism in so far as these levels of reality, what might be called sound-worlds, are ruled by or even equated with deities. The nature or characteristics of a deity, its location and function, are contingent upon the level of the universe in which it occurs. This idea of the identification of deity with layer of the cosmos can best be illustrated by reference to the cosmology of the thirty-six *tattva*-s which, although part of the six-fold way, constitutes a complete system in itself. This cosmology and its system of correspondences is found, for example, in the root text of the Trika, the *Mālinīvijayottara Tantra* (M V T), and pervades the later works of Abhinavagupta and other Śaiva exegetes. Indeed this system is not exclusive to the monistic Śaivas but is also inherited by the dualistic Śaivas, the main doctrinal rivals of the Trika.

In this scheme, the cosmos is divided into five broad categories or regions called *aṇḍa*-s (spheres, literally 'eggs') and *kalā*-s (particularity), each of which contains a number of *tattva*-s which are the principles underlying the different worlds of the cosmos and the substance (*vastu*) which constitutes those worlds (see fig. 1). Worlds comprising and governed by *tattva*-s exist within broader spheres of the cosmos. The MVT says that there are one hundred and eighteen worlds in all (MVT 2.61; TA 11.51–53), though other texts such as the *Svacchanda Tantra* mention two hundred and twenty-four (S V T 4. 198–200). Arguably we have in these correspondences a number of different cosmologies being grafted on to each other; indeed these texts are good examples of what Gombrich calls 'the Indian tendency not to supercede new cultural elements but to juxtapose them with the old in a hierarchical ranking' (Gombrich 1975: 112). This can be seen here in the MVT with its system of *aṇḍa*-s, each of which is governed by a deity, Īśvara, Rudra and so on, and which is lined up with the five goddesses called the *kalā*-s, some of whose names perhaps indicate a connection with the five elements.

The way of the *tattva*-s (*tattvādhvan*) is divided into the pure course (*śuddhādhvan*) and the impure course (*aśuddhādhvan*), the former being beyond the pollutions (*mala*) of individuality (*āṇava*), subject-object distinction (*māyīya*) and action (*kārma*) which become operative in the impure course below *māyā*. The term *māyā*, which might be rendered 'magical illusion', takes on a specific meaning in Śaivism as the critical transition point between one important region of the cosmos, the pure course, and another, the impure course. Moreover it provides the substance of the bodies of beings in the impure course.

In this system, which comprises the twenty-five Sāṃkhya categories plus eleven Śaiva ones, the *tattva*-s which are levels of the cosmos are associated with deities. More specifically, the higher up the cosmic scale, the more are deity and world identified, whereas in the lower *tattva*-s they are more distinct. Thus the Śiva and Śakti *tattva*-s are ambiguous in so far as they are considered to be both the top of the cosmos and as transcending it. Therefore the MVT places

Figure 1 Śaiva cosmology according to the *Mālinīvijayottara Tantra*
(2.36–58) and Abhinavagupta's *Paramārthasāra:*
Transcendent Paramaśiva, the body of consciousness.

AṆḌA	KALĀ	TATTVA	ŚAKTI	EXPERIENT
	Avakāśa/ śāntyatīta	(1) Śiva	Cit	Śiva
		(2)Śakti	Ānanda	
		(3) Sadāśiva	Icchā	Mantramaheśvara
Śakti (ruled by Īśvara)	Utpūyinī/ śānta	(4) Īśvara	Jñāna	Mantreśvara
		(4) Śuddha Vidyā	Kriyā	Mantra
Māyā (ruled by Rudra)	Bodhinī/ vidyā	(6) Māyā (3 malas of āṇava, māyīya, kārma)		Vijñānakala Pralyakala
		(7) kalā (8) vidyā (9) rāga (10) kāla (11) niyati ⎫ (12) puruṣa		Sakala
Prakṛti (ruled by Viṣṇu)	Āpyāyinī/ pratiṣṭhā	(13) prakṛti (14) buddhi (15) ahamkāra (16) manas		
		(17)–(21) jñānendriyas (ears, skin, eyes, tongue, nose) (22)–(26) karmendriyas (speech, hands, feet, anus, reproductive organs) (27)–(31) tanmātras (sound, touch, form, taste, smell) (32)–(35) bhūtas (space, air, fire, water)		
Pṛthivī (ruled by Brahmā)	Dhārika/ nivṛtti	(36) earth (pṛthivī)		

no worlds in this category which is beyond worlds. Beings in the pure course below Śakti, namely Sadāśiva, Īśvara, Śuddha Vidyā and their powers of Icchā, Jñāna and Kriyā, govern their levels of reality and are the substances which constitute those levels (PH: 7). At this very high level of the cosmos deity and world are one. For example, Sadāśiva, the highest clearly manifested being and level, has a predominant sense of subjectivity or I-ness (*ahantā*) and an awareness of apparent objectivity (*idantā*) as yet indistinct (*asphuṭa*). He is aware of the identity of subject and object characterized by the sentence 'I am that' (*aham idam*; ssv: 11). At this level therefore, there can be no distinctions between the 'person' of the deity, his 'body' and 'world'; distinctions here are only potential or incipient. The 'person' of Sadāśiva is identical with his 'level' of the cosmos which is also his 'body'. By contrast, in the lower *tattva*-s being and world are more distinct, though never completely separated. For example the *tattva*-s which constitute the group of senses (*karaṇavarga*) or faculties of cognition (*jñānendriya*-s), i.e. hearing, seeing, touching etc., are animated by a group of deities (*karaṇeśvarīvarga*; SN: 31; PH: 8). Indeed, in the 'Hymn to the Circle of Deities Situated in the Body' (*Dehasthadevatācakrastotra*) attributed to Abhinavagupta, the deities of the five senses, the mind (*manas*), ego (*ahaṃkāra*) and intellect (*buddhi*), are identified with the eight mothers (*mātṛkā*-s).[6]

But let us return for a moment to the idea of the cosmos as levels of sound. The identification of sound with levels of the cosmos and with deities is clearly illustrated by the idea of *mantra* which refers firstly to an expression in empirical language given to an adept during initiation, to be repeated in order to gain release. Secondly, *mantra* refers to a higher level of the cosmos as is illustrated by the six-fold way, and thirdly, it refers to a deity (*devatā*). For example, the three highest kinds of experient beneath Śiva and above *māyā*, who exist at the level of the three pure *tattva*-s Sadāśiva, Īśvara and Śuddha Vidyā, are called the Mantramaheśvaras ('Great Lords of Mantra'), Mantreśvaras and Mantras. Thus the eight Mantramaheśvaras or Vidyeśvaras experience the world or level of Sadāśiva by whom they are governed (*adhikāra*), the Mantreśvaras experience the world of Īśvara and so on. These beings, sometimes collectively referred to as Mantras, are individual only in an attenuated sense and Kṣemarāja says of them that their bodies comprise space (*ākāśa*), manifold sound (*vicitravācaka*) and differentiated awareness (*paramarśa*). Indeed he says that the Mantras, being above the level of *māyā*, are without individual or subtle bodies and therefore possess omniscience, in contrast to the bodies of beings below *māyā* which are not omniscient (SN: 46). Thus these beings are not clearly differentiated from the world they inhabit; their consciousness, body and world merge together.

Given that these higher Mantra *devatā*-s are not clearly distinguished from their worlds, they are nevertheless regarded as distinct entities: there are eight Mantramaheśvaras with names, such as Anantabhaṭṭaraka, who is their head, Vyomavyāpin and so on (SN: 46). What then differentiates them? The answer is that they possess the pollution of individuality (*āṇavamala*) as a trace (SN: 23). The dualist Śaiva text, the MG, says that these beings are differentiated by their degree of impurity and that they have to be in some sense impure in order to perform their functions (MG: 128) delegated by Śiva, of creation (*sṛṣṭi*), maintenance (*sthiti*), destruction (*saṃhāra*), concealing (*tirodhāna*) the light of Śiva and bestowing grace (*anugraha*) through the medium of human teachers or gurus. So what differentiates one Mantra body from another is each one's field of activity and, according to the MG, their degree of impurity.

The Mantras are regarded as Paramaśiva's organs or faculties, and their only purpose is the fulfilling of Paramaśiva's will and the bestowing of grace to embodied ones. Once that is done according to Kṣemarāja, once freed from their own authority, called a pollution (*adhikāramala*; SN: 46; MG 4.3–4), their bodies are tranquillized (*śāntarūpa*) and they merge (*saṃpralīyante*) with Śiva, along with the minds of those who are devoted to them (*ārādhaka*-s; SK 1 and 2). The Mantras are higher beings who emerge out from the pure consciousness of Paramaśiva and merge back into it, along with their devotees, once they have fulfilled their function. That is, the Mantras through human teachers and their gross representations as sacred formulas, are means whereby bound beings are freed from the limitations of their *māyā*-formed and *karma*-determined bodies and can merge with Paramaśiva.

We have therefore a clear picture of these higher beings with partially particularized bodies of sound, made of Śakti and having a certain sphere of influence or authority. These beings are not constrained by either *māyā* or *karma*, being above the *māyātattva* in the pure course. Below them are beings known as Vijñānakalas, who only have the pollution of individuality (*āṇavamala*), Pralyakalas, who have the pollutions of individuality and *karma* (which propels them into future rebirths), and the Sakalas who have all three pollutions of individuality, *karma* and subject-object differentiation (*māyīyamala*). This latter category includes lesser deities as well as human, animal and plant life, whose bodies are made of *māyā* and determined by *karma*.

All these beings, however, are interpreted as a projection of pure consciousness or a contraction (*saṃkoca*) of that innate essence (*nijarasa*). A deity is therefore a condition of contracted consciousness, as is his body and world. Indeed the degree of contraction or concealment (*gopayitvā*) determines the place of a deity in the cosmos: the meaning of a deity is contingent upon its place in the total structure.

THE TWELVE KĀLĪS

I have so far shown that the Śaiva concept of deity, specifically the deity's nature, location and function, is determined by its place in the cosmical hierarchy. I have also tried to show that the levels of the cosmical hierarchy are regarded as levels of sound and that deity and sound are inseparable. I now intend to show that the monistic Śaiva concept of deity is also 'psychologized', that is, interpreted in terms of the dynamics of consciousness.

In speaking about cosmology the texts use terminologies which are either Śakti or Śiva orientated, by which I mean ways of talking about the cosmos as the manifestation of a female power (namely Sakti) or the emanation of a male consciousness (namely Śiva). Sometimes these ways of talking are combined, and while the cosmos is referred to as Sakti, its source is referred to as Śiva. The cosmology of the thirty-six *tattva*-s is predominantly Śiva language; Sadāśiva, Īśvara and Śuddha Vidyā are male deities and the *tattva*-s are spoken of as emanations or appearances (*ābhāsa*-s) of Śiva's consciousness.

This Śiva terminology is one way in which the monistic Śaivas speak of manifestation. At the esoteric heart of the Trika, however, we find that Śakti terminology predominates; the cosmos is made up of twelve emanations, the twelve Kālīs (see fig. 2), who are spoken of as manifestations either of the trembling (*manthan*) Bhairava, a terrifying form of Śiva, or as manifestations of Śakti as Kālasaṃkārṣiṇī, a form of the terrible Goddess Kālī. The origin of this doctrine and its psychological interpretation must be located in the ecstatic cremation-ground (*śmaśāna*) traditions, specifically a tradition called the Krama, and the practice of its visionary yoga. Sanderson has shown how this goddess Kālasaṃkārṣiṇī and her projection as the twelve Kālīs becomes incorporated into Trika doctrine, finding her way into the heart of Trika liturgy and being projected back by Abhinavagupta on to earlier texts such as the MVT, though this Kālī terminology is absent from the text itself (Sanderson 1986: 193–204). These twelve emanations or Kālīs are interpreted psychologically, being identified with the projection and contraction of consciousness.

According to Kṣemarāja the 'wheel of power' (*sakticakra*), a term designating the totality of the universe, comprises these twelve Kālīs, the twelve goddesses of consciousness (*ciddevī*) who garland the trembling Bhairava, the Lord of the wheel (*cakreśa*) who is their cause (*hetu*). These goddesses manifest Bhairava's play (*krīḍā*) through the four acts of initial exertion (*udyoga*), the appearance (*avabhāsana*) of the cosmos, the tasting (*carvaṇa*) or experiencing of it and its destruction (*vilāpana*; SP: 6). The trembling Bhairava, equated with Paramaśiva and pure consciousness, shakes off these circles of power which are likened to waves. The *Vijñānabhairava*, a Śaiva text on yoga, says: 'As waves from water, waves of flame from fire, or rays from the sun, so these waves of the universe (*viśvabhaṅgya*) break out (*vibhedita*) from me, Bhairava' (VB 110).[7] These manifestations, these goddesses which make up the wheel of the universe, are waves on the ocean of Śiva – or Kālasaṃkārṣiṇī – and are essentially identical with that pure consciousness. Furthermore, these deities represent the projection and withdrawal of consciousness back into itself, which occurs not only on a macrocosmic scale, but also within the individual Śaiva practitioner; their final withdrawal representing his final liberation from the cycle of birth and death.

Although Kṣemarāja uses Śiva terminology, namely Bhairava, for their essence and source, the Krama tradition, from whence the twelve Kālīs originate, and indeed Abhinavagupta himself, refer to their source as the Goddess Kālasaṃkārṣiṇī, the Destroyer of Time, or the Nameless One (*anākhya*), also called the secret fourth (*turya*) power Mātṛsadbhava (the others being the goddesses Parā,

Figure 2   The Twelve Kālīs of the Nameless Wheel (*anākhyacakra*)

	object of cognition (*prameya*)	1) Sṛṣṭikālī 2) Raktakālī 3) Sthitināśakālī 4) Yamakālī
Kālasaṃkārṣiṇī or Bhairava	means of cognition (*pramāṇa*)	5) Saṃhārakālī 6) Mṛtyukālī 7) Rudrakālī 8) Martaṇḍakālī
	subject of cognition (*pramātṛ*)	9) Paramarkakālī 10) Kālāgnirudrakālī 11) Mahākālakālī 12) Mahābhairava- caṇḍograghorakālī

Aparā and Paraparā; Sanderson 1986: 199–200). These twelve Kālīs are interpreted by Abhinavagupta as designating both cosmological and psychological processes. He writes that they represent the totality of manifestation and, while occurring on a vast macrocosmic scale, they are yet present in all appearances. Thus he says that they appear in the twelve phases of the moon, the twelve initial vowels of the Sanskrit alphabet which represent cosmogonic manifestation as sound, the twelve signs of the zodiac (*rāśi*), and are also present in mundane objects such as pots (*ghaṭa*) and cloth (*pata*; TS: 30). More importantly, they are homologized by Abhinavagupta with a classification of the process of cognition, and he divides them into three groups or stages of development, namely the object (*prameya*), subject (*pramātṛ*) and means (*pramāna*) of cognition (TS ch 4; TA 4. 171–72; Sanderson 1986: 198). These can be seen in fig. 2. The cosmology of the twelve Kālīs is thus interpreted psychologically by Abhinavagupta, thereby illustrating an important point that these hierarchical cosmologies are also regarded as states of consciousness.

The passage in Abhinavagupta's *Tantrasāra* describing the twelve Kālīs shows how they manifest the cosmos (the first two) and then reabsorb the cosmos, which is seen as the imploding of consciousness into itself, leaving no vestige of either individual experiencer or world of experience. Throughout, Abhinavagupta uses the verb *kalayati* which can mean both 'projects' and 'reabsorbs', depending on context. He establishes a quasi-etymological link between *kal* and *Kālī*, enumerating the various meanings of *kal*, and therefore implicitly of the Goddess herself, as movement (*gati*), projection (*kṣepa*), cognition (*jñāna*), enumeration (*gaṇana*), the production of experience (*bhogikaraṇa*), sound (*śabdana*), and the bringing about of dissolution within one's own self (*svātmalayīkaraṇa*; TS: 30). He thus conveys the meaning of *kal* as the projection and withdrawal of the cosmos from and into pure consciousness. This shows that the twelve Kālīs are states of consciousness projected and withdrawn by the absolute, which descend as the various layers of the cosmos and produce experience; they provide a context in which experience can occur, namely an experiencer, a world of experience and means of experiencing.

Only the first four Kālīs are concerned with the projection, maintenance and withdrawal of the in any sense 'objective' cosmos. With the first Kālī, Sṛṣṭi, we have the initial emanation from the pure consciousness of Kālasaṃkārṣiṇī, though as yet there is no externality, no distinction between subject and object, but only an internal projection, meaning that the subject-object distinction is only a latent possibility. Only with the second Kālī, Rakta, occurs the manifestation of objectivity (and therefore distinct subjectivity) which Abhinavagupta calls 'quivering externality'. Raktakālī assumes the appearances of the worlds and is thus a force which constrains beings into their particularity. Rakta is destroyed by Sthitināśa, the destroyer of the condition of supporting. She represents the withdrawal of objectivity and the cessation of external fluctuation, which Abhinavagupta refers to as the cessation of the trembling of the waves (*Kramastotra* 17). With the fourth Kālī, Yama, who devours Sthitināśa, there is the complete withdrawal of any trace of objectivity.

The cycle of the objects of cognition is thereby completed. That is to say the manifestation, sustaining and withdrawal of the cosmos is achieved in these four stages, the last two of which are stages of withdrawal. The following cycle therefore appears:

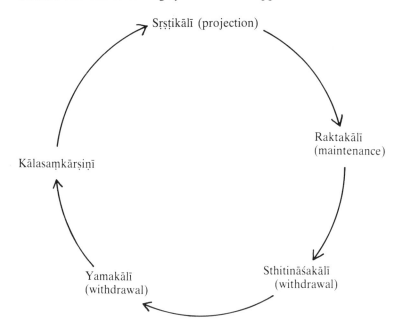

The remaining Kālīs are concerned with the withdrawal of projection and the destruction of any sense of individuality or limited subjectivity. They can be seen as refinements of the last Kālī in the cycle of objectivity, that is, representing the stages of the withdrawal of consciousness between Yamakālī and Kālasaṃkārṣiṇī.

I shall not give a detailed account of each of the Kālīs. Suffice it to say that, having withdrawn the objects of experience, the Kālīs then withdraw the means of cognition, that is, they destroy the cognition which knows externality along with the senses and the power which animates them. Thus if Sthitināśa and Yama destroy the objectivity of manifestation, i.e. what appears as external to consciousness, then Saṃhāra destroys the cognition that knows even that destruction. Finally the cognition of being an experiencer is destroyed and any residual trace (*vāsanā*) of individuality (*āṇava*) is withdrawn until, with the last two Kālīs, any trace of a tendency towards expansion (*vikāśa*) is checked and all sense of time (*kāla*) disappears (*Kramastotra* 26). Even Mahābhairavacaṇḍograghorakālī is herself devoured by Kālasaṃkārṣiṇī – though the relation between them is one of identity – and consciousness finally implodes in upon itself like, to use a modern metaphor, an imploding black hole.

The cosmos is now reabsorbed into the pure consciousness of Kālasaṃkārṣiṇī within the Śaiva practitioner; all duality is abandoned and liberation is achieved, conceived as possession of or absorption into (*samāveśa*) pure consciousness (*saṃvit, caitanya*).

In the twelve Kālīs we see the central ideas of the monistic Śaivas concerning deities and their relation to cosmology. The general picture here is clear. Kālasaṃkārṣiṇī (or Bhairava) projects herself as the twelve Kālīs (indeed iconographically they are depicted as being identical with her, surrounding her; Sanderson 1986: 198) who constitute the universe, then withdraws them into herself. First, we have here the idea that consciousness projects the universe in a number of stages; secondly, that these stages are identified with deities, namely the twelve Kālīs. Thirdly, these deities are also levels of sound and, fourthly, they produce the individual experient and his world of experience which they ultimately destroy; the twelve Kālīs give rise to the individual's experience, constitute that experience and finally devour it, or in Kṣemarāja's terminology they exert (*udyoga*), manifest (*avabhāsana*), taste (*carvaṇa*) and finally destroy (*vilāpana*) experience. This is not obvious in the context of everyday or worldly transaction (*vyavahārika*), but is an esoteric understanding of the human condition. Thus Abhinavagupta says that this process is hard to comprehend as it is very secret (*atirahasya*; TS: 30).

I have tried to illustrate the monistic Śaiva understanding of polytheism; that the nature, function and location of deities is determined by the cosmical hierarchy, and how they interpret these various cosmological schemes, which probably represent diverse traditions, in the light of their monistic metaphysics. Indeed the establishment of a monistic doctrine over against the dualism of their close rivals, the Śaiva Siddhānta, was one of the main objects of their textual exegesis. The monistic Śaivas are therefore polytheists in the sense that they maintain the reality of the hierarchical cosmos and the community of beings within it, yet finally they are monists in the sense that all external appearances (*ābhāsa*-s), which include all the gods, are but waves on the ocean of Paramaśiva; projections of consciousness within consciousness.

NOTES

1. The terms heterodox and orthodox are not relative in the context of Tantrism. As Sanderson 1985: 211 note 61 observes, Tantric traditions juxtaposed themselves against the orthodox Vedic tradition in a conscious way.
2. One way of explaining the relation between them might be to say that the Trika is a system of initiation and liturgy, the Spanda is a tradition of yoga and textual commentary, while the Pratyabhijñā is the articulation of monistic Śaiva theology concerned with the presentation of arguments.
3. SN: 10: . . . *cidātma bhagavān nijarasāśyānatārūpaṃ jagad unmajjayati.*
4. MM 25: *styānasya kramavaśād ikṣuvrasyeva śivarakāśasaya / gula piṇḍā iva pañcāpi bhūtāni madhuratāṃ na muñcanti /*; cf. Abhinavagupta PS 26. Also the Pañcarātra text the *Jayākhyasaṃhitā* 4.104: 'As sweetness standing in sugar cane is perceived as formless, likewise God within one's own body is the unchanging supreme self' (*mādhuryam ikṣusaṃstham ca amūrtam upalabhyate / evaṃ svadehagaṃ devaṃ paramātmānamavyayam //*).
5. This is also true of Vedic religion. Heesterman (1957 p.6) writes: 'The point at issue for the Vedic thinkers is not to disentangle and differentiate conceptually different entities and notions but to realize, to know, their connections'.
6. The eight mothers (*mātṛkā*-s) are also identified with cosmic levels of sound expressed as the fifty letters of the Sanskrit alphabet (in contrast to the apparently random letters of the *mālinī* system of the MVT). See SSV 1.22; 2.3.
7. VB 110: *jalasyevormayo vahner jvālābhaṅgyaḥ prabhā raveḥ / mamaiva bhairavasyaitā viśvabhaṅgyo vibheditāḥ.*

REFERENCES

Texts and Translations

Dehasthadevatācakrastotra, attributed to Abhinavagupta in Pandey 1935: 952. Ed. with a French translation by L. Silburn, *Hymnes de Abhinavagupta*, Paris: E.de Boccard, 1970.

Jayākhyasaṃhitā. Ed. E. Krishnamacharya, Gaekwad's Oriental Series no. 54, Baroda 1967 (1st edn 1931).

Kramastotra by Abhinavagupta. In Pandey 1935: 948–51.

KSTS   Kashmir Series of Texts and Studies.

MM   *Mahārthamañjari* with *parimala* by Maheśvarānanda. Ed. M. R. Śāstri, KSTS 11, 1918. French translation by L. Silburn, *La Mahārthamañjari de Maheśvarānanda*, Paris: E.de Boccard, 1968.

MVT   *Mālinīvijayottaratantra*. Ed. M. S. Kaul, KSTS 31, 1921.

MG   *Mṛgendrāgama, Sections de la Doctrine et du Yoga, avec la vṛtti de Bhaṭṭanārāyanakaṇṭha et la dīpikā d'Aghoraśivācārya*, French translation of the *Jñāna* and *Yogapadas* by M. Hulin. Pondichery: Institut Français d'Indologie, 1980.

PS   *Paramārthasāra* by Abhinavagupta with *vivṛti* by Yogarāja. Ed. J. C. Chatterji, KSTS 7, 1916.
            English translation by L. D. Barnett in the *Journal of the Royal Asiatic Society of Great Britain and Ireland*, London 1910.
            French translation by L. Silburn, *La Paramārthasāra*, Paris: E. de Boccard, 1957.

PH   *Pratyabhijñāhṛdaya* by Kṣemarāja. Ed. J. C. Chatterji, KSTS 3, 1911. English translation by Jaideva Singh, Delhi: Motilal Banarsidass, 1963.

SS   *Śivasūtra* by Vasugupta. See SSV.

SSV   *Śivasūtravismarśinī* by Kṣemarāja. Ed. J. C. Chatterji, KSTS 1, 1911.
            English translation by Jaideva Singh, Delhi: Motilal Banarsidass, 1979.
            French translation by L. Silburn, Paris: E. de Boccard, 1980.

SP   *Somaśambhupaddhati*. Ed. and French translation by H. Brunner-Lachaux, 3 vols, Pondichery: Institut Français d'Indologie, 1963, 1968, 1977.

SK   *Spanda Kārikā* by Vasugupta or Kallaṭa with the *vṛtti* by Kallaṭa. Ed. J. C. Chatterji, KSTS 5, 1916.

SN   *Spandanirṇaya* by Kṣemarāja. Ed. M. S. Kaul, KSTS 42, 1925. English translation by Jaideva Singh, Delhi: Motilal Banarsidass, 1980.

SVT   *Svacchandabhairavatantra* with *uddyota* of Kṣemarāja, KSTS 7 vols. 1921–55. Reprinted 4 vols, Delhi: Motilal Banarsidass, 1986.

TA   *Tantrāloka* by Abhinavagupta with *viveka* by Jay-
        aratha. 12 vols, ed. M. R. Śāstri and M. S. Kaul,
        KSTS, 1918–38.
        Italian translation by R. Gnoli, *La Luce delle Sacre
        Scritture*, Turin: Boringheri, 1972.
TS   *Tantrasāra* by Abhinavagupta. Ed. M. S. Kaul,
        KSTS 17, 1918.
        Italian translation by R. Gnoli, *L'Essenza dei Tantra,*
        Turin: Boringheri, 1960.
VB   *Vijñānabhairava* with commentaries of Kṣemarāja
        and Śivopādhyāya. Ed. M. R. Śāstri, KSTS 8, 1918.
        English translation by Jaideva Singh, Delhi: Motilal
        Banarsidass, 1979.
        French translation by L. Silburn, Paris: E. de Boc-
        card, 1961

Secondary sources

Alper, H. (1979) Siva and the Ubiquity of Consciousness: the
    Spaciousness of the Artful Yogi, *Journal of Indian Philos-
    ophy* 7: 345–407.
Dyczkowski, M. (1988) *The Doctrine of Vibration*. New York:
    SUNY Press.
Gombrich, R. (1975) Ancient Indian Cosmology, in C.
    Blacker and M. Loele (eds.), *Ancient Cosmologies*.
    London: Allen and Unwin.
Heesterman, J. C. (1957) *The Ancient Indian Royal Conse-
    cration*. The Hague: Mouton.
Pandey, K. C. (1959) *Abhinavagupta: an Historical and Philo-
    sophical Study*. Benares: Chowkhamba Sanskrit Series
    (1st edn 1935).
Sanderson, A. (1985) Purity and Power Among the Brahmans
    of Kashmir, in M. Carrithers et al. (eds), *The Category of
    the Person*. Cambridge: CUP.
—(1986) Maṇḍala and the Āgamic Identity in the Trika of
    Kashmir, in A. Padoux (ed.), *Mantras et Diagrammes
    Rituels dans l'Hindouisme*. Paris: Centre National de la
    Recherche Scientifique.

JOHN C. L. GIBSON

Language about God in the Old Testament

In describing the nature and activity of the deity whom they called
Yahweh, the writers of the Old Testament were as apt to use
language which strikes us as polytheistic as to use language which
we would accept as monotheistic. Modern Old Testament scholarship, confronted with such a language mix, is uneasy; it senses a
problem and, as is its academic wont, it looks for a historical
solution. Monotheism becomes the final stage in a religious development which began with ancient Israel's religion being little
distinguishable from the religions of their polytheistic neighbours.
For the stage in between, the term *henotheism* is often used: other
gods might exist, but for Israel only one God mattered. I do not
doubt that there is truth in this reading of the evidence; but it is by
no means the whole truth.[1] Left unasked is the question whether the
ancient Israelites were as uncomfortable with the language mix I
have mentioned as the modern scholar is. The answer must surely
be that they were not. In this paper, therefore, I would like to
eschew too much historical probing and simply look at Old Testament theological language as it comes to us. I am assuming, in
effect, that the writers of the Old Testament knew very well what
they were doing when they combined in their descriptions of Yahweh what we would regard as both polytheistic and monotheistic
features.
    Let us begin our investigation with the *Shema* (Deuteronomy
6:4): 'Hear, O Israel: The Lord our God is one Lord'. Here at least
it would seem that we have something unambiguously monotheistic. But the statement is not at all as clear in Hebrew as it appears to
be in English. 'The Lord' is a title which was at some point in Israel's
history – we are not sure when – substituted for the actual name of
Israel's God, Yahweh, which was as time went on considered too
holy to say out loud. It is 'Yahweh' which is in the text. Moreover, as
commonly in nominal sentences of this kind, there is no copula in

the Hebrew; 'is' has to be supplied by the translator as he thinks appropriate. Properly, therefore, the English translation I have cited (it is taken from the Revised Standard Version, as are the other quotations in this paper) ought to go 'Yahweh our God is one Yahweh', which does not seem to me to mean very much. The most commonly suggested alternative is 'Yahweh our God, Yahweh is one', which keeps us pretty firmly within a monotheistic ambit. But equally possible is 'Yahweh our God, Yahweh is the only one', in which case the statement could simply be drawing attention to Yahweh's uniqueness as compared with other deities. A third possibility is 'Yahweh is our God, Yahweh alone'; and there also the existence of other gods is implicit, though the emphasis is on Yahweh's sole claim to Israel's allegiance.

I am inclined to favour the last of these translations, on the grounds that the *Shema* was a declaration of faith, intended to set Israel apart from other nations, an invitation to them to confess on every possible occasion (see the following verses) their devotion to the God who had delivered their ancestors from Egypt and brought them to Sinai to hear his Law. But I would not wish a nuance of Yahweh's distinctiveness over against other gods to be overlooked; it must be there too; for, as we shall shortly find out, a very large proportion of Old Testament descriptions of God contain an element of comparison with other gods, and in not a few of them the phraseology used can strike our modern ears as distinctly embarrassing.

One of the cooler of such descriptions, with which Deuteronomy 6:4 must be linked, is the first of the Ten Commandments. We possess the Ten Commandments in two full recensions (in Exodus 20 and Deuteronomy 5) and one more problematic recension (in Exodus 34). There are significant differences between these recensions, but they do not in the case of the two full recensions affect the first two commandments, which are in both almost identical and also in both belong to a separate category, since they alone of the ten are put into the mouth of God. They read with their preamble, in which Yahweh is also the speaker:

> I am the Lord your God, who brought you out of the land of Egypt, out of the house of bondage.
> You shall have no other gods before me.
> You shall not make for yourself a graven image, or any likeness of anything that is in heaven above, or that is in the earth beneath, or that is in the water under the earth; you shall not bow down to them or serve them; for I the Lord your God am a jealous God . . .

The people of Israel here also acknowledge their relationship with the deity who had become known to them when they were slaves in Egypt; and the relationship is defined as an exclusive one, making room for no other deity. Furthermore, this God is so unique in his nature that no plastic image of any kind can be permitted to represent him. Other gods, however, are mentioned, as they were not in the *Shema*. But equally this time the words are more slippery than they seem. The Hebrew of the first commandment is literally, 'There shall not be for you other gods in front of me'. It does not say 'except me' but 'in front of, over against me', a spatial description which seems to draw unnecessary attention to the presence of other deities. At the same time, however; it does not say 'you shall not worship', though that is what it means; it avoids expressing directly the possibility that any Israelite could do such a thing.

The essential thrust of the first commandment is, then, that Israel must worship only Yahweh and turn its face against the worship of other gods. The second commandment then follows neatly: Israel must not in worshipping Yahweh make idols to represent him as the worshippers of other gods did ('you shall not bow down to them or serve [i.e. worship] them' refers to such idols, not to other gods). And it is to this commandment that the words about Yahweh being jealous are attached. He is not so much jealous of them worshipping other gods (did the formulator think that this would accord them too high a status?) as he is of them confusing his true nature by bowing down before images of him that could only be derived from things in his own creation. This God was not to be confused with what he as creator had made; and there may be an added nuance: he was not to be confused with anything that men had made and therefore were tempted to think they had some control over.

These two confessional statements – that in the *Shema* and that in the first two commandments – are rather special. They show us orthodox and very subtle theological minds at work trying to encapsulate the essence of Israel's faith.[2] It is a pity that modern commentators on the Old Testament do not usually match their subtlety. It is not subtle to categorise the *Shema* as all but, if not quite, monotheistic and therefore later, and higher on the scale of theological development, than the first commandment where the emphasis is still mainly henotheistic. Nor is it subtle to speak of the formulators of these statements as struggling to escape the restraints of the polytheistic language of their environments, as though with a last heave they would be where we are. Or rather, if there is subtlety in these assessments, it is our subtlety, not that of the formulators, for they are too patently based on our judgement of what the Old Testament writers ought to be saying. What should intrigue us about these passages is not the inability, but the reluctance, of their formulators

to dispense with comparison. They want to abase other gods but by
no means to get rid of them; for that would not, in the polytheistic
age in which they lived, serve their purpose. Their subtlety (as
distinct from ours) consists in the way in which they manipulate
polytheistic language; they cannot but allow other gods some kind
of real existence, but in doing so they make sure that they contrast
them with Yahweh to their permanent disadvantage.

Let us now consider some descriptions of God that come, not
from studied official prose, but from the freer world of poetry; and
let us start, as we have done with prose, with Hebrew poetry at its
seemingly most monotheistic, with Second Isaiah. This is the
pseudonym of an unknown prophet in the period of the Babylonian
exile, whose work survives in chapters 40–55 of the present biblical
book of Isaiah. Something very akin to monotheism is often
detected in his writings, and he is usually credited with having
attained an even higher rating than the *Shema* on the scale I have
mentioned; as in 43:10 with its apparently carefully honed wording:

> 'You are my witnesses', says the Lord,
>   'and my servant whom I have chosen,
> that you may know and believe me
>   and understand that I am He.
> Before me no god was formed,
>   nor shall there be any after me.'

Or as in 46: 5–7, with its magnificent polemic against idols:

> To whom will you liken me and make me equal,
>   and compare me, that we may be alike?
> Those who lavish gold from the purse,
>   and weigh out silver in the scales,
> hire a goldsmith, and he makes it into a god;
>   then they fall down and worship!
> They lift it upon their shoulders, they carry it,
>   they set it in its place, and it stands there;
>   it cannot move from its place.
> If one cries to it, it does not answer
>   or save him from his trouble.

The first of these passages seems to say pretty plainly that no other
gods except Yahweh have ever existed or shall exist, and the second
that the idols other nations worship are in reality no more than bits
of precious metal. But we should hesitate before leaving it at that.
There is the comparative language of the first couple of lines of the
second passage to be taken into account; and we find this kind of

language frequently in Second Isaiah (no less than three times, for instance, in chapter 40, at verses 12ff., 18 and 22). But even more illuminating, there is 41:22–4 where Yahweh summons the gods of the nations to his presence and challenges them to produce their credentials:

> Tell us the former things, what they are,
>   that we may consider them,
> that we may know their outcome;
>   or declare to us the things to come.
> Tell us what is to come hereafter,
>   that we may know that you are gods;
> do good, or do harm,
>   that we may be dismayed and terrified.
> Behold, you are nothing,
>   and your work is naught.

The 'tell us' with its plural pronouns implies a meeting of the heavenly council to which these gods have to report and justify themselves. The picture is in essence the same as in Psalm 82 – and that psalm has been called 'one of the most difficult passages in the Old Testament as far as the use of the term monotheism is concerned' (Wright 1950: 30). There is no escaping the impression that for the prophet and his exiled audience these gods do very much exist. We should therefore regard the other two passages as more rhetorical than theological. The prophet is trying to revive the spirits of a downcast people who, if we only think for a moment of their situation, must have stood in very genuine awe of the gods of their conquerors, and to convince them that their God, Yahweh, far from having been worsted by these gods, was more powerful than they were and was about to intervene on behalf of his own and lead them home to Zion. It is the arrogance and exaggeration of faith that we hear in the first two passages I have cited, not a systematic theologian at work concerned to put his thoughts about God into the most appropriate conceptual terms. If we want to get near to Second Isaiah's real state of mind on the issues that concern us in this volume, we should interpret these two passages in the light of the third, where the gods of the nations are tangibly there, in front of Yahweh before he calls them 'nothing'.

With my next quotations (which are, like Psalm 82 already mentioned, taken from lyric poetry), the language of comparison comes clearly and robustly out into the open.

The victory song in Exodus 15 recounts the overthrow of Pharaoh's chariots in the waters, and then goes on (verse 11):

> Who is like thee, O Lord, among the gods?
> Who is like thee, majestic in holiness,
>   terrible in glorious deeds, doing wonders?

As we now have it, this poem is later than the event it celebrates, for
there is a reference to the Philistines in verse 14 and to the building
of Solomon's Temple in verse 17; but if anything in it belongs to an
earlier version, this rather crude verse does. Yahweh is but one
among other gods; and the crudity is not mitigated if an emendation, based on the Septuagint (Greek) translation, is accepted for
the second line: 'majestic among the holy ones'. If this was the
original text (and it is supported by the parallelism), the term 'gods'
could be given the meaning 'angels', and the reference would be to
the divine beings who surround Yahweh's throne in the heavenly
council and who are not generally (*pace* Isaiah 41: 22ff. and Psalm
82) allowed to have any independence over against him. I am
inclined to accept the emendation, but to argue on the contrary that
in this verse 'gods' should be allowed to interpret 'holy ones'; for
what would be its point if Yahweh were being contrasted with
entities which were but picturesque extensions of himself?

Psalm 89:5–7 is even more extravagant in its wording:

> Let the heavens praise thy wonders, O Lord,
>   thy faithfulness in the assembly of the holy ones!
> For who in the skies can be compared to the Lord?
>   Who among the heavenly beings is like the Lord,
> a God feared in the council of the holy ones,
>   great and terrible above all that are round about him?

These 'holy ones' and 'heavenly beings' (a weak rendering; for the
Hebrew is literally 'sons of gods' or even 'sons of God') are likewise
members of Yahweh's court or council, and likewise they cannot be
denuded of menace. It may by and large be true that when the Old
Testament writers use the polytheistic terminology associated with
this assembly, making Yahweh into the 'Lord of hosts' and 'a great
King above all gods' (Psalms 95:3), it is their intention to enhance
his majesty and holiness. Thus in Psalm 103:19–21 these gods
become his 'angels', his 'hosts' and 'his ministers that do his will'
and, as in Psalm 148:1–2, their chief task is to sing his praises. But in
this psalm, as in Exodus 15, there is an unmistakable whiff of
rivalry; the other divine beings are not simply playing a supporting
role but have to be put in their place. It is as though they are being
warned not to overreach themselves and reminded that, when it
came to the crunch, they would not succeed. In Exodus 15, the
implicit thought is that they could not have done what Yahweh had

done in delivering his people from Egypt and harnessing wind and wave on their behalf. In Psalm 89 it is, in the immediately following verses, Yahweh's creation of the world that is the subject of celebration; and that too involved a battle and a victory, for cosmos did not emerge until chaos in the shape of a 'divine' monster called Rahab (in Psalm 74:12–17 it is called Leviathan) had been slain.

It will perhaps by now be evident why I devoted so much of the earlier part of this paper to arguing that a comparative dimension ought not to be removed from formulations like the *Shema*, however sedulously they may appear to us to avoid polytheism, and to countering the too easy modern assumption that Second Isaiah's rhetoric is at basis monotheistic. These passages may steer clear of the lurid linguistic furniture of the passages from lyric poetry that we looked at next; but the message of the two sets of passages is essentially the same. Other gods are threateningly real in the problems they pose both for Yahweh and for his people Israel; but he is King of heaven no less than of earth, and is as able to deal with other gods as he is to deal with their human counterparts like Egypt and Babylon; and that is why he alone is worthy of Israel's undivided allegiance. The desire to contrast Yahweh with other gods so that he may be seen to be incomparably superior to them is endemic to Old Testament religious language in all its stages, and it is wrong of modern scholars to want it to disappear with the passage of time. As long as we do not grasp that fundamental point and insist on fitting ancient Israel's religion into an evolutionary scheme based on a movement from polytheism through henotheism towards monotheism we will miss what makes it tick. It is the incomparability of its God, a notion that can only be got across by using the vocabulary of comparison.[3]

NOTES

1. For a relatively moderate statement of this position see Ringgren 1966: 66–7, and for a much more radical one Garbini 1988: 59ff. For rare protests against such an evolutionary understanding see Wright 1950 and Lohfink 1982: 135ff., both of which I found helpful in preparing this paper.

2. For a recent treatment of this 'essence' see ch. 1, sect. 6 ('The characteristic features of Yahwistic faith') in Schmidt 1983: 53ff.

3. The most thorough treatment of Yahweh's incomparability is Labuschagne 1966; see also Schmidt 1983: 177ff. Two related matters which I would have liked to develop are: how the kind of passages I have been looking at bear on the

issue of the 'One' and the 'Many' which was prominent in
several of the discussions at this conference; and how
Israel's religious language is able to unite within itself vo-
cabularies which are in neighbouring cultures restricted to
different deities. On the first of these see Johnson 1942, and
on the second Gibson 1984 and Schmidt 1983: 136ff. On the
notorious 'us' passages in Genesis 1:26 and 3:22 see my own
(Gibson 1981) and other commentaries. On the tangential
problem of what seems to be a dualism of good and evil
within Yahweh's nature, see Lindström 1983.

REFERENCES

Garbini, G. (1988). *History and Ideology in Ancient Israel.*
London: SCM Press.
Gibson, J. C. L. (1981). *Genesis, Volume 1.* Edinburgh: The
Saint Andrew Press.
    (1984). The theology of the Ugaritic Baal Cycle. *Orientalia*
    53.202–19.
Johnson, A. R. (1942). *The One and the Many in the Israelite
Conception of God.* Cardiff: University of Wales Press.
Labuschagne, C. J. (1966). *The Incomparability of Yahweh in
the Old Testament.* Leiden: Brill.
Lindström, F. (1983). *God and the Origin of Evil: A Contex-
tual Analysis of Alleged Monistic Evidence in the Old
Testament.* Lund: GWK Gleerup.
Lohfink, N. (1982). *Great Themes from the Old Testament.*
Edinburgh: T. and T. Clark.
Ringgren, H. (1966). *Israelite Religion.* London: SPCK.
Schmidt, W. H. (1983). *The Faith of the Old Testament: A
History.* Oxford: Basil Blackwell.
Wright, G. E. (1950). *The Old Testament against its Environ-
ment.* London: SCM Press.

J. G. HOWIE

Greek Polytheism

Polytheism is not confined to the religions and literatures of Greece and Rome, but it is in them that Westerners generally first encounter the phenomenon; and the literary texts that generally first come to mind are the *Odyssey* and the *Iliad*, which have usually been read in that order.

In these two texts there are a number of gods, endowed with strong personalities (such as Hera, the implacable enemy of the Trojans and forerunner of Virgil's Juno) and closely identified with different aspects of the physical and mental worlds (like Poseidon, god of the sea, and Athena, the companion of the clever Odysseus in both epics). They take sides with contending mortals and strive against each other on those mortals' behalf. They are willing to heed prayers not only for help but also for vengeance. A god can also plead with another god on behalf of a mortal, interceding for him in the same way as a saint does in some varieties of Christianity. In these ways they are able to show their gratitude for sacrifices and other forms of worship, and may sometimes, but not always, heed prayers that cite such obligations. Thus, in the *Iliad*, Chryses successfully prays to Apollo for vengeance, citing sacrifices and temple-building as obligations (1.37ff.) and in the *Odyssey*, Athena assiduously intercedes on Odysseus' behalf (1.45ff., 5.5ff.), while in the *Iliad* Poseidon urges upon Hera, who like himself is a supporter of the Greeks, that the Trojan Aeneas must be saved because he has given gifts deserving of gratitude and is not fated to die before Troy (20.297ff.); he then miraculously saves him (20.344). On the other hand, not even Zeus is able to save his pious worshipper, Hector, because, as Athena points out, he has long been destined to his fate (22.179ff.); and, earlier in the poem, Zeus has similarly been unable to save his own son Sarpedon (16.431ff.). Yet at least both heroes' bodies are preserved for burial. Priam sums up the question of

divine obligations in his response to the news that Hector's body has
been preserved: 'So it is worth giving proper gifts to the gods; for
they have remembered their gratitude to my son even in his fate of
death' (*Iliad* 24.425ff.).

These words are addressed by a grateful mortal to a god
(Hermes) in disguise in the final book of the *Iliad*; and it is
reasonable to suspect that they have some wider, exemplary, significance. That significance becomes clear when we remember
that the main divinities in the two epics are gods who in historical
times had cults with sacrifices, which were performed at cult
centres and from which priests and indeed sometimes whole communities benefited (see the *Homeric Hymn to Apollo* 526ff.
for Delphi's dependence on the god's cult). Might we therefore
see Priam's words, couched as they are in such positive and general
terms, as exemplifying a teaching that in the contract between man
and god (that is, cult), fate is one of the bits of small print? It would
appear so. Both Bacchylides (3.25ff.) and Herodotus (1.90f.) in-
voke fate to account for the fall of Croesus, Delphi's munificent
patron, in the historical period, thus confirming the impression
created by the setting of Priam's words that they are intended as
exemplary.

We have seen that Homer's way of defending the cult of the gods
against complaints of inefficacy is also employed by two authors of
the Classical period. Moreover, the pantheon of gods whose cult is
thus justified is the same one; and already Homer (*Iliad* 15.187ff)
presupposes a way of accounting for that pantheon's reign under
Zeus's supremacy, which is expounded in full by Hesiod in the
Theogony, and accepted by Classical authors such as Aeschylus
(*Agamemnon* 160ff.): namely, the Succession Myth. This is the cue
for my approach in the present paper. Briefly, I propose to treat as a
single, flexible (and no doubt in some respects still developing)
system the divine and heroic mythology of Greek literature, as
represented by Homer, Hesiod, Pindar, Bacchylides, and Attic
tragedy and, moreover, to show how the traditional forms of prayer
and hymnic predication, which are related to those in the Bible[1], can
be said to be illustrated and validated in principle in Greek mythical
narrative in the same way as moral principles and other generalisations are.

The basic account is in the *Theogony* of Hesiod. Remarkably
enough, the prooemium of this work alludes to the existence of
poetical accounts and lays claim to superior veracity, and moreover
does so by exploiting the audience's familiarity with conventions of
hymnic predication (27ff.):

Country shepherds! Evil disgraces! Mere bellies!
We know how to tell many falsehoods resembling truths;
And we know, when we are willing, how to declare things [that
are] true.

In their epiphany, the Muses address the poet with characteristic
divine scorn (West 1966:160, Richardson 1974:243f.; cf. e.g. Isaiah
6.9) and declare their own powers (first-person hymnic predication), both their negative and their positive powers (another regular
hymnic feature; for both compare Exodus 20.2 and 5f.): they know
how to deceive as well as how to tell the truth, and it all depends on
their own desires (again this fickleness is traditional in hymnography; see West 1966: 163). The Muses are the traditional source of
inspiration and therefore of authority for the poet. When in a
prooemium they are made to say that they can deceive, it is the
author's way of saying in the most unexceptionable way that when
other poets tell a certain story or offer a certain version of it, what
they say may not be true even if they are genuinely inspired and that
both they and their audiences may be genuinely deceived, so that
the present author has a right to tell a different and no less inspired
version of his own. In other words, hymnography is so familiar to
Hesiod and his audience that he is able to use it as a vehicle for
recommending his own story of the rise of the gods. Hesiod's
concern to preface his account in this way is a clear indication that
his is not the first such account and that others were already known
to his audience.

There are a number of factors in Hesiod's overall account which
are of particular relevance to my discussion. First, there is a process
of differentiation in the creation of the world, a differentiation
which is presented in the form of genealogical relationships brought
about through sexual and asexual reproduction; and these activities
are presented as an irresistible compulsion. In Hesiod's account,
one of the very first entities existing in the universe is Eros; and his
hymnic praise of Eros (120ff.) foreshadows the influence which that
god is to have in the story (a use of hymnic praise paralleled by
Sophocles' praise of the same power in *Antigone* 786ff. and his
praise of the related power, Aphrodite, in the *Trachiniae* 497ff.).

Secondly, there is a clear distinction between certain abstract
entities, on the one hand, and the gods, on the other; and the latter
are all ultimately descended from Earth. One effect of this arrangement is certainly that greater plausibility is given to the notion that
heroes are descended from gods through unions with mortals. The
heroes that emerge from such unions have their adventures (in
which Greek myth is almost uniquely prolific – Kirk 1974: 215) in

the *Spatium Mythicum* (for which see von Leyden 1952), and they serve as the basis for many important historical family and national claims.[2] The fundamental importance of these figures is clear from the archaic poet Hesiod's care to include them in his account of the successive races (the Myth of the Five Races, *Works and Days* 109ff.), even though their inclusion disrupts the pattern of a succession of races associated with metals. The late fifth-century historian Thucydides is careful to include the pragmatic substance of the heroic age in his rationalising account of the development of Greece, converting the age of heroes into a crest in the line of development of military power in Greece, which was then followed by a decline (Howie 1984: 516–18).

The most impressive evidence of the importance of Earth's role is provided by the opening of Pindar's sixth *Nemean* ode (1–7):

There is one race of men and one race of gods. From one mother we both draw our [first] breath. What separates [us] is that [our] power is entirely divided, so that the [human] race is nothing and [for the other race] the brazen sky abides, a seat secure for ever. Yet we do resemble the immortals in something, be it in a great mind or in form, even though we do not know to what finishing-line fate has written that we must run by day or in the watches of the night.

Here the physical and mental affinities between men and gods are traced back to their common origin from Earth. The difference is that men are subject to death (tactfully expressed by implication) and they are unable to foresee what is in store for them. A further, implicit, point is that fate plays a vital part in men's dealings with the gods.

Thirdly, Zeus's power is founded on the willingness of other gods to support him by advice or active help against any other god or gods or any other power, or indeed against the pattern of events that overtook his grandfather Ouranos and his father Cronus. In other words, in Greek polytheism the other gods may from time to time find it necessary to ensure the stability of Zeus's order. After his victory over his father Cronus, Zeus's order is threatened by his own union with Metis (which might have produced a son greater than Zeus) and is saved by the advice of Ouranos (the Sky) and Earth, as we learn from Hesiod's *Theogony* (886ff.). A similar story is told of the danger of a marriage with Thetis in Pindar's eighth *Isthmian* ode (26ff.), where the danger is averted by Themis (the goddess of law); and in the *Iliad* Zeus is threatened by a conspiracy of other gods, including Athena, and it is Thetis's advice that saves him (1.396ff.).[3] In one well-established story, Zeus's son Hercules' help is needed against a concerted attack by a brood of children of the Earth, the Giants (see e.g. Pindar's first *Nemean* ode 67ff.). After Zeus's defeat of Earth's monstrous child Typhos, yet another threat to his power, Zeus engenders creatures embodying the positive side of life such as the Graces and the Muses.

There is an illuminating presentation of Zeus's order thus consolidated in the opening of Pindar's first *Pythian* ode (1–33a), which can be summarised as follows:

Pindar praises the lyre as joint possession of Apollo and the violet-haired Muses, obeyed by dancers and singers, inducing even fierce Ares the war god to desert his spears and soften his heart, since her darts can even enchant the minds of the gods through the skill of Apollo and the deep-bosomed Muses. The eagle on Zeus's sceptre slumbers under a cloud the lyre has cast over him, held down by her volleys. But all those creatures that Zeus does not love are terrified when they hear the Muses' voices, including the hundred-headed Typhos, who made war on the gods and is now held fast by the cliffs off Cumae and by Mount Etna. The poet then describes the natural phenomenon for which the monster serves as aetiology: the rivers of fire with their glowing smoke by day and the rocks rolling through red flame by night. It is the monster that sends up these frightful springs of fire, a wondrous portent to behold and a wonder to hear from witnesses. It lies bound under the peaks and the plain, its back goaded by its very bed. The poet ends with a fervent prayer to Zeus: 'May it be possible, O Zeus, may it be possible [for us] to find favour with thee, who watchest over this mountain, this brow of a fruitful land.' And with that he passes to praise of the victor who has founded a city as a neighbour to [the god's] mountain and made it famous with a victory at Delphi.

Pindar here describes the positive power of Zeus's order, represented by the lyre, which for early Greek authors served as a symbol of culture and civil concord (see e.g. *Pythian* 4.293ff., 5.65ff. and *Iliad* 1.601ff.). The Muses are its joint possessors; and, like the Graces and the Seasons, they were only conceived after Zeus's victory over Typhos. When the poet passes to the creatures unloved by Zeus and frightened by the goddesses' song, the prooemium reveals itself as praise of Zeus himself, whose positive powers are now followed by his negative powers, as manifested by his ability to imprison a hundred-headed monster that might otherwise have ruled the world (*Theogony* 836ff.). Such an application implicitly inspires relieved gratitude and acceptance of Zeus's order, but it also inspires fear; and it is in that spirit that the god is directly addressed.

The order thus established does not merely provide the foundation for the traditional Greek pantheon and the distribution of powers as exercised by its members on land and sea and in the air, over mortals' struggles to feed and defend themselves and over arts, crafts, and culture. Zeus's order is also the foundation for his authority and power as guarantor of justice. Hesiod himself reserves this aspect for a separate poem, the *Works and Days*. That poem opens (1–10) with hymnic praise of Zeus's vast positive and negative powers over the individual mortal, stressing the ease with which he wields these powers and effects complete reversals (both typical hymnic predications; see Krischer 1968: 5–8). Hesiod makes Zeus the father of Dike, or Justice, and stresses the importance of success in earning one's living if one is to practise justice. Aeschylus unites in one ode Zeus's power to help a worshipper, his victory in the Succession Myth, and his establishment of a moral order for mortals (*Agamemnon* 160ff.). Likewise, Pindar's picture of Zeus's order in the *Pythian* ode (see above) serves as the opening for a poem praising the rule of law under Hieron, the tyrant of Syracuse, and his son, Deinomenes, king of the city of Aetna, stressing the value of 'harmonious' civil concord and a settled constitution, and concluding with moral advice for the two rulers. The virtue of Zeus as defender against forces of disorder and brutality, as exemplified by the monstrous Typhos, can be seen from the way Pindar equates his achievement and his order with Hieron's continuing efforts (75) to defend the freedom of Greek communities in Sicily against the Phoenicians and the Etruscans. In his *Prayer to the Muses* (*fr*.13: West 1972), the Athenian statesman Solon expounds Zeus's role as the enforcer of divine retribution, whether immediate or deferred. The distribution of power and the moral authority of Zeus, the supreme god, as established in the events recounted in the *Theogony* and reflected in the *Iliad*, constitute a common moral and religious background for the representation of both the heroic age and the contemporary world by the archaic and Classical Greek poets.

It is clear from discoveries made over the last few decades that the traditional story of the establishment of Zeus's order is ultimately based on an Ancient Near Eastern scheme, of which examples survive from the Assyro-Babylonian culture, from the Hittites, and from the Phoenicians (West 1966: 18–31); and this scheme is commonly known as the Succession Myth, because of the way in which kingship over the gods passes through the hands of several successive gods, and the line of succession is characterised by violence. In the Assyro-Babylonian[4] and Hesiodic versions the supreme god now reigning and celebrated in the poem can be seen as the avenger of earlier gods in the story (*Enuma Elish* Tablets II.23,

III.10, 58, 116, 138, IV.13 in Pritchard 1969; *Theogony* 209f.), thus consolidating his moral claim to power as no mere usurper.

We do not possess any Greek version earlier than Hesiod, but we can still see something of the development and rationale of the traditional Greek version. In the Greek pantheon the supreme god is the father of some of the most powerful gods; in the *Iliad* and the *Odyssey* Zeus's fatherhood of these gods enables him to impose his will with the authority of the head of a household, though there are passages where he resorts to a threat (*Iliad* 8.10ff., 15.18ff.) or challenge (*Iliad* 8.19ff.) reflecting overwhelming superiority in physical power. This role as head of the divine family makes him a convenient justificatory divine parallel for the primacy of the father in early Greek moral teaching. In Pindar's sixth *Pythian* ode, a strongly didactic poem in praise of Thrasybulus, nephew of Theron, the tyrant of Acragas in Sicily, the young man is praised for his devotion to his father, Xenocrates, and is said to follow the teachings once imparted by the Centaur Chiron to Achilles when he reared him on Mount Pelion: to honour Zeus most among the gods and never to deprive his parents throughout their fated life-span of a like honour (*Pythian* 6.19ff.). There is no doubt that the poet is openly citing an earlier and widely familiar didactic work known as the *Precepts of Chiron* (*frr.* 283–5: Merkelbach–West 1967).

The effectiveness of a weather-god is demonstrated in the convincing way in which the natural fear of the elements can be harnessed to create the requisite awe (cf. Exodus 19.19 and 20.18 in association with the Ten Commandments).[5] Thus evil weather on land or sea can be presented as a punishment from Zeus (*Iliad* 16.384ff., *Works and Days* 247), and the thunderbolt serves as convincing instrument of instant intervention, as when it is used to prevent the distinction between life and death being violated by destroying at a single stroke both the healer Asclepios and the man he raised from the dead (Pindar *Pythian* 3.57f.). The same fear is exploited in *Pythian* six, when Zeus is described in the paraphrase of Chiron's precept as the lord of lightning and thunderbolts, stressing his most terrible sanction against the individual transgressor.

Some indication of the process by which Zeus became guardian of justice in general may be offered by Hesiod's *Works and Days*. Hesiod makes Zeus's relationship with justice a genealogical one: he is the father of the virgin goddess Dike (Justice), the violation of justice is presented as if it were the physical violation of a woman (220ff.), and Zeus intervenes when she tells her father how she has been wronged (256ff.). In Hesiod's own day this picture was probably all the more striking because of the jealously guarded position of unmarried daughters in an ancient Greek household (a position

which continued right into recent Greek peasant society; see Walcot 1970: 69–72). Aeschylus seized on this relationship and attempted to explain the name of Dike as *Dios kore*, Zeus's daughter
(*Libation-Bearers* 948ff.), doubtless on the analogy of the real
Greek title of the *Dios kouroi*, Zeus's sons, Castor and Pollux,
long-standing household gods (Nilsson 1940: 68–9 and ill.29; 1955:
406–11). At a later point in the *Works and Days*, Hesiod warns
against wronging guests/hosts, suppliants, a brother (through adultery with a sister-in-law), orphans (? through being a dishonest
guardian to a relative's children), or a parent, saying that *Zeus
himself* is angered by such conduct and ultimately punishes it
(327ff.). As regards some of these offences, he is clearly acting in his
capacities as *Zeus Xenios* (guardian of hosts and guests – and even
beggars according to *Odyssey* 14.57f.), *Zeus Hikesios* (guardian of
suppliants), and perhaps also as *Zeus Genethlios* (guardian of
family relationships, Pindar *Pythian* 4.166f.), and there is no inter-
mediary. Zeus has a number of other titles marking him as a
household god, such as *Zeus Ktesios* (protector of household property, who could be represented as a house snake – see Nilsson 1940:
67–9 and ill. 26; 1955: 403–6, pl.27.1) and *Zeus Herkeios* (god of the
surrounding fence; see Nilsson 1940: 67–8; 1955: 402–3). From this
domestic role – perhaps through a role as household god of the king
(cf. Nilsson 1954: 417–23) – his more general responsibility for
justice in public life could have been built.

We can also see that Hesiod's concern to exalt Zeus caused him to
attempt to eliminate some features that were based on his very role
as supreme god and father of the gods in Greek myth before
Hesiod's own time. Thus Hephaestus, the divine smith, who is
regularly represented as crippled and is one of Zeus's children by
Hera in both the *Iliad* (1.577ff.) and the *Odyssey* (8.310ff.), did not
appear to Hesiod to be a worthy son for Zeus and so he revised the
god's origin by making him a flawed piece of asexual reproduction
by Hera inspired by a desire to emulate Zeus's giving birth to
Athena (his daughter by Metis) out of his own head (*Theogony*
924ff.). To effect his revision, Hesiod employs the motif of emulation, an established motif for aetiologies[6] and therefore highly
suitable as an explanation of Hephaestus' strange appearance.
Again, Hesiod was most unhappy about Zeus's role in the aetiology
of the common Greek sacrificial ritual, whereby the gods were
awarded only the thighbones wrapped in fat and the edible meat
went to the mortal worshippers (for the ritual and its origins see
Burkert 1983: 1–48). It is clear from Hesiod's own reference to the
story in the *Works and Days* that in the version already current in his
day Zeus was successfully deceived by Prometheus the Titan

(member of the same generation of gods as Zeus's father Cronus): when gods and men separated, Prometheus had the task of apportioning the shares of sacrificial victims between them; he dressed the thighbones up with fat to make them look attractive and hid all the good meat in the skin, and Zeus chose the attractive thighbones.

The division of meat between men and gods makes perfect sense if we consider men's need for food and their concern to have some ritual to induce the continuing supply of animals (West 1966: 306), but it can seem odd to anyone considering the dignity of the gods. The answer was to have an aetiological story (perhaps already involving emulation, as in *Theogony* 534) that would account for something so strange on the face of things.[7] In both the *Works and Days* and the *Theogony* this trick by Prometheus sparks off a vendetta with Zeus. In the *Theogony*, Zeus responds by creating woman and the poet then expatiates on the woe that that signifies for mortal males. In the *Works and Days*, the vendetta is lengthier. Its subsequent stages are: the withdrawal of fire from men by Zeus; its theft in a fennel stalk by Prometheus; the creation of woman in the form of Pandora by Zeus; the acceptance of this dubious gift on men's behalf by Epimetheus (Afterthought), in spite of warnings from his brother Prometheus (whose name can be interpreted as Forethought) to accept no gift from Zeus, followed by Pandora's fatal opening of the great jar (through female curiosity, a motif occurring also in the story of Adam and Eve in Genesis).[8] In the *Theogony*, whose general theme is Zeus's supremacy, Hesiod contrives a dialogue between him and Prometheus (543ff.): Zeus comments ironically (*kertomeōn*; cf. *Iliad* 5.419, *Odyssey* 13.326f., Sophocles *Philoctetes* 1235, Theocritus 1.62) on the partisan division, Prometheus with a slight smile (a suppressed version of the motif of a smile or a laugh in an intellectual contest[9]) invites Zeus to choose whichever portion his feelings command him to and Zeus, knowing what he will find and already planning his revenge, chooses the thighs and finds that they are mere bone, commenting that Prometheus did not *forget* a cunning trick (i.e. he did not see Zeus's warning to *abandon* it; cf. *Works and Days* 275). The word for the partisan character of the division, which would have left men to starve altogether if Zeus had chosen otherwise, is the adverb *heterozelōs*, 'with eagerness for one side'. In other words, Zeus has seen both the apparent partiality in the attractive thigh-portions and the real partiality in the hidden meat and is commenting on both, but Prometheus does not see the ambiguity of Zeus's comment[10] nor his implicit warning and presses ahead, thus showing himself to be less intelligent than Zeus (for Zeus's anger at seeing what he knows he will find cf. Hephaestus' anger in *Odyssey* 8.304). These revisions by Hesiod of the role of Zeus as supreme god as it was in current versions are likely to be the sort of changes he has in mind when he makes the Muses speak as they do in his prooemium.

There are two other features of Hesiod's treatment of Zeus which may not reflect innovation by Hesiod himself but are still suggestive of the ways in which the Succession Myth and Zeus's supremacy came to fit in with Greek culture. In his account of the overthrow of Zeus's two predecessors, Hesiod relates the two key incidents to a number of places in Greece, with the effect that statements are made shedding lustre on individual communities and their cults in a mutually corroborative manner. Thus when Ouranos is castrated by Cronus, the severed members are cast like a polluted object into the sea and within them grows the love-goddess Aphrodite, who is carried close to the island of Cythera before landing on Cyprus. The poet then relates epic titles of the goddess to his story by way of further proof (*Theogony* 154–206). The birth of Zeus is related to two other communities: the god's mother goes secretly to Lyctos in Crete, either just before or after the birth, and Cronus is deceived into swallowing a stone wrapped in swaddling-clothes instead of his child; later, after Cronus has been tricked into regurgitating all his children, Zeus places the stone, which was also vomited up, in (Apollo's shrine in) Delphi, where a stone purporting to be that stone was exhibited in antiquity (see Pausanias 10.24.6) 'as a wonder for mortals' (*Theogony* 453–500). Thus the birth of Zeus is related to Crete, where indeed there was a vegetation-god who died and was reborn and birth-caves were shown (West 1966: 291, 297–8), and to Delphi, whose cult is thus made to be especially honoured by Zeus and to be (by implication) very old indeed. Here Hesiod presents a divine myth as founded on mutually supportive statements creditable to various Greek communities (Howie 1984: 531–4). This is in line with the underlying general construction and interrelationship of Greek divine and heroic myths (Howie 1984: 504f., 531f.) so as to form a framework consistent in chronology by genealogical reckoning and place in terms of the movements of the characters (Kirk 1974: 268), generally acceptable in the archaic and Classical Greek-speaking world and already presupposed in the Homeric epics (Kakridis 1972; Willcock 1978: X–XII). At the same time, Hesiod's treatment of another aspect of fundamental Greek beliefs again indicates the way in which the organisation of divinities and divine myth in terms of a pantheon ruled by Zeus was made acceptable. Cronus's castration of Ouranos must have been a deeply disturbing notion for societies in which the most terrifying beliefs were fostered in defence of family ties, particularly the duties of children towards parents. In Hesiod's account, it is from

Ouranos's very blood as it mingles with the ground on which it falls that the Furies, the implacable underworld avengers of parents, are engendered; Zeus, Cronus's son, is brought safely to birth with the help of Ouranos; and by defeating and imprisoning his own father, Zeus carries out the vengeance prophesied by Ouranos at the time of his castration. The Greeks were a highly superstitious people (Thucydides 7.50.4 and 79.3, Theophrastus, *Characters* 16, 'The Superstitious Man'; Nilsson 1940: 102–20). As far as possible, Hesiod attempted to harness this superstition to his moral views within the framework of Zeus's order, making famine, diseases, wars, and storms at sea (*Works and Days* 242ff.) the instruments of Zeus's punishment and fostering a belief in thirty thousand watchers in Zeus's service (252ff.), to take their place in a supernatural world populated by many horrors of folk belief such as Empusa, the destructive seducer of men, and Mormo, the child-snatcher (Nilsson 1940: 91). His praise of Hecate, a goddess certainly associated with witchcraft and corpses in the Classical period, shows, possibly in a consciously exemplary manner, how an individual god was placed in the system expounded by him and also reflected by the Homeric poems: to paraphrase his account (409–52):

> Hecate is the daughter of two Titans, Perses and Asteria. She is greatly honoured by Zeus, having a share of earth, sea, and sky, and is most honoured among the gods. If a mortal sacrifices to her and propitiates her and calls to her, great honour will easily attend him if she accepts his prayers favourably, for she has the power. She has a share of all the honours allotted to the Titans, the earlier gods, and Zeus did not deprive her of those allotted to her then; and though an only child she has all the more honour through Zeus. To any mortals she is willing to she gives great help. She sits beside kings in courts, and whoever she wishes is outstanding in the assembly. She helps anyone she wishes to be victorious in war. She helps contestants in games so that they easily win and bring honour to their parents. If fishermen pray to her and to Poseidon she easily gives them a good catch – and snatches away any that appears if she so wishes in her heart. She increases livestock in conjunction with Hermes. Herds of cattle, goats, and sheep, if she is willing in her heart, she makes great from few – or fewer from many. Thus, though her mother's only child, she is honoured with privileges among all the gods. Moreover, Zeus made her a *kourotrophos*, a nurturer of the young that have seen the light of dawn since her own birth. Thus she has been a *kourotrophos* from the beginning, and such are her honours.

Hesiod's praise relates Hecate's powers to the Succession Myth and subordinates her to Zeus and his order. She is conjoined with other gods (Poseidon and Hermes). She exercises her powers with the ease characteristic of the gods and has divine powers of reversal; her powers have a negative as well as a positive side. Praise of her powers is qualified by the proviso that she has to be willing. She is one of the gods charged with nurturing the young to maturity (West 1966 on *Theogony* 347; Price 1978). As a virgin goddess she is well qualified to be a *kourotrophos* (Price 1978: 2, 202f.).

Hesiod's way of associating Hecate with another god in some of her activities is paralleled by, for example, the association of Apollo and the Muses in Pindar's praise of the lyre (*Pythian* 1.1ff.) or his praise of the birth-goddess Eileithyia as sitting as assessor with the Fates (*Nemean* 7.1). In this way a minor god (and his or her cult) can be associated in the sphere of influence of a greater one and, bluntly speaking, responsibility for failure as well as success of the worshipper can be shared. Another way in which responsibility can be shared is for one god to intercede with another. In addition to the examples in epic, Bacchylides makes Artemis intercede with Hera to release the daughters of King Proetus of Argos from the madness inflicted on them after laughing at Hera's temple (11.40ff., esp. 95ff.). Herodotus's account of the Delphic oracle reports that all that Athena's pleading with Zeus could obtain for Athens was the 'wooden wall', which was interpreted as the navy (7.141f.). Conversely, the favour of one god is not always sufficient. Hippolytus's devotion to the virgin Artemis did not save him from the vengeance of Aphrodite, whom he scorned (Euripides' *Hippolytus*). Thus in the common Greek religious view events might be influenced by the collaboration or conflict of personal gods under Zeus's reign within the limitations of fate; and it was possible for Pindar in his sixth *Paean*,[11] performed at Delphi, to praise Apollo as having made every effort within these limitations, abundantly manifesting both his positive and his negative powers:

Apollo, the far-shooter, in the guise of Paris, shot Achilles and at once deferred the taking of Troy by slaying that trusty bulwark of the Greeks. How often he strove against white-armed Hera, pitting his might against her! And how often against Athena! Great sufferings would never have come to pass and Achilles would soon have sacked the land of Dardanus had not Apollo been guarding it. But Zeus did not dare undo what was fated: that for the sake of Helen, Troy should vanish in the flames. And when with great weeping they had laid Achilles on the pyre, messengers sailed to Skyros and brought back Neoptolemus, who utterly sacked Troy. But after

that he saw neither his mother [on Skyros] nor the Myrmidons'
horses under his command in his ancestral fields [in Thessaly].
He landed in Molossia near Mount Tomaros, escaping neither
the winds nor far-shooting Apollo. For the god had sworn that
because he slew the aged Priam at his own altar of *Zeus
Herkeios* where he had cast himself [as a suppliant], Neoptolemus should reach neither home nor old age. And so Apollo
killed him while he was quarrelling over the rightful honours
in [the god's] own precinct beside the broad [stone] navel [of
the earth]. (*Paean* 6 (*fr.* 52 f. 78–119: Snell–Maehler 1975,
abridged)

Here, Apollo's positive efforts to defend Troy are unsuccessful
because of fate, despite his efforts against the gods championing the
other side, while his negative powers are fully successful in his
punishment of Neoptolemus for the impiety of his slaying of Priam.
The Epic presentation of the Troy tale, reflected here, was realistic
and provided a striking *exemplum*. Taboos against slaying or raping
suppliants of the gods such as Priam on the altar of *Zeus Herkeios* or
Cassandra clinging to a statue of Athena[12] are conspicuously
broken, along with other rules concerning sacrilege, so that such
taboos are not allowed to give the contemporary audience any false
hope that the horrors of the sacking of a city (see *Iliad* 9.590–595)
can somehow be eluded if their city ever falls. Instead, they are
upheld only in the sense that the violators are punished by the gods
by storms or even death at sea such as befell Locrian Ajax for the
rape of Cassandra (Alcaeus *fr.* 298; Voigt 1971) or landing far from
home as Neoptolemus and others did and, in Neoptolemus's case,
himself dying at an altar by signal poetic justice (Pausanias 4.17.4).
In the prologue of the *Trojan Women*, a play which fully reflects the
horrors of a captured city, Euripides shows Athena and Poseidon,
who had supported the Greeks, planning the Greeks' punishment at
sea. In the *Agamemnon*, Aeschylus associates Agamemnon's death
with the sacrilege at Troy and the shipwreck of much of the returning Greek fleet. At the same time, the *Paean*'s version is compatible
with the claim of the Molossian kings (explicitly acknowledged in
his seventh *Nemean* ode) that Neoptolemus reached Epirus and was
their ancestor.

Pindar is thus drawing on Epic, including the *Iliad*, for the material for this praise of a god at a major cult centre, and yet he places
the god under the authority of Zeus and fate and shows him in
conflict with other gods under the same dispensation. Logically,
material for similar praise of other gods could be drawn from the
Iliad, mutatis mutandis, such as in fighting for the Greeks themselves rather than the Trojans. After all, we see Hera doing her best

for the Greeks – especially in Book xIV in her seduction of Zeus –
and Athena, and Poseidon. It is certainly arguable that in these
efforts the gods can be seen fully satisfying their obligations to their
worshippers, just as they did in saving Hector's body. Pindar's
praise of Apollo carries our argument somewhat further. In historical times, Epic was recited at religious festivals, and in the *Odyssey*
Demodocus is shown prefacing an Epic recital by praise of a god:
when invited to sing of the Wooden Horse of Troy, 'he began with a
god and revealed the [theme of his] song, taking up the story where
the Greeks burnt their tents and sailed off' (8.499ff.). Thus Epic was
directly associated with worship. The collection of *Homeric Hymns*
represents the type of hymn sung before an Epic recital (Boehme
1937: 24ff.; cf. Pindar *Nemean* 1.1–3); and in some of the acknowl-
edgedly early ones it is clear that the narratives contained in them
are related to hymnic praise, in the sense that the audience can see
enacted in them aspects of the god that could also be the theme of
direct praise.[13] Thus the god's disguise in the *Homeric Hymns* to
Aphrodite, Demeter, and Dionysus provides an occasion for an
epiphany and a first-person hymnic predication or in Aphrodite's
case a dramatically appropriate equivalent[14], and in the narrative in
the *Homeric Hymn to Demeter* both the positive and the negative
powers of the goddess are clearly exhibited. (We may compare the
way Apollo's cheerful dissimulation in Pindar's *Pythian* nine pre-
pares the ground for dramatically motivated second-person praise
of the god by Chiron.) Thus Greek audiences were accustomed to
the presence of hymnic elements in implicit form in the narrative
parts of hymns in direct praise of the gods, such as those preceding a
recital of Epic. It may therefore be argued that the role of the gods
in the *Iliad* is so arranged that it not only functions as a sort of
exemplum, illustrating the powers and limitations of the gods and
justifying their cult, but also serves as a composite celebration of
their powers, a joint hymn, as it were, to them all.

The emotional impact of the divine side of Homeric Epic and, by
extension, of the gods of polytheism on Greeks of the Classical
period cannot easily be guessed. It may be significant, however, that
Pindar strives for a strongly emotional effect in a passage that
depends on a combination of cultic and poetic polytheism, at the
conclusion of a poem in which he has consistently striven to impart
both intellectual interest and moral authority to heroic poetry,
especially as regards its relationship with claims of states and families founded on the past through mythical and other hereditary
links (Howie 1984: 520–29). This is the seventh *Nemean* ode,[15]
whose mythical part is in praise of the heroes Ajax and Neoptolemus, both descended from Zeus's son Aeacus of Aegina, the home

of the victor. Appropriately, a positive view is taken of Neoptolemus. In a concluding prayer, Pindar turns to the aspirations of
father and son for the future: kindly treatment for the father in old
age, marriage and children for the son and continuity of the line
with retention of their current privilege (a deliberately vague term,
as in *Odyssey* 7.150, here to make the prayer of more universal
significance for the audience) and the hope of better, together with
continuing fundamentally good fortune, that is of the healthily
varied sort appropriate to mortals (54ff.) At the same time, the
passage provides moral instruction for the young victor and for all
other young people reached by a poem whose general acceptability
and moral validity is intended to secure it a wide circulation. Having
praised his work as providing a splendid crown for the young victor,
the poet changes to a solemn tone:

But, when speaking of Nemea [where the victory was won],
remember Zeus [the divine patron of the games] and whir
quietly the murmur of hymns that say so much. It is fitting to
speak of the King of the Gods on this spot [probably the
Aiakeion, the shrine of Aeacus] with gentle voice. For men tell
how he begot Aeacus in Aegina with seed the mother [the
eponymous Nymph Aegina] received, so that he might be the
city-ruler of my nation of good name [Thebes] and – O Hercules – thy well-disposed guest-friend and brother.   (80–86a)

If there is such a thing as one man getting benefit from another,
we would say that a neighbour who has shown love to his
neighbour with constant mind is a gratification worth everything. If a god, too, were to uphold this [principle] then, O thou
that didst subdue the Giants, Sogenes would wish to dwell in
thy care with good fortune, keeping a tender heart towards his
father in his forefathers' blessed in possession [and] godly
street. For he has a house with precincts of thine on either side
as he goes forth, like a four-horse chariot with its two, yoked,
pairs.   (86b–94)

O blessed one, it befits thee to persuade Hera's husband [Zeus]
and the owl-eyed Maiden [*kora*, Athena]. Thou hast the power
often to give aid against difficulties hard to traverse. It befits
thee to fit together for them a life securely strong and in-
terweave it with a sleek old age in such a way that [their life]
remains fortunate. And may their children's children ever have
the same privilege as now and a better one later.   (95–101)

My heart will never say that I dragged Neoptolemus about with
unturning words [i.e. incapable of adaptation to the different

places[16] a man, particularly a poet, may visit]. But ploughing up
the same thing three or even four times is a lack of [poetical]
resource [cf. *fr. adesp.* 947a; Page 1962], like the idly-barking
'Corinth(us) [is] Zeus's [own]' [said] to [or: by?] children.
(102–5)
In this final prayer there is both a plurality of gods and heroes
appealed to, and a plurality of purposes. The poet begins by urging
reverent language at the local hero Aeacus' shrine and speaks with
awe of how the supreme god begot him with the eponymous nymph
of the island. Then Panhellenic heroic myth (Hercules was also a
son of Zeus; Aeacus's sons Peleus and Telamon served as Hercules's allies; cf. Pindar *Nemean* 4.20ff.: an Aeginetan's victory at
games in Thebes applauded by Thebans because of Telamon's
alliance with Hercules) and possibly also recent history (when
Thebes and Aegina were allied against Athens and the cult images
of the sons of Aeacus were received into Thebes as allies – Herodotus 5.80f.; Howie 1984: 528 n.130) are employed to forge a link
with Hercules, the supreme god's mightiest son who was assumed
into Olympus after his death (*Nemean* 1.69), and was viewed both
as a hero and as a god (*Nemean* 3.23: *herōs theos*, the hero-god),
and to ask for his aid. The grounds for this request are related both
to local cult and to Panhellenic myth. The family home is close by
two shrines of Hercules (perhaps one for Hercules as hero and
another for him as a god; for the familiarity of such pairs of shrines
see the *dixa Herakleia* in Herodotus 2.44.5), so that on the one hand
Hercules and the poet's patrons are neighbours (for this bond cf.
Zeus's relationship with the city of Aetna in *Pythian* 1 cited above)
and (obviously pious) worshippers, and on the other hand Hercules
as a god is the neighbour of Zeus and the other gods on Olympus
and they are beholden to him for his help against the Giants in the
last threat to Zeus's order (see e.g. *Nemean* 1.65ff., where his life on
Olympus is also mentioned). These are the claims of gratitude (of
worshipper on god and of god on higher god) and Hercules's claims
are like those of Thetis with Zeus in *Iliad* 1 on Achilles' behalf,
inasmuch as both averted a threat to Zeus's whole order.

The prayer is made in young Sogenes' name and the poet acts as
intercessor with Hercules on the grounds that Hercules was born in
Thebes, asking Hercules in his turn to act as intercessor, and placing
the grounds for these gods' obligations to Hercules in a relative
clause, a form often used in hymnic praise. The prayer is twofold:
the son asks for Hercules's help so that he can live where his
ancestors have lived under divine protection. At the same time, he
joins with it a prayer that he may do so while caring for his father in a
kindly manner (cf. *Pythian* 6 for the emphasis on filial duty; for the

duty to look after ageing parents see also Hesiod, *Works and Days* 187f., where it is said that failure to fulfil this obligation is one of the evils that will lead to the destruction by Zeus of the present human race of Iron); built into the prayer is a promise on the son's behalf to look after his father in his old age (comparable with blessings linked conditionally with requests such as that of Chryses in *Iliad* 1.17ff.). Thus the basic prayer involves a traditional moral obligation for Sogenes.

Other aspects of the prayer further deepen its significance. The designation of Sogenes' home as 'his ancestors' blessed in possession [and] godly street' alludes to Zeus and Apollo. The adjective *euktemon*, 'blessed in possession', from *ktēma*, 'possession', alludes to Zeus *Ktēsios*, the protector of the household property; and the noun *agyia*, 'street', alludes to Apollo *Agyieus*, the god of the aniconic apotropaic column placed outside individual houses in the street (Nilsson 1940: 79–80, ill.30; 1955: 544, pl.34.4). These allusions suggest divine protection, a suggestion reinforced by the adjective *zatheos*, 'godly', which refers in the first instance to the house's particular position near the shrines of Hercules. But these allusions also include status as a settled citizen. The allusion to Zeus and Apollo, when taken together with the reference to Sogenes' ancestors, *progonoi*, suggest the title *patrōos*, ancestral, which is found applied to both Zeus and Apollo. At Athens an archon-elect had to undergo a scrutiny, *dokimasia*, in which he was asked whether he had an Apollo *Patrōos* and a Zeus *Herkeios* and where their sanctuaries were and whether he had family tombs and where they were (Nilsson 1940: 66–7, 82–3; 1955: 57, who identifies Apollo *Patrōos* as the *Agyieus* in front of the house). The allusions in the prayer thus both appeal for divine protection and assert long-standing citizen status.

In the second part of the prayer, the reference to Zeus as husband of Hera reminds the audience of Hera's role as goddess of marriage (Nilsson 1955: 429–33) and the reference to Athena as *kora* is reminiscent of her role as *kourotrophos*. As a virgin goddess she is well qualified to be one (Price 1978: 2, 202–3), and in Aegina she seems to have been identified with the local *kourotrophos* goddess Aphaia, in whose temple sculptures were found celebrating the aid Athena gave to Greeks such as Hercules and the Aeacids against barbarians (Welter 1954: 37–40).[17] Moreover, Athena was also associated with health in general,[18] so that her influence extends to Thearion's hope for a 'sleek old age'. Thus the terms of the prayer emphasise Thearion's and Sogenes' status as citizens, and allude to the former's hopes of continuing health and the latter's hopes of marriage and children safely brought to maturity. These hopes echo

the thanks expressed in the poem's opening invocation of Eileithyia, the goddess of childbirth and herself a *kourotrophos* (Price
1978: 191), for Sogenes's birth and safe childhood. At the same
time, the references to all three gods, when taken together, have
other relevances. They remind the audience of the close association
of Athena and Hera on behalf of the Greeks in the *Iliad* and of the
association of Athena and Zeus both in Epic (as in *inter alia* her
intercessions with Zeus against the Trojan Hector in the *Iliad* and
for Odysseus in the *Odyssey*) and in their role as protectors of cities
with the titles Zeus *Polieus* (Nilsson 1955: 153–4, 417) and Athena
Polias or *Poliouchos* (Nilsson 1955: 433–438). Zeus had a special tie
with Aegina. He was the lover of the island's nymph and father of
Aeacus, who had once interceded with him on behalf of all Greece
in a time of drought, a story which served as *aition* for his cult as
Zeus *Hellanios*, god of all the Hellenes, with a shrine on Mount
Oros (Isocrates 9.14f.; Apollodorus 3.12.6.9f. etc.; Radt 1958: 133,
n.1; Nilsson 1940: 7). Hence Pindar's prayer has a bearing on the
welfare of the whole community, upon which the individual welfare
of Sogenes and Thearion obviously depend.

Hercules, the intercessor, is praised as subduer of the Giants,
creatures who were believed to have perished through their own
violence,[19] so that they serve as a negative moral *exemplum* for the
young Sogenes.[20] When the address is renewed, Hercules is
reminded of his power *often* to give aid. The word *alka* (warlike
defence or aid) alludes to his role as an apotropaic god invoked as a
defender against evil, *alexi-kakos*.[21] The word *often* serves as a
tactful reminder that the god cannot *always* prevail on his worshipper's behalf (cf. West 1966 on *Theogony* 420). Pindar's choice
of the term *alka* also accommodates a reference to Hercules's
military prowess and specific power to help in war. Thus the prayer
invokes a variety of powers and functions related to the aspirations,
duties and concerns of the young citizen.

The modest pride, the aspirations, and the fears of father and son
are all enfolded in a protective web of divinities of Epic poetry and
of common Greek, local, and domestic cult, making them exemplary and sympathetic figures.

Yet the poet does not end on this note. He gives an assurance that
his heart will never say that it has (in this or any other poem past or
future) dragged the Aeacid hero Neoptolemus about by speaking of
him in a way not adapted to his audience. (If he treats him differ-
ently in his *Paean* for the Delphians, whether earlier or later, he is as
good as his word.) This conclusion tells much about the mixture of
piety and inventiveness with which heroes were treated by a poet
and about the way people could react to a mythical claim involving

even Zeus, if it was not skilfully presented. The reference to Neoptolemus after the prayer is best compared with the ending of a
Homeric Hymn like *Demeter* 491–5, where the poet asks Demeter
and Persephone for a pleasant livelihood in return for his song and
promises to remember them in another one. Pindar adapts this form
of exchange in *Isthmian* six, where he prays as an intercessor with
Clotho and the other Fates for future success for the victor's father,
whom he describes as a man dear to him, and adds an address to the
Aeacids. In this he says he will never set foot on Aegina without
praising them, an assurance that corresponds to that in *Demeter*.
Moreover, he then passes to a myth in which Hercules prays that
Telamon will have a fine son, thus showing how a hero, in this case
Hercules, can serve as an intercessor. Hence, formally, the assurance in *Nemean* seven 102ff. concerning the Aeacid Neoptolemus is
intended to make quite sure of the good-will of Hercules by insisting
that he neither has done nor will do any harm to this descendant of
Hercules's guest-friend Aeacus in this or any other poem, though he
must adapt to suit his varying audiences.

The lively terms in which Pindar concludes have a bearing on my
earlier remarks on the systematic and mutually supportive character of
Greek myth. The Corinthian claim is used as a counter-example,
showing the pitfalls to be avoided in making mythical claims. The claim
embodied in the phrase *Dios Korinthos* is a claim of close connection
with Zeus and of Zeus's paternity of the city's eponymous hero. The
phrase seems to have been associated with repetitiousness in actions or
words (Leutsch-Schneidewin 1839 and 1851: I,63; II,368) and idle
threats (Schol. Plato *Euthydemus* 292E; Greene 1938: 123), and an
undiplomatic remark that 'Zeus's Corinth(us)' would brook no de-
fiance was said to have been the last straw for the Megarians oppressed
by Corinth's Bacchiad rulers (Demon *FGrHist* 327 F 19; Jacoby 1964).
At the same time, we are told by Pausanias (2.1.1) that only Corin-
thians seriously claimed that Corinthus was a son of Zeus. I therefore
would argue that Pindar in effect contrasts with the Corinthian slogan
the varied associations enjoyed by even the grim Neoptolemus, who, as
an Aeacid, is likewise descended from Zeus and is moreover associated
with a variety of communities and claims in Greece (cf. *Nemean* 4.44–
56), ensuring wide interest in the poem (see 64ff. and Howie 1984:
528–9). The poet prefers myths that are well-integrated into the system
and afford scope for the sort of inventiveness permissible in the *Spatium Mythicum*.

Myth is a familiar source of *exempla* for exhortations and conso-
lations. Greek heroic myth can be used for both. Hercules, the son
of Zeus, is exemplary in his endurance of suffering (e.g. Aeschylus,
Agamemnon 1040f., Sophocles, *Philoctetes* 1418ff). Great heroes in

the *Iliad* are destined to die. These heroes are intended to serve as *a fortiori exempla* for consolation, as is particularly clear from the dialogue between Zeus and Hera before the death of Sarpedon in Book XVI and from Pindar's statement in *Isthmian* seven (31ff.) that a relative of the victor followed the example of Hector and other epic heroes (not only in the *Iliad*) in sacrificing his life in battle. Heroes such as Achilles, Ajax, Nestor, and Odysseus were also correctly understood as serving as *exempla* in other positive traits (Xenophon *Symposium* 4.6).

On the other hand, the value of the Greek gods for positive *exempla* is limited. Their wrath has to be implacable against the scoffer or the non-worshipper. The Old Man in Euripides' *Hippolytus* (114ff.), and Cadmus in the same author's *Bacchae* (1348), are sadly mistaken in their pleas that a god should be less easily moved to anger than a mortal. That is the effect intended by the poet. Observance of the cult has to be seen as a categorical imperative (see Aphrodite's own significantly general remarks in the prologue to the *Hippolytus*, 3–8). The remarkable sex-drive of gods and heroes is a vital motor for myth, especially for those serving as the bases for genealogical claims. Hence to Hercules, the greatest son of Zeus, is attributed the largest progeny of all (Grote 1888: 1,89).

Nevertheless, polytheism means that gods can figure in more stories and can serve as figures of *a fortiori* consolation. Just as Zeus loses his son Sarpedon in the *Iliad* and grieves bitterly, so Demeter loses her daughter Persephone to a grim and remote husband. The *Iliad* even shows Aphrodite being consoled by her mother Dione on her wound by cataloguing other gods wounded by mortals (5.382ff.). Though the myths she cites may have been recherché even for Homer's original audience, the fact is that through learning or inventiveness the poet is able to show gods resorting to consolation in the same way as mortals have to do. The exemplary value of polytheistic myth is also reflected in cult in the three temples of Hera in Stymphalus in Arcadia (for which see Pausanias 8.22.2 and Burkert 1985: 123, n.34). These were sacred to Hera as Virgin, Spouse, and Widow (*Chera*). The local aetiological myth explained that, after a quarrel with Zeus, the goddess returned to her old guardian, Temenus, in Stymphalus and he erected these temples to her. The third title may be applied to her because it can sometimes be used for a woman separated or otherwise without a husband and not bereaved (LSJ *s.v.*). Nevertheless, its general significance is assured by the two other titles. Thus the quarrels of King and Queen of Heaven in Epic provide an *aition* to make plausible a (consolatory) comparison between bereaved (and separated) women and the Queen of Heaven.

Greek polytheism, coupled with its anthropomorphism, made mythical claims more convincing in a certain sense, and provided scope for *a fortiori* forms of consolation and for the presentation of a god as one of several such powers not always in harmony and as subject to a supreme god and to fate. But it was a view that was easily vulnerable to criticism and ridicule. Thus in the early fifth century BC Xenophanes of Colophon ridiculed Greek anthropomorphism (*frr.* 15 and 16: Diels-Kranz 1951; Freeman 1948: 22) and claimed that Homer and Hesiod had actually attributed to the gods everything that was shameful among mortals: stealing, adultery, and mutual deception (*fr*.11: Diels-Kranz 1951; Freeman 1948: 22). Xenophanes thus attacked elements of myth necessary for the divine machinery in Epic (cf. Hera's deception of Zeus in *Iliad* 14), genealogical claims (Zeus begot Hercules by imposture and adultery), and aetiology (as in Prometheus's contest with Zeus). In the fourth century BC Plato (*Republic* 3.388) attacked Homer's presentation of the gods and heroes in distress over death, citing Thetis's distress at her son Achilles's fated death (*Iliad* 18.54), Zeus's distress at the death of Hector (22.168), and Achilles's and Priam's distress at the deaths of Patroclus (18.23f.) and Hector (24.414f.). There the religious and consolatory aspect of the divine examples is ignored, as is the moral value of the human examples, since both Achilles and Priam bear some responsibility for their losses.

If we look at our more recent heritage in the West, we find that the clock has turned back. Christianity, which officially shares the monotheism of Judaism, in fact offers striking parallels to the Classical myths in its scope for consolatory *exempla* and actually gives the modern reader some insight and empathy with the ancient Greeks as regards the implications and emotional impact of some myths. Prometheus pays the penalty for man's salvation and advancement. Men must advance but Zeus is not necessarily their friend (cf. Lloyd-Jones 1971: 33) and could, if they were wicked enough, destroy them – as indeed Hesiod threatens in his prophecy concerning the (present) race of Iron, and as Prometheus says he wished to do on first assuming power (*Prometheus Bound* 231ff.). This implacability on the part of the supreme god is saved from compromise by the fact that Prometheus has to pay the penalty. It is tempting to see Prometheus as in this respect comparable with Jesus, dying for men's sins. Hercules, the favourite son of Zeus (see *Iliad* 19.95ff.), labours mightily to clear the world of monsters, and yet he dies in hideous agony (see his own complaint in Sophocles, *Trachiniae* 1010ff.). Despite his assumption into heaven, he is cited by Achilles in a speech of consolation to his divine mother Thetis as an example of how even the children of the gods must die. Hercu-

les's anguish after all his labours provides a similar sort of consolatory pathos to Jesus' sufferings on the cross. Again, Demeter's long
grief may be compared with Mary's for Jesus (Nilsson 1940: 54), as
may indeed Zeus's grief for his son Sarpedon (*Iliad* 16.458ff.).

NOTES

My sincerest thanks are due to the Editor, Dr G Davies, to
Profesor A. J. Beattie for helpful discussion, to Professor E.
K. Borthwick for advice on many points, to Professor G.
Steiner of Marburg for bringing to my attention and providing
me with a copy of Benito (1969), and above all, to Dr R. C.
McCail for subjecting the whole paper to his scrutiny. Some
parts of this paper go back to a paper delivered in 1980 in
Sheffield at the Fifth International Colloquium on Aegean
Prehistory. For all views expressed here I am alone
responsible.

1. For the typical Greek forms see Norden 1923: 143–76.
2. For modern north Melanesian parallels with that distinction and with the use of myths for claims, see Malinowski
   1926: 26–30.
3. On these two examples see Köhnken 1975 and Braswell
   1971 respectively.
4. See the translation in Pritchard 1969 and the translation
   and extensive introduction in Sandars 1971: 11–110.
5. Kirk 1970: 90, citing R. Pettazzoni, says that the chief
   deity of most peoples tends to be a weather-god representing sky or rain, wind or thunder.
6. Compare already the myth of Enki and Ninmah, summarised by Kramer 1961: 103–5 and Kirk 1970: 105–7 (with
   good remarks on the aetiological aspect), and the introduction and full translation by Benito 1969: 9–19 and
   34–44. Hera's failure to rival Zeus may be compared with
   Ninmah's to rival Enki in its implications for the power of
   these two male gods. For the implications for Ninmah,
   compare Benito 1969: 18.
7. Compare, for example, the aetiological myths for local
   sacrificial rites in Rhodes and Paros in Pindar, *Olympian*
   7.45ff. and Ps.-Apollodorus 3.15.7.
8. The effect of Hesiod's story of a battle of wits is comparable with that in the myth of Enki and Ninmah, at the
   end of which the author declares, 'Ninmah could not rival
   the great lord Enki' (line 140; see Benito 1969: 18 and 44);
   cf. *Theogony* 613–16.
9. Thus Zeus laughs outright in anticipated triumph in Hesiod *Works and Days* 59, while in *Pythian* 9 Chiron smiles
   with his brow relaxed when teasingly tested as a prophet

by Apollo. Hades, too, smiles with [unfurrowed] brow when tricking Persephone into staying part of every year in the underworld in the *Homeric Hymn to Demeter* 357f.

10. For ambiguity used in a trick in an aetiological myth cf. Hades' deception of Persephone the *Homeric Hymn to Demeter* 360–69, esp. 364, as interpreted by Richardson 1974: 269. Compare also Hera's deliberate exploitation of the unintended ambiguity of Zeus's words in her trick to subordinate Hercules to Eurystheus in *Iliad* 19.95–133. Knowingly ambiguous language serves in Theogony 543ff. as a sign of power. Compare the series of ambiguities used by Dionysus as he leads Pentheus, who had refused to recognise his divinity, on to his final destruction in Euripides *Bacchae* 955–70.

11. This is a highly controversial poem. There is a full edition and commentary by Radt 1958.

12. The two offences are presented together by the Kleophrades Painter *circa* 480 BC; see Arias and Hirmer 1962: pl.125.

13. Euripides *Bacchae* has a similar effect, clearly with the intention of reinforcing the cult. It is like a Homeric Hymn presented on the stage. The god goes about in disguise, finally identifying himself at the end of the play in an epiphany (Dodds 1960: 234–5 on 1329). His powers of reversal are exhibited in the rejuvenation of Cadmus and Teiresias through worship (188–90), and his positive and negative powers are exhibited throughout the play, strikingly in the juxtaposition of the scenes of his female worshippers at peace and at war (677–774; concluding with an appeal by the messenger to recognise such a god).

14. For typical features of epiphanies and a collection of examples, including those in the *Homeric Hymns* and Homer, see Richardson 1974: 207–9 and 251–2. Lovely Aphrodite hardly needs to name herself (see 176–86, 286–8 and for some of her powers, 249–51).

15. Like *Paean* 6, this is a controversial poem; for a recent full commentary in English see Carey 1981.

16. Cf. Theognis 213–18, Pindar *fr.*43 Snell–Maehler 1975, Clearchus of Soli *fr.*75 Wehrli 1948. Cf. lines 50–52 and 64–9 and Howie 1984: 528f.

17. Pindar wrote an ode to Aphaia for the Aeginetans under her own name according to Pausanias 2.30.3 (*fr.*89b: Snell–Maehler 1975).

18. In Athens, Athena had the title Athena *Hygieia* as early as the end of the sixth century BC. In the temple of Athena, *Alea* ('refuge'; 'shelter'; 'warmth' are all attested senses of the term; see LSJ *s.v.*), in Tegea in Arcadia the goddess's statue was flanked by Asclepios and his daughter Hygieia (Pausanias 8.47.1), whose statues were by the fourth-century Scopas of Paros.

19. For the Giants as examples of violence see *Odyssey* 7.58–60, Bacchylides *fr*.15.50–63 Snell–Maehler 1970 (perish through *hybris*), Pindar *Pythian* 8.8–18 (Porphyrion, king of the Giants, linked with Typhos in perishing through *hybris*). For Pindar (*Nemean* 1.63–69) Hercules's victory over them was a triumph for justice and the order of Zeus.

20. Cf. also the coupling of Tityus and the enormous Otus and Ephialtes as negative *exempla* in Pindar *Pythian* 4.90–92, a poem which also ends with morally instructive prayer attributed to a young man, the exiled Damophilus.

21. Nilsson 1940: 78f.; 1955: 544. The reference to Hercules's victory over the Giants may have a further point. Weinreich 1915 has collected examples from later antiquity of a form of apotropaic inscription over house-doors to the effect that Hercules *Kallinikos*, the 'glorious victor', dwells within and therefore let no evil enter. Nilsson assumes that the form goes back to Classical antiquity.

REFERENCES

Arias P. E. and M. Hirmer (1962). *Greek Vase Painting*. London: Thames and Hudson.

Benito C. A. (1969). 'Enki and Ninmah' and 'Enki and the World Order', University of Pennsylvania Ph.D. thesis, Ann Arbor USA, and High Wycombe UK: University Microfilms.

Boehme R. (1937). *Das Prooimion, Bausteine zur Volkskunde und Religionswissenschaft* 15 Bühl.

Braswell B. K. (1971). Mythological Innovation in the *Iliad, Classical Quarterly* 21, 16–26.

Burkert W. (1983). *Homo Necans*, translated by P. Bing. Berkeley, Los Angeles, and London: University of California Press.

—(1985). *Greek Religion Archaic and Classical*, translated by J. Raffan. Oxford: Basil Blackwell.

Carey, C. (1981). *A Commentary on Five Odes of Pindar*. Salem, New Hampshire: The Arno Press.

Diels H. and W. Kranz (1951). *Die Fragmente der Vorsokratiker*. 6th edn Berlin: Weidmannsche Verlagsbuchhandlung

Dodds E. R. (1960). *Euripides' Bacchae*. Edited with introduction and commentary by E. R. Dodds. 2nd. edn Oxford: Oxford University Press.

Greene W. C. (1938). *Scholia Platonica, Philological Monographs* 8, American Philological Association.

Grote G. (1888). *A History of Greece* (ten-volume edn). London: John Murray.

Howie J. G. (1984). Thukydides' Einstellung zur Vergangenheit: Zuhörerschaft und Wissenschaft in der *Archäologie*. *Klio* 66, 502–32.

Jacoby F. (1964). *Die Fragmente der griechischen Historiker Teil IIIB*. Leiden: E. J. Brill.

Kakridis J. T. (1972). Probleme der griechischen Heldensage. *Poetica* 5, 152–63.

Kirk G. S. (1970). *Myth: Its Meaning and Function in Ancient and Other Cultures*. Berkeley, Los Angeles: University of California Press; Cambridge: Cambridge University Press.

—(1974). *The Nature of Greek Myths*. Harmondsworth: Penguin Books.

Köhnken A. (1975). Gods and Descendants of Aiakos in Pindar's Eighth Isthmian Ode, *Bulletin of the Institute of Classical Studies* 22, 25–36.

Kramer S. N. (1961). Mythology of Sumer and Akkad, in S. N. Kramer (ed.), *Mythologies of the Ancient World*. Garden City, New York: Doubleday, 93–137.

Krischer T. (1968). Sapphos Ode an Aphrodite. *Hermes* 96, 1ff.

Leutsch E. and Schneidewin F. G. (1839 and 1851). *Corpus Paroemiographorum Graecorum* I (Göttingen 1839) and II (Göttingen 1851). Repr. 1965, Hildesheim: G. Olms.

von Leyden W. (1952). Spatium Historicum. *Durham University Journal* 13, 89–104.

LSJ = Liddell H. G. and R. Scott (1940). *A Greek – English Lexicon*. Ninth edition rev. Sir H. S. Jones with R. McKenzie. Oxford: Oxford University Press.

Lloyd-Jones H. (1971). *The Justice of Zeus*. Berkeley, Los Angeles and London: University of California Press.

Malinowski B. (1926) *Myth in Primitive Psychology. The Sir James Frazer Lecture*. London: (reprinted by Negro Universities Press, West Port (Connecticut) 1976).

Merkelbach R. and M. L. West (1967). *Fragmenta Hesiodea*. Oxford: Oxford University Press.

Nilsson M. P. (1940). *Greek Popular Religion*. New York: Columbia University Press (reprinted in 1960 with the title *Greek Folk Religion*, New York: Harper Brothers).

—(1955) *Geschichte der griechischen Religion* I, 2nd edn. Munich: C. H. Beck.

Norden E. (1923) *Agnostos Theos*. Berlin: Teubner (4th edn, repr. 1956, at Stuttgart: Teubner).

Page D. L. (1962). *Poetae Melici Graeci: edidit D. L. Page*. Oxford: Oxford University Press.

Price T. H. (1978). *Kourotrophos: Cults and Representations of Greek Nursing Deities*. Leiden: E. J. Brill.

Pritchard J. B. (1969). *Ancient Near Eastern Texts relating to the Old Testament*; Third Edition with Supplement. Princeton: Princeton University Press. (The *Enuma Elish* is translated by E. A. Speiser under the title of *The Creation Epic*, 60–72, with supplements by A. K. Grayson, 501–3.)

Radt S. L. (1958). *Pindars Zweiter und Sechster Paian*. Amsterdam: Hakkert.

Richardson N. J. (1974). *The Homeric Hymn to Demeter*. Oxford: Oxford University Press (2nd corrected impression: 1979).

Sandars N. K. (1971). *Poems of Heaven and Hell from Ancient Mesopotamia*. Harmondsworth: Penguin Books.

Snell B. and Maehler H. (1970). *Bacchylidis carmina cum fragmentis post B. Snell ed. H. Maehler*. Leipzig: BSB B. G. Teubner.

—(1975) *Pindarus: pars II: fragmenta, indices: post B. Snell ed. H. Maehler*. Leipzig: BSB B. G. Teubner.

Voigt E.-M. (1971). *Sappho et Alcaeus: Fragmenta: edidit Eva-Maria Voigt*. Amsterdam: Polak & Van Gennep.

Walcot P. (1970). *Greek Peasants Ancient and Modern*. Manchester: Manchester University Press.

Wehrli F. (1948). *Die Schule des Aristoteles III Klearchos*. Basel: Schwabe

Weinreich O. (1915). De dis ignotis quaestiones selectae. *Archiv für Religionswissenschaft* 18, 1–52, esp. 8–15 and 46–50.

Welter G. (1954). Aiginetica XXV–XXXVI. *Archäologischer Anzeiger* 1954 24–48, esp. 37–40.

West M. L. (1966). *Hesiod Theogony edited with Prolegomena and Commentary*. Oxford: Oxford University Press.

—(1972). *Iambi et Elegi Graeci ante Alexandrum Cantati*, ed. M. L. West, 2. Oxford: Oxford University Press.

—(1978). *Hesiod Works and Days edited with Prolegomena and Commentary*. Oxford: Oxford University Press.

—(1988). *Hesiod Theogony and Works and Days: A new translation*. Oxford: Oxford University Press.

Willcock M. M. (1978). *The Iliad of Homer Books I–XII*, edited with Introduction and Commentary by M. M. Willcock. London: Macmillan Education Limited.

L. B. VAN DER MEER[1]

The Evolution and Structure of the Etruscan Pantheon

Although much has been written about Etruscan religion, by Thulin, Taylor, Clemen, Pallottino, Bloch, Pfiffig, Dumézil and Colonna, little attention has been paid to a possible development of polytheism in the historic period of Etruscan civilisation, the last eight centuries BC.[2] We know the names of more than eighty divinities, many of whom were 'imported' from the Greek (e.g. Apulu and Artumes), the Italic (e.g. Menerva) and Roman world (e.g. Vetis), in different periods and places.

In view of the evolution of Greek religion, which has strongly influenced the Etruscans, at least from the sixth century BC, and possibly from the Villanovan period, onwards, it seems probable that Etruscan religion must have undergone an evolution. Greek religion, according to the famous study of Gilbert Murray, had at least five stages: Saturnian; Olympian; philosophical religions like Stoicism and atheistic Epicureanism in the fourth century BC; a Hellenistic period with special attention paid to Tyche, the divinity of fate; and a Roman period with revivals of so-called paganism, especially in late antiquity (Murray 1935). Probably the Saturnian and Olympian pantheon was even preceded by a cult of theriomorphic gods in prehistoric times, judging from the epithets of some gods.

As far as can be seen, an identical development cannot be traced in Etruria. We can use archaeological and epigraphic evidence for this research, like the Mummy Wrappings of Zagreb and subsequent Greek and Roman written sources. The latter are partly contemporary with Etruscan civilisation and partly from a later, even much later, date and thus have been influenced and tainted by non-Etruscan thinking, philosophy and theology.

We can distinguish at least five stages in Etruscan religion. I should like first to give a general, global outline.

In the orientalizing period, and sometimes in the archaic period,

TURAN AND THE CIRCLE OF LOVE

1. Kylix from Narce (VII BC; TLE 29):

TURANIRIA ACHAVISUR   ITHAVUŠVA

THALANA THANR ALPNU ZIPNA

TURAN   THANR   THALNA   ACHVIZR

ZIPANU ALPANU ACHUVIZR THANR

Figure 1

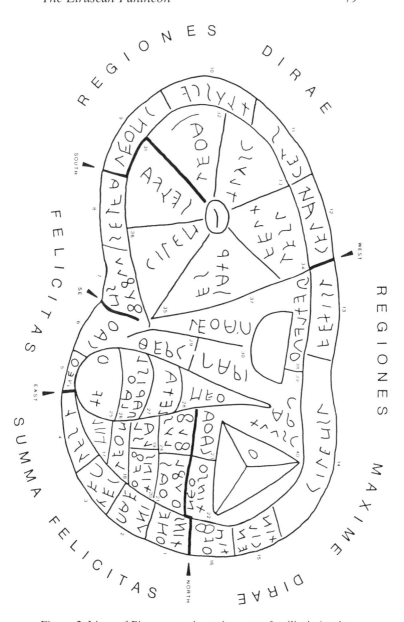

Figure 2 Liver of Piacenza: orientation; pars familiaris (regions
1–8) and pars hostilis (regions 9–16).

gods could be worshipped in the form of animals. In the sixth century we observe a growing and accelerating process of assimilation between Etruscan and Greek gods, a syncretism which was stimulated by the presence of Greek merchants in harbours (*emporia*) like Gravisca. Ex-votos for Aphrodite and Turan, Demeter and Vei were found together in their respective cult rooms of the Gravisca sanctuary (Torelli 1977). Greek traders and immigrants in Etruria came from everywhere: Corinth, Athens, Aegina, Asia Minor, etc. Another, politically inspired, form of syncretism about 500 BC is afforded by the sanctuary at Pyrgi, where Vel Thefaries, ruler of Caere, established a cult in honour of Uni Astre (Iuno Astarte), because of his political alliance with the Carthaginians.

In the fifth century Italic gods, especially from the Umbrian world, as for example Fufluns and Selvans, appear in inscriptions and visual arts. In the fourth century some very clear examples of relationships between gods, indicated by visual pairs, by epithets, and by names in the nominative followed by epithets in the genitive (for example Turmś Aitaś, the Etruscan Hermes of Hades) may be observed. Some mirrors show constellations of gods which we might call spheres, circles sometimes dominated by a principal god such as Turan. In the sphere of the underworld, symptoms of anxiety are dominant. Tuchulcha, Charun and Vanth, the last two often as a visible couple, then appear for the first time. The fear of the unpleasant aspects of underworld life can probably be explained by the political situation, the invasions of Celts in the north and Romans in the south of Etruria. It is interesting to note that the earliest representations of Charun appear at Bologna (Sassatelli 1980), and those of Vanth in South Etruria, clearly inspired by South Italian Furies.

In the Hellenistic period the secondary gods (e.g. Lasa) begin to play a more important part. This means that the great gods from the classical period, Turms, Turan, Menerva, Apollo, seem to disappear or are replaced by minor divinities. It seems very probable that the old aristocratic élite gradually lost its position, its mythological knowledge and its gods. An important phenomenon, not only in Etruria, is the appearance of the divinities of fate, Athrpa (Atropos), Nortia, and Cilens probably influenced by the Fortuna cult at Praeneste in Latium. The most important documents of the time (about 100 BC) are the Bronze Liver of Piacenza and the famous Mummy Wrappings of Zagreb. The Liver clearly presents a real polytheistic system, used by *haruspices*, and was probably made about 100 BC in the vicinity of Cortona. Neither document mentions the formerly important gods such as Apulu, Artumes, Sethlans, Turan and Turms. I will return to this question later on.

With the extinction of Etruscan civilisation, its gods did not all die. We know for certain that at least Nortia, a goddess of fate, was still worshipped at Bolsena in the third century AD.

THE STRUCTURE OF THE PANTHEON. GENEALOGICAL BACK GROUNDS

The world of the Etruscan gods is not easy to analyse, because, like Roman religion, it hardly had a mythology. As far as is known the Etruscans did not have an author like Hesiod who wrote down a *Theogony*. The loose structure of the pantheon can be explained by the fact that numerous gods were originally local gods: for example, the Demeter-like Vei at Veii, the Apollo-like Soranus (Etr. Suri) at Soracte, and Voltumna (Etr. Veltune) in the national *Fanum Voltumnae*, which may be in the vicinity of Volsinii veteres. In addition, some gods probably were cultivated and worshipped by one aristocratic family. The fact that some gods have a gentilitial origin may be illustrated by the Hellenistic *Tomba della Tassinaia* at Chiusi, belonging to the Tiuza family, who clearly worshipped the moon-goddess Tiu/Tiv(r).[3] That such a practice already existed in the archaic periods is testified by aristocratic theonymous names like Uselna, Laranii etc. The origin of the custom may have been Italic because, as Varro writes, the Sabine family Aurelii (Auselii) worshipped especially Ausel, the Sun. The strong gentilitial character of some gods can be deduced from their epithets, especially from the fourth century BC onwards, for example Lasa achununa and Selvans sanchuneta (a family of Umbrian origin!). A third reason may be that many names of gods are in fact abstractions and personifications. I would like to demonstrate this by the name of Thesan, who is undoubtedly the equivalent of Eos, the Greek goddess of dawn. The ending -an indicates a *participium praesens*, like Turan, whose name means 'the Giving one'. The root thes- in Thesan can be explained by an adverb in a votive inscription, which runs: . . . *tez.alpan turce ('merito libensque dedit')*, and by the words *tesne rasne* in the text of the Cippus of Perugia, which mean 'by Etruscan Right' or by 'Public Right'. The chief of the kitchen servants in the *Tomba Golini I* at Orvieto is called *tesinth tamiathuras* (the chef, the ordering person of the housekeepers). The word thes- must therefore mean something like order and right. The goddess Thesan indeed has the function of goddess of order, because she indicates a cosmic movement, the rising of the sun. Although the goddess did not appear before *c.*500 BC in votive inscriptions, her cult must have been much older. Already in the seventh century BC aristocratic women call themselves *Thesa(n)thei(a)*. A fourth reason for the loose structure may be that some gods were worshipped only on special occasions in local ritual calendars. An example is afforded by Culsu, a gate deity who according to votive inscriptions and the Mummy Wrappings was worshipped in August, like the gate divinity Portunus at Rome (Rix 1986).

Even if there are many abstract deities and personifications, can we nevertheless discover family ties in the Etruscan pantheon? One would expect so because epigraphic documents show a clear interest in ancestral cults on the one hand and in family relationships on the other. Inscriptions call some gods *ati* (mother, e.g. Catha, Cel, Turan), *tatanu* (grandmother, e.g. Cel), *sians* or *sans* (father, e.g. Maris and Tec(vm)), *clan* (son) and *cliniiar* (sons). Of course this does not prove anything. We know from Roman religion a Iupiter, a Diespater, a Marspiter and so on, who certainly do not bear the *epiclesis* 'pater' because of their fathership. It is striking that no deity is called *puia*, which means wife! Some Etruscan divinities, like Ati Catha (Mother Dawn), do not have children. The same goes for Turan Ati (the goddess of love). If a god or goddess has children, it can, almost without exception, be explained by the influence of Greek religion and mythology. One of the earliest examples is offered by a votive inscription on an Attic red-figure kylix by Oltos (*c*.500 BC), which runs: *itun turuce venel atelinas tinas cliniiaras*: 'Venel Atelinas gave this to the Sons of Tin'; these are the Dioskouroi (*TLE* no. 156). About fifty years later, a mirror depicts the battle between Laran and Celsclan (son of Cel). In fact we know from votive bronzes that Cel was venerated as Ati (mother), quite probably as mother goddess of earth. Because Laran looks like the Greek Ares it seems very likely that Celsclan is an Etruscan translation of Gegenes, a son of Ge (Mother Earth) that is, a giant, as Colonna has pointed out (Colonna 1976–7). Another even later example of a mother-son relationship under Greek influence is offered by a mirror from Volterra of about 350 BC showing the adoption of Heracles. The story is explained by an inscription: *eca tva ichnac hercle unial clan thra:sce*: 'this shows how Heracles became son of Uni', or 'Heracles as son of Uni sucked (his mother's breast)' (*TLE* no. 399).[4]

An original native genealogy of Etruscan gods cannot be demonstrated, although there might be one exception. At the end of the second century BC Festus (542, L 359) wrote about the most important prophet of Etruscan theology: *Tages nomine Genii filius nepos Iovis, puer dicitur disciplinam aruspicii dedisse duodecim populis Etruriae*, 'Tages called the son of Genius, grandson of Iupiter, a boy – they say – has given the discipline of foretelling to the twelve peoples of Etruria'. At first sight the statement might be a Roman

invention, because earlier Roman sources like Cicero and Ovid
state that Tages rose (*sponte sua*) from a furrow ploughed by a
peasant.[5] Festus may be using an Etruscan source, certainly if Epiur
on a famous mirror from Vulci at Paris, dated about 330 BC, could
be interpreted as Tages. It would show Hercle as Genius presenting
his son to his father Tin (Zeus). Madame Rebuffat, however,
interprets Epiur as an obsolete form of Greek Euphorion, the
posthumous winged son of Achilles and Helen, who was not beloved by Zeus (Rebuffat-Emmanuel 1973: 521–3).[6] There are three
arguments against this hypothesis: the transition from Euphorion to
Epiur; the absence of Achilles; the presence of Hercle who does not
have a place in the Euphorion myth. Epiur probably is not an
Etruscan word, because the Etruscan ending -ur indicates a plural.
It may be a loanword from Greek. One could conjecture a relation
with the Greek word *epos*, because the Umbrian word *vepur* derives
from *epos*, too. Epiur would mean the Speaking One, the incarnation of revelation (Morandi 1982: 89 1. 41). All written
sources testify that Tages is a teaching *haruspex*. It is quite striking
that a mirror at Hamburg shows Hercle with a baby boy in the
presence of Menrva and Leinth, the personification of Death.[7] That
Death is about to fetch the boy becomes understandable in the light
of Censorinus' statement that Tages died on the day of his birth,
after the revelation of the *ars haruspicina* (Isidorus Etymologiarum
lib. VIII, 9, 34). The lower exergue of the Hamburg mirror shows
Catmithe (Ganymedes), the boy who was beloved by Zeus, so there
may be a congruence between the main scene and exergue. Another
mirror from Vulci presents Hercle lifting up Epiur from the earth,
which may indicate the discovery or the apotheosis of the boy.[8] Of
course the question remains why the Epiur story on the Paris mirror
has been combined with a Trojan story in the lower zone. The
reason is that Tages is related to Tarchon, the founder of Tarquinia
and other Etruscan cities. The famous Pavatarchies mirror from
Tuscania, dated about 300 BC, and a story told by Johannes Lydus
make clear that Tarchon (Tarchunus) found Tages during ploughing (Johannes Laurentius Lydus, *De ostentis*, prooemium, 3). On
the mirror they are flanked by gods, the apolline Rathlth and the
national god Veltune, whom I mentioned above. Pavatachies on the
mirror is a boy, *pava* (cf. Greek *pais*, *paFis*, *paFos*), called Tarchies,
which transcribed in Greek and Latin became Tages by popular
etymology (*Ta ges* = things from earth). Lydus also says that
Tarchon was an associate of Aeneas, as is also told by Virgil.[9] And
in fact a mirror at Cambridge shows the king of Troy, Priam, and
Tarchies or Tarchunus.[10] So both zones on the Epiur mirror have a

common Trojan background. It seems probable, therefore, that Hercle on the Epiur mirror is actually Genius, the father of Tages.

If Epiur does not come from the Greek word *epos*, one might suppose a connection with the Greek adjective *ephorios*, 'a person from the limit', for Tarchon the city founder may have discovered the baby-prophet during the ritual ploughing of a furrow during the foundation of the city of Tarquinia. Curiously enough, Columella (*De re rustica* X, 346) writes: *hinc caput Arcadici nudum cute fertur aselli Tyrrhenus fixisse Tages in limite ruris*, 'hence Tyrrhenian Tages is said to have set up the head of an Arcadian ass-colt at the edge of his fields', which points to a boundary activity. Even Isidorus speaks about a prophecy on the boundary (Isid. *Etym.* lib. 8, 9, 34): *hic* (sc. Tages) *ex oris aruspicinam dictavit, et postea non apparuit*. The words *ex oris* have been considered as corrupt but they are authentic if we assume that the *orae* refer to the *primigenius sulcus*.

From a recent publication by Colonna we know that the Etruscan word *farthan* means 'genius'. We know some examples, for instance *Maris harth sianś* (cf. Marspiter), and *farthan nethunsl*, the Genius of Nethuns according to the Mummy Wrappings. The Etruscans clearly did not know a father of Neptunus, an imported Umbrian divinity, so they invented an abstract anonymous father. Another example in the Mummy Wrappings is *farthan aiseraś seuś* (probably the genius of an underworld goddess). So much for the exceptionally few family ties we can discover.

AUTOGENESIS

There is another story of divine birth in the fourth century BC, about a god who seems to generate and regenerate from death, probably to symbolize the dying and growing of nature. A mirror from Bolsena (now in the British Museum) probably shows three life periods of the god Maris: Mariś *husrnana* (a childish Maris) lifted up by a Menerva *kourotrophos* from a vase; Mariś *halna* (a Maris growing up) on the arm of Amamtunia (the Nurse of Turan); and Mariś *isminthians* (probably a Maris of Death, because this Maris is called after Apollo Smintheus, god contra pestilence or causing death) on the leg of Turms, a god who often has the function of *psychopompos* (Hermansen 1984; van der Meer 1988). That Maris *husrnana* is lifted and not baptized, becomes clear by the fact that the fluted crater at Bolsena had the function of a cinerary urn.

The mirror is a visual rendering of a story told by Aelianus, archpriest at Praeneste, who writes that a certain Mares, the oldest of the Ausonians, a kind of centaur, died three times and lived three times. His longest life lasted 123 years, that is the length of the fifth of the ten Etruscan *saecula*, probably the fourth century BC, the time of our mirror (Censorinus, citing Varro, *De die natali* 17.6). It demonstrates that Maris and Mares go back to a common, probably Italic, myth. Maris certainly was a polyfunctional god, but not of the first rank. He presents himself rather as an assistant of Turan and other gods. His epithets betray this aspect, for instance Maris *tiusta*, which means Maris servant of Tiu/Tiv, the Moon goddess. This combination brings us to the interrelations or networks of divinities, especially in the fourth century BC.

SYSTEMS, CIRCLES AND SPHERES BEFORE *C*.100 BC

Now we turn to the question of whether there might have been any polytheistic systems or structures before 100 BC, which is the date of the Piacenza Liver.

There are some indications that already in the seventh century BC a cluster of gods can be discovered. For clarity's sake, attention should first be paid to a group of bronze mirrors from the fourth century, representing love scenes between Turan and Atunis. One of them, now in Leningrad, shows on the border six floating divinities in a circle. Four of them are indicated by inscriptions: Alpan, Achvisr, Munthch and Mean. Probably there was even a second Munthuch (only the final letters -uch are visible; ES IV, pl. 322). The Leningrad mirror presents part of a circle of gods belonging to the principal divinity of love, Turan. Now it is striking that an inscription (*TLE* no. 29) on the foot of a kylix from Narce, dated in the seventh century BC, mentions not only Turan, or more probably Turanir(ia), but also Achaviŝur, and Ithavuŝva. Unfortunately the text is written without punctuation, so that a translation of the interpretation is a hazardous undertaking. The inscription starts with a question: *ipas'* : *ikam*, that is: 'of' or 'for whom am I'? One would expect the name of the owner. However the long inscription clearly gives instructions to sacrifice to the gods mentioned, judged by imperatives like *ar, nuna*. Turan seems to have been one of the most important gods in the seventh and sixth centuries. Another vase, the famous *bucchero aryballos* Poupée, from the same period, mentions *aisera turannuve*, which means the turan-like goddess or, less probably, goddesses (*TLE* no. 939).[11] There is no doubt that Achaviŝur and Ithavuŝva originally were considered as a collective in view of the endings -ur and -va. So probably Turan-ir or Turan-ir-ia is a plural too. Unfortunately we have no epigraphical representations from the early period, but the mirrors, about three hundred years later, represent Achaviŝur and Ithavuŝva as individual gods. It reminds us of the Jewish name Elohim, which linguistically is a plural, but the bearer in reality was experienced as a single being.

At first sight the goddess Ithavusva in the Narce inscription does not seem to belong to Turan's circle, because a fourth century mirror represents her as a goddess of birth, in this case under the name Ethausva, together with Thanr. That Ethausva belongs in fact to Turan's sphere can be deduced by analogy. Another birth-scene shows Thanr and Thalna in a role comparable with the Greek Eileithuiai. The latter frequently appears in love scenes. Of course one could argue that Ethausva and Thalna are polyfunctional, belonging to the spheres of both love and birth. The latter option may be preferred, because three mirrors of the same size (diam. 18.3 cm), and probably from the same workshop, show, although in changed positions, more or less the same sets of love goddesses, to which Thanr and Thalna belong (fig. 1: ES IV, 1, pl. 324, 324A):

thalana	thanr	alpnu	zipna
zipanu	alpanu	achuvizr	thanr
turan	thanr	thalna	achuvizr

A second circle of gods which has its roots in earlier centuries is formed by visual pairs like Laran–Maris, Maris–Preale, Laran–Letham (ES IV, 1, pl. 284,1 and 284,2; V, 59, pl. 49). Their protective, rather martial function is illustrated by their flanking positions in mirror scenes. They are clearly the local bodyguards of Olympian gods. These combinations of local gods occur two centuries earlier, about 500 BC, in a completely different context, the text of the Capua Tile. This is a ritual calendar of the Icni family, in which gods are listed that had to be worshipped because of deceased forefathers (*apher*; *apa* = father). In lines 18 and 19 successively Larun (probably in April) and Lethams (certainly in May) receive the same kind of sacrifice (*ilucu*). Professor Pallottino has pointed out that the Capua text has much in common with the Roman *parentalia* and *larentalia*, also festivities connected with the ancestral cult. The subordinate position of gods like Laran and Letham makes it very probable that Roman authors reckoned them to be in the category of *Penates* (household gods). Arnobius (*Adv. gentes* 3, 40) quotes four categories: *Penates* of Iupiter, of Neptunus, of the *inferi* (underworld gods) and of mortal men. However strange this late statement may be, it explains that *penates* like Laran and Letham operate both in the upper- and the underworld. The comparison suggests too that the Roman Lar and Etruscan Laran may have a common origin, as has been thought before. The quadripartition of *Penates* can probably also be found in the sixteen-partite-margin of the Piacenza Liver, as we shall see later on.

A third circle of gods, this time related to the cosmic order, is offered by a mirror in the Vatican (Vatican MEG 12645), which shows a conversation between Thesan (Eos), Usil (Sun) and Nethuns, who together symbolize the travelling of the sun during day and night (ES I, pl. 76). Although there is no earlier epigraphic evidence, the terracotta antefixes of temple B at Pyrgi according to von Vacano show successively the series of Phosphoros, Thesan, Usil, Leukothea, Hercle and Nyx, which testify that a cosmic system of divinities existed already about 500 BC in visual arts (von Vacano 1980).

The examples of visual clusters of gods in the fourth century appear to have a tradition of two or even three centuries. Therefore at least between *c*.500 and *c*.300 BC there were small systems, based on concepts of love, birth, protection and light. They testify to some continuity and conservatism in Etruscan religion.

Many inscriptions in the fourth century BC show a linking of gods. There are two forms: 1) the combination of two names, one in the nominative and one in the genitive, for instance Marśhercles. Because Maris is not a son of Hercle, we have to consider him as an assistant. It seems probable that this type of combination is due to Italic or Roman influence. The *Tabulae Iguvinae* afford some parallels, for instance Vesune Puemunes Pupřices (Vesona Pomoni Popdici), interpreted by Pfiffig and others as Vesona, *cultus* partner of the vegetation god Pomonus. It is striking that a similar couple, Vesuna and Fufluns, gods of vegetation and light can be seen on a mirror from Castelgiorgio, a place not far from the border between Umbria and Etruria (ES V, pl.35). Gellius (*Noctes Atticae* 12, 23, 1) gives us a list of similar pairs: for example *moles* Martis, *nerio* Martis, *salacia* Neptuni, which are abstractions, forces of Mars and Neptunus, who later were considered as divine partners (cf. Gellius N.A. 13, 23, 10: *'Nerio' igitur Martis vis et potentia et maiestas quaedam esse Martis demonstratur*).

2) Another form is the name with an epithet, for instance, Maris tiusta, Maris of the Moon. In the light of the foregoing, Maris is to be held as a god dependent on the Moon, active in the sphere of the moon. The same holds good for Tinia *calusna*, a Iupiter active in the reign of Calu, god of the underworld. As far as can be seen the double names never testify opposition. The combinations are homogeneous.

HELLENISTIC PERIOD

The process of clustering gods in verbal or visual pairs based on a common background did not stop after the fourth century BC. Even

in the second century BC examples can be found, like the famous
ex-voto statues from Cortona, dedicated by the same person to
Culsanś and Selanś (Selvans) close to a city gate of Cortona. From
recent studies by Krauskopf and Rix, we know that the word culs-
must mean 'gate'.[12] The surname Tularia of Selvans makes clear
that he also is a divinity of boundaries (De Simone, forthcoming).
Both ex-votos must have been associated by the concept of boundary. And as Heurgon has pointed out, the pair Catha-Pacha (Pacha
= Gr. Bakchos) in inscriptions was born of the coupling of two solar
deities (Heurgon 1957).

These new dyads bring us to the most detailed system in the
Etruscan world, the Bronze Liver of Piacenza. It is a real microcosm, the margin of which reflects the macrocosm, sixteen-partite
heaven, which according to Pliny had four sectors, four very favourable in the north-east and four favourable regions in the south-east,
four terrible in the south-west and four very terrible in the north-
west (figure 2). The four cardinal points are marked by gods, who
are associated with the concept of boundary, Tin (region 16), Tul
(connected with Lvsa in region 4), Selva (in region 8, and Cul
(Culsu, connected with Lvsa in region 12). Even the quadripartite
system of Arnobius' *Penates* is visible. Tin (Iupiter) resides in
region 1, Neth (Neptunus) in region 5, Letham in region 9 and Vetis
in region 13. The Liver does not present a chaotic constellation.
Given the information above, it is easy to see that there are at least
pairs of associated gods: Usil-Tiv, Catha-Fufluns, two couples
which are interrelated because they symbolize the rising of sun and
moon in the east; Mari(s)-Letham, Maris-Hercle, who together
seem to form a trio; Tin-Uni and so on. But most interesting is the
tendency towards hierarchy in the pantheon. Around the north
point, Tin (to be compared with Zeus) occurs three times, although
he has to share his power. He occurs in three regions because he
throws one favourable and two more or less unfavourable types of
lightning (Seneca, QN 11, 41). He shares his power with Nethuns
(1), with Thufltha (16) and with Cilens (15). The last two are both
females. I would suggest that Thufltha, in one votive inscription an
adjective applied to Aisera (which means goddess), is a divinity of
punishment and Cilens one of fate, who can be compared with
Fortuna. There is unfortunately only one representation of Cilens,
dressed in a heavy mantle flanking Mera (Menerva), on a terracotta
slab from a temple of Bolsena, possibly the temple of Nortia,
goddess of Fate. Other representations in the Italic world show
Menerva only in the company of Fortuna, once even with a Fortuna
dressed in a heavy mantle again (Van der Meer 1987, 90–96). If my
interpretation is right, the Liver testifies a tendency notable in the

whole Hellenistic world, the stressing of the force of Tyche/Fortuna, goddess of blind chance.

Another document from the same period, the Mummy Wrappings of Zagreb, clearly shows both the hierarchic phenomenon and the stressing of the idea of fatality. The main gods are Crapsti, Aisera and Nethuns (Pfiffig 1963). If we realize that Crapsti can be a hypostasis of Tin (cf. the Umbrian Iupiter Grabovius), and that Aisera can be an underworld goddess, it is clear that the ritual calendar is dominated by gods similar to the highest ones of the Liver. It is therefore no accident that the formula that 'yearly, monthly and daily sacrifices had to be made at sanctuaries of Cilth, goddess of city and districts' is frequently repeated. If Cilth is identical with Cilens – which seems very likely because of the common root cil- – , the supreme divinity was the goddess of Fate.

Neither Liver nor Mummy Wrappings, as I said before, mentions some famous gods of the archaic and classical periods, like Turan and Menerva. Minor gods take their place, for example Lasa instead of Turan. Because the same process is visible on mirrors of low quality, which after 300 BC generally show only the *Dioscuroi* or a Lasa, we have to conclude that the disappearance of the old aristocratic gods was due to a process not only of *Entmythologisierung* but also of democratisation, including an extra appreciation of the lower gods. But there were ranks and degrees: even Charun got epithets in the second century BC. In the *Tomba dei Caronti* at Tarquinia we see a Charun four times, respectively with the epithets *thune* (the first), *huthis* (the fourth), and *chunchulis*, which refers to the dangerous death god Tuchulcha (Pallottino 1962).

To sum up the results of my enquiry: the Etruscan pantheon originally showed a very loose structure. In the fourth century BC we see societies and pairs of gods, some of whom appeared to have existed already in embryo two or three centuries earlier. The forming of double divine names was probably influenced by Italic and Roman religion. There are no real genealogical ties between the deities, unless they have been influenced by Greek models. About 300 BC a break is visible, probably because of social revolutions which led to a growing influence of a middle class. The old gods of the aristocracy make way for lesser deities. The growing number of dyads results in a very complicated system that was governed by the *modus operandi* of *haruspices*, a microcosm divided into a *pars hostilis* and *pars familiaris*, visible on the Bronze Liver of Piacenza.

NOTES

1. I am indebted to Miss Sheila Girardon and Dr Glenys Lloyd-Morgan for the correction of the English text.
2. The most extensive bibliographies on Etruscan religion are given by Pfiffig (1975) and by van der Meer (1987).
3. Richard (1976): 915–25; about Selvans sanchuneta see Colonna (1966): 165–72.
4. *TLE* no. 399; Florence Museo Naz. Arch. inv. no. 72740.
5. Cicero, *De divinatione* II, 50–51; Ovid *Metamorphoses* XV, 552–59. As for the evaluation of literary sources and the Pavatachies mirror, see Wood (1980): 325–44.
6. I. Mavleev, Epiur, LIMC III, 1 s.v.; de Simone (1968) I, 61, n. 72 suggests a derivation from Gr. *epiouros* (guardian) which does not make sense.
7. Hamburg (Walter Kropatscheck Collection). Hornbostel (1980): 255–6.
8. ES II, pl. 181.
9. Virgil, *Aeneid* 8, 506; 10, 153, 290; 11, 727, 746. About the etymology of *pais* and *puer* see Bonfante (1981): 313–14; M. Talocchini, REE (1978): 343–5 n. 97.
10. Colonna (1980): 161–79; Maggiani (1986) 26 (unpublished inscription on a sors: *aplu.putes/tur.farthns*).
11. M. Pallottino, REE (1958): 235–6; idem, REE (1960): 479–84.
12. I. Krauskopf, Culsans/Culsu, LIMC III, 1 s.v.

REFERENCES

Bonfante, G. (1981). Pais. *Parola del Passato*, 36, 313–14.
Colonna, G. (1966). Selvans sanchuneta. *Studi Etruschi* 34, 165–72.
—(1976–7). La dea etrusca Cel e i santuari dal Trasimeno. *Rivista Storica dell'antichità* 6–7, 45–62.
—(1980) Note di lessico etrusco. *Studi Etruschi* 48: 161–79.
de Simone, C. (1968). *Griechische Entlehnungen im Etruskischen*. Wiesbaden: Harrasowitz.
—(forthcoming). Intervention in *Atti del Secondo Congresso Internazionale Etrusco (Florence 1985)*. Florence: Olschki.
ES = *Etruskische Spiegel*. ed. E. Gerhard.
Hermansen, G. (1984). Mares, Maris, Mars and the archaic gods. *Studi Etruschi* 52, 147–64.
Heurgon, J. (1957). Influences grecques sur la religion étrusque: l'inscription de Laris Pulenas. *Revue des Etudes Latines* 35, 106–26.

Hornbostel, W. (1980). *Aus Gräbern und Heiligtümern*. Mainz am Rhein: von Zabern.

Maggiani, A. (1986). La divination oraculaire en Etrurie. *Caesarodunum* 56: Tours: Université de Tours (CNRS), 1–48.

Morandi, A. (1982) *Epigrafia Italica*. Rome: 'L'Erma' di Bretschneider.

Murray, G. (1935). *Five Stages of Greek Religion*. London: Watts and Co.

Pallottino, M. (1952). Un ideogramma araldico etrusco. *Archeologia Classica* 4, 245–7.

Pfiffig, A. J. (1963). Studien zu den Agramer Mumienbinden. Der etruskische Liber Linteus. *Denkschr. Oest. Ak. der Wiss. phil. hist. Klasse* 81. Graz: Oest. Ak.

—(1975). *Religio etrusca*. Graz: Akad. Druck- und Verlagsanstalt.

Rebuffat-Emmanuel, D. (1973). *Le miroir étrusque*. Rome: École française de Rome.

REE = Rivista di epigrafia etrusca (in *Studi Etruschi*).

Richard, J. C. (1976). Le culte de Sol et les Aurelii à propos de Paul. Fest. p. 22L. *Mélanges J. Heurgon* II, 915–25. Rome: École française de Rome.

Rix, H. (1986). Etruskisch culs* 'Tor' und der Abschnitt VIII 1–2 des Zagraber Liber Linteus. *Vjestnik* 3rd series 19, 17–40.

Sassatelli, G. (1980). Una nuova stele felsinea. *Studi Zuffa* 107–37.

TLE = *Testimonia Linguae Etruscae*, ed. M. Pallottino (1868). Florence: 'La Nuova Italia' Editrice.

Torelli, M. (1977). Il santuario greco di Gravisca. *Parola del Passato* 32, 398–458.

van der Meer, L. B. (1987). *The Bronze Liver of Piacenza*. Amsterdam: J.C. Gieben.

—(forthcoming 1988) Maris' birth, life and death on two Etruscan mirrors. *Bulletin Antieke Beschaving* 63, 115–28.

von Vacano, O. W. (1980) Ueberlegungen zu einer Gruppe von Antefixen aus Pyrgi. Forschungen und Funde. *Festschrift Neutsch.* 463–75. Innsbruck: Verlag des Inst. f. Sprachwiss, der Universität Innsbruck.

Wood, J. R. (1980). The myth of Tages. *Latomus* 39, 325–44.

G. LLOYD-MORGAN

A Mirror for the Goddess: Dedications of Mirrors at some Graeco-Roman Sanctuaries

Although mirrors have been found on prehistoric sites in the Near East and eastern Mediterranean area from the third millennium and earlier,[1] our evidence for their use becomes much more extensive from Greek classical times on. Mirrors have been found in civilian domestic contexts (Maiuri 1932: 252, 260, 350–54, 452, pl.XLVII, XLVIII, LIXB, fig.104, 135–6), in military bases[2] and in funerary deposits.[3] From the early first century AD onwards they have also been found outside the frontiers of the Roman Empire (Lloyd-Morgan 1980: 103–05; Minns 1913: 266, 378, 420, 426, 430). Much less well-known are the mirrors in shrines and sanctuaries dedicated to the major deities and lesser immortals. It is particularly unfortunate that many examples from early excavations, now in museums and other public collections, have no provenance, merely the laconic 'bought in Rome', or 'from Leptis Magna'.

Some precious evidence for gifts of mirrors to shrines and temples can be found in contemporary literature. Lucius Apuleius writes of the Temple of Juno at Samos:

> . . . famous from Antiquity: to reach it, if I remember aright, one must follow the shore for not more than twenty furlongs from the city. The Treasury of the Goddess is extraordinarily rich, containing great quantities of gold and silver plate in the form of platters, mirrors, cups and all manner of utensils . . .
> (*Florida* 15: Teubner II, 19)

Excavations at well-known religious centres can also be fruitful, as for example those carried out at the Sanctuary to Hera and Apollo at Argos. Some thirty-three mirrors in varying states of preservation were identified, one of which was inscribed in an archaic script: 'Aristeia offered me on behalf of Ekethaio' (Waldstein 1905: 264–6, 332 pl.XLVI no.1581). Sadly, the name of the goddess is not given, though there are many other inscriptions and graffiti which make it quite clear that she was the recipient. There is a late sixth-century BC mirror-handle from the *temenos* of the Sanctuary of Hera Limenia at Perachora which does provide us with a good example. The inscription has been translated as recording the gift of the mirror by Chrysanthis to Hera (Payne 1940: 180, pl.80, 13; 1962: 401, pl.170 no.167). Amongst the twenty or so mirrors found during the excavations is an Egyptian one which was dated to about 700 BC with 'earlier and later limits as 750 BC and 650 BC' (Payne 1940: 142–3, pl.46). One face is engraved with a representation of the goddess Mut in a temple, and the surviving hieroglyphics have been read as: 'Lady of Heaven who gives Life, Prosperity and Health . . .'. It seems probable that it was an exotic antique when it was given to the Greek goddess.[4] Not unexpectedly, mirrors have been found at Olympia, where Hera as Mother of the Gods was worshipped in her own temple adjacent to that of Olympian Zeus. These mirrors include not only the usual solid bronze examples, such as might well have been found in daily use, but also tiny votives of sheet metal.

Hera is not the only goddess in the Graeco-Roman pantheon to receive gifts of mirrors. One mirror inscribed to Brauronian Artemis was dedicated by Hipulla and was found within the eponymous Sanctuary at Brauron in Attica (Oberländer 1967: 185, no.273; fig.4 251–2; also 134 no.200, uninscribed). Another, dedicated to Artemis Limnatis, was found at the Temple to Artemis at Triphylia in Elis (Oberländer 1967: 43, 252 no.50, 251 fig.4; also the uninscribed no.57, p.46). There are also several unprovenanced examples to Limnatis[5] and Artemis (Oberländer 1967: 252 and 251, fig.4).

By contrast Athena does not appear to want or need mirrors, if Callimachus, writing in the third century BC, is to be believed: '. . . ὄισετε μηδε κάτοπτρον' – 'bring not, ye companions of the Bath, for Pallas perfume nor alabaster (for Athena loves not mixed unguents), *neither bring ye a mirror*' ('On the Bath of Pallas', *Hymn* V, 1.17; Loeb translation). There is a mirror from Sparta, however, which is thought to date to around the mid-sixth century BC, with an inscription which has been read as a dedication to Athena by Euonyma (Oberländer 1967: 32 no.42, 252, 253, and 250, fig.4).

Two reliefs from Sklavochori near Sparta, which were found in 1803 by George Hamilton Gordon, the fourth earl of Aberdeen, have provided further evidence for the offering of mirrors and other feminine items to a goddess (Walker forthcoming). One relief (BM 1861. 5–23.2, 69 cm × 107 cm) was dedicated by 'Claudia Ageta (daughter) of Antipatros, Priestess', and shows not only a mirror of first-century type with a handle in the form of a Hercules club

(Lloyd-Morgan 1978: 231, 233 n.23; 1982: Group J 44; Craddock 1983: 131–3, pl.XXV, 134 n.16–34), but also two pairs of sandals, a hair-net, combs, strigil, perfume bottles, cosmetics and other items of the *mundus muliebris*. The left-hand border, which is well preserved, shows a tightly packed bundle of laurel leaves with a central binding, paralleled by one seen on the border framing the figures on a pinax from Eleusis and dedicated to the goddesses by Ninnion (NM Athens. Beazley 1941: 4, fig.4). The other relief (BM 1861.5–23.1, 89 cm × 89 cm) was dedicated by 'Anthouse (daughter) of Damainetous, assistant priestess', and like the slab of Claudia Ageta has a make-up box, comb, perfume bottles, sandals and a mirror. It also includes a hair-net and a triangular shaped loin-cloth with ties at the side. There are representations of a spindle wound with thread, and what is probably a short distaff. More interesting, from a ritual viewpoint, is a torch, symbol of Demeter and connected especially with the cult of the Goddess at Eleusis. The representation of a small chest and two vessels in the three surviving corners of the slab could be seen as either representations of items utilised in cult practice, or the objects of everyday use equally appropriate to the use of mortal woman.[6] Further finds from the area since the reliefs were first discovered have revealed inscriptions and votive offerings all dedicated to Demeter and suggest the presence of an important Sanctuary to Eleusinian Demeter at the modern village of Kalyvia. Even though the mirrors themselves, with the other toiletries, have not survived, we have the slabs as precious evidence that during the second century AD at least, it was thought appropriate for this Goddess also to receive the gift of a mirror.

Mirrors are most closely associated with, and are one of the attributes of, Venus/Aphrodite. She is seen, appropriately, in an engraved scene inside the lid of a Greek hinged lid-mirror of the fourth century BC, with a little winged Cupid standing beside her as she dices, or perhaps plays knuckle-bones, with Pan (BM 1888.12–13.1); as a silver statuette from the Kaiser Augst Treasure dated to the first half of the fourth century AD, with a mirror in her right hand and a lock of gilded hair in her left (Augst, Museum Augusta Raurica, 62.52, ht 12.7 cm: Laur Belart 1963: 33, fig.23, no.23); on mosaics as far apart as those from the wine-bar of Alexander Helix at Ostia (Reg.IV, Is.VII: Becatti 1953: 205 no.391, pl.CXII), the Roman Villa at Rudston, Yorkshire (Richmond 1933: 4–5, fig.1 – now in Hull); and in other major fields of the arts as well as in miniature. Cupid/Eros, as son of the goddess, can be found as one of her attendants – as in the Ostia mosaic noted above, or holding up a mirror for her as she arranges her hair.[7] Sometimes other attendants associated with her carry a mirror, perhaps typified by a delicate, almost androgynous, statuette of a Ganymede (?), now in the British Museum (BM 1848.8–3.44; Lloyd-Morgan 1974: 85–6). The evidence from paintings, sculpture and figurines is complemented by the literature. Indeed, the very act of dedicating a mirror at a temple to one of the deities is nicely represented amongst the dedicatory epigrams of the *Palatine Anthology*. The most famous one is upon the dedication by the celebrated courtesan Laïs of her mirror to Aphrodite, the best example being attributed to Plato and probably dating to the Hellenistic period.

> I, Laïs, whose haughty beauty made mock of Greece
> I who once had a swarm of young lovers at my doors
> dedicate my mirror to Aphrodite,
> since I wish not to look on myself as I am
> and cannot look on myself as I once was.
> (*Palatine Anthology* 6:1, Loeb edn)

There are three other exercises on the same theme by Julianus, but these do not have quite the same impact or elegant economy of words (*Palatine Anthology* 6:18, 19, 20). Two other verses, whether they are literary exercises or not, list the items that Nicias 'past her fiftieth year', and Calliclea respectively dedicate to Cypris/Aphrodite (*Palatine Anthology* 6:210, 211). These items include not only a bronze mirror, but also other things such as sandals, anklet, hairnet, comb and bosom-band, echoing some of the gifts so carefully depicted on the two relief slabs noted above from the Shrine of Demeter, now in the British Museum.

Other companions of Venus/Aphrodite also appear on, or with, mirrors. A tiny lead model of a mirror now in the Römische-Germanisches Zentral Museum, Mainz (0.16490, ht 5.5 cm, said to be from west Hungary) is decorated in low relief on the reverse with the Three Graces. It may well have been a votive offered to the goddess or the Graces themselves as a humble gift. Similarly, a Nymphaeum at Saladinovo, southern Russia on the Black Sea, dated to between the second and fourth centuries AD, yielded not only several reliefs of three nymphs – one may show one of them carrying a mirror – but also three small lead mirrors each bearing a retrograde votive inscription on the reverse in three lines (figure 1. Dobrusky 1897: 12, figs.1–3; Hoddinott 1975: 196 pl.125).

Turning to Italy, the evidence for the early periods is not so clear as that found in the archaic and later levels of the Greek sanctuaries. The celebrated Sanctuary of Diana at Nemi, however, has produced fragments of mirrors which are now in the Villa Giulia Museum at Rome; and from excavations in the 1880's there is an

Etruscan mirror-handle of the well-known third-century BC type
with stylised animal's head terminal and stylised acanthus leaves in
the upper section (MacCormick and Blagg 1983: 56, no. N647,
fig.11; compare *CSE* Italia 1,1, Bologna, 445 no.22). It is also
interesting to note that Lake Nemi, on the shores of which the
sanctuary was situated, was named in Roman times 'Speculum
Dianae' – 'the Mirror of Diana' – confirming once again that, like
Greek Artemis in her various aspects, so too Diana in Italy,
especially at Nemi, could properly be gifted with mirrors for her use
and adornment.

Although no mirrors have yet been found in Etruscan shrines and
temples,[8] there are engraved bronze mirrors showing domestic
scenes where goddesses and immortal ladies use them (for example,
Thetis adjusting her hair in a mirror which shows her reflection: *ES*
5, 123, p.96). An engraved scene on a rectangular bronze cista from
Praeneste, now in the Villa Giulia but formerly in the Barberini
Collection, shows two winged deities, often loosely referred to as
Lasas, at their toilette. The one on the left holds a hand-mirror,
which shows her own reflection, despite the distracting attentions of
a satyr who hides beneath the huge basin on an ornamental stand,
whilst her clothed sister watches. A fourth to third century date is
suggested (Giglioli 1935: 54, pl.CCXCV).

France, and especially Provence and the southern Rhône valley,
has been especially rich in finds of mirrors of the Roman Imperial
period (for example, the extensive finds of mirrors from Vaison-la-
Romaine suggest something of the extent of production and exchange – Sautel 1926: II, 296–311 – but not all sites have yielded up

Figure 1 Lead votive mirror from the Nymphaeum at Saladinovo,
S. Russia: reverse side with inscription (after Dobrusky 1897 fig.3)

quite so many well-preserved examples). Some of the heavier Hellenistic mirrors have also been found within the region (for example, Nîmes, Musée Archéologique 007.2.45; Orange Museum, unnumbered and incomplete lid-mirror on display in March 1972), a legacy perhaps of the long-standing trade connections with Greece from the time of colonisation, if not before. It should not be surprising, therefore, to learn that a modest series of square lead frames for glass mirrors of the Roman Imperial period have been found in southern France, with dedicatory inscriptions as an integral part of the decoration, in similar fashion to the Saladinovo finds noted above. These inscriptions are also in Greek, some referring to Selene and others to Aphrodite (figure 2; Barruol 1985).

Thus from inscribed mirrors, finds from shrines and sanctuaries of deities, as well as representations in art and literary references, it can be seen that there is a useful body of evidence for gifts to divine ladies and their general association with mirrors. This can be used to help with the interpretation of other finds. One relatively straightforward example from France is the hoard of silver found near the village of Notre-Dame-d'Alençon (Maine-et-Loire) in 1836. This consisted mainly of silver vessels and at least two mirror discs (Barratte 1981: 70–71, no.39, pl.XXXa – inv. Bj2064, d.12.3 cm;

Figure 2 Lead frame for glass mirror with dedicatory inscription to Selene found at Saint-Come-et-Maruejols (Gard) (after Barruol 1985 fig.1) twice life size.

71–2, no.40, pl.XXXb – inv. Bj36, d.14.6 cm), with two supports that may have belonged to the mirrors (Barratte 1981: 70, no.37, pl.XXIXf – inv. Bj2069; no.38, pl.XXIXg – inv. Bj2066). Graffiti on some of the vessels and the smaller mirror disc give the name of the dedicatee as the goddess Minerva. Presumably, as with the dedication of the mirror to Athene at Sparta mentioned above, she was seen as a less war-like, more feminine goddess than the Pallas Athene of the Callimachus Hymn, and possibly in this instance had been equated with a native deity. No other legible names have been read other than those of the donors.

Another hoard found slightly earlier, at Backworth in Northumbria in 1812, was partly dispersed, but at present consists of a collection of jewellery, five gold rings, one silver ring, two gold chains, one gold bracelet, one pair of silver gilt fibulae, three silver spoons and about two hundred and eighty coins. These last suggest that the date of deposit of the hoard should be around AD140. The coins and jewellery were packed into a silver patera with an inscription on the handle which has been read as 'To the Mothers (given by) Fabius Dubitatus'. The disc of a silver hand-mirror, sadly damaged, probably datable to the first century AD, had been used as a makeshift lid when the hoard was buried (Hawkins 1851: BM 1850, 6 – 1.2, d.13 cm.). Although only one item has survived with a dedicatory inscription, as with the Notre-Dame-d'Alençon hoard it seems highly likely, as indeed Hawkins suggested when he published the collection, that jewellery, coins and mirror as well as the patera itself were all originally dedicated to the Mother Goddesses.

Thus apart from one anomalous dedication by a certain Polyxena of a mirror to 'Zeus and Kremata' at Dodona (Oberländer 1967: 139 no.219, no.12 fig.4; 250, 253),[9] it appears that virtually all mirrors were gifted to goddesses, whether they belonged to the Graeco-Roman pantheon and were honoured at major sanctuaries; or whether they were local deities assimilated into that pantheon in the smaller shrines of far-flung provinces of the Roman Empire. It follows therefore, that where we have offerings of mirrors in temples and other holy places, we may expect to find a goddess, either as the chief object of devotion or playing a subsidiary role as consort, sister, or companion to a male deity. These dedications can be found in sanctuaries such as the one in Kopilovtsi near Pautalia in Bulgaria, where lead mirror-frames are reported to have been found (Hoddinott 1975: 182 n.34); or the highly important sanctuaries of Möhn (Hettner 1901: 21, no.3, 4, fig.IV.79) and Dhronecken near Trier (Hettner 1901: 48–9, no.16–22, fig.V.15–18 and 12–14). In Britain, excavations at Collyweston Great Wood, Northamptonshire, produced foundations of two polygonal Celtic temples with an incomplete first-century hand-mirror disc within the area of the *temenos*, thus suggesting the presence of a goddess (Knocker 1965: fig.12). Similarly, excavations in the Iron Age and Roman temple at Hayling Island, Hampshire, yielded not only jewellery and other feminine knick-knacks which would have been offered by female votaries, but also mirror fragments. This suggests that even if the principal deity was male, as witnessed by chariot equipment and weaponry in the Iron Age phase, a goddess companion was also present (Downey 1978: 86–7; Downey *et al*. in Rodwell 1980: 290, 293).

Mirrors at sanctuaries and holy places were not only tokens of gratitude for favours received. We have one precious record in Pausanias of a mirror being used for divination at the Sanctuary of Demeter at Achaia.

> There was a spring that was an infallible oracle not for all purposes but for the sick. They tie a mirror on to some thin kind of cord, and balance it so as not to dip it into the spring, but let the surface of the mirror just touch lightly on the water. Then they pray to the Goddess and burn incense and look into the mirror, and it shows them the sick man either alive or dead. The water is as truthful as that. (VII, 21.4–6. See also Delatte 1932.)

Mirrors could have a more sinister side when used for fortune-telling or magic. Apuleius, who wrote the *Florida* and the better known *Golden Ass*, had to defend himself at Sabratha in AD157, not only on the suspicion that he had enticed Aemilia Pudentilla, a wealthy widow into marriage, and causing the death of his stepson and former pupil Pontianus, but also having a mirror for magical purposes (*Apologia* 13–16). By his wit and eloquence he cleared his name and reputation, but the suspicion that mirrors were dangerous implements, not to mention a device of the devil, lingers on powerfully in the writings of some of the early Church Fathers. Tertullian's *de Cultu Feminarum* I.1.3 sees them as an incitement to licentiousness. There are medieval representations of the Whore of Babylon of Revelations 17, 18, showing her combing her hair and holding a mirror in a wicked, luxurious manner, very much after the style of Venus seen in Classical art: an especially fine example is found in the Tapestry of the Apocalypse ordered by Louis I of Anjou from Nicholas Bataille of Paris, from the designs of Hennequin of Bruges and woven between 1375 and 1380, now in the Château d'Angers (Maine-et-Loire). It is pleasant to report, therefore, that in AD 625 Pope Boniface, when writing to the Christian queen Aethelburga, wife of Aedwin of Northumbria, sent not only his blessings but also 'a mirror of silver and an ivory comb inlaid with gold . . . and we pray your highness to accept this gift in that same spirit of loving kindness as it has been sent by us . . .' (Bede, *History* 2, XI).

Although the drift towards pantheism in the later Roman Empire saw various gods being depicted with a multiplicity of attributes other than their own (Weisshäupl 1910), it is Venus in all her aspects who is the one deity associated primarily with the mirror (for example, bronze no.829 in the British Museum: Venus adjusting her sandal and leaning on a trellis supporting a variety of attributes, with Cupid holding a mirror; Weisshäupl 1910: 193, pl.109–11). Even in the ostensibly Christian court of Honorius, Claudianus could still (in AD 398) write the Epithalamium for the wedding of the Emperor to Maria, daughter of Stilicho, and make reference to the goddess:

Venus was on her throne having her hair combed
. . . Her face eagerly sought the mirror's opinion
that image was reflected by the palace walls
and where ever she looked she was pleased by the sight . . .
        Epithalamium of Honorius and Maria, ll.97–8, 105–08

NOTES

1. Mellaart 1965: 88, pl.54 notes finds of obsidian mirrors from some of the richer female burials at Çatal Hüyük with dates around 6000 BC; Clarke and Piggott 1965/1970: 204–05, fig.58 illustrate one of the Royal Tombs at Alaça Hüyük dated *c*. 2400–2200 BC with a 'copper mirror'; Lilyquist 1979 gives evidence for metal mirrors of copper or copper alloy which appear consistently from the third millennium BC onwards, some of which might be as early as the First Dynasty.
2. For example, a number of fragments of Roman mirrors of the first century AD have been found within the *castra* at Chester: Lloyd-Morgan 1977: 51, no.1,2; 52, no.5, pl.4; nos.6, 9, 11. Juvenal (*Satires* II.99–109) suggests that on campaign during the Civil Wars of AD 69, Otho carried and used a mirror as part of his military equipment.
3. Smetius 1678: 118 is the earliest description of modern times of the find of a mirror in a Roman burial, in this instance found in a sarcophagus at Nijmegen, NL, on 13 February 1645. Simonett 1941 also records a number of mirrors found in the following cemeteries; Muralto Passalli, Grave 4; Villa Liverpool (unter) Grave 12, Grave 24; Muralto Branca, Grave 2; Minusio Cadra, Grave 15.
4. For a discussion of dedications of mirrors to Egyptian god-

desses see Husson 1977. Witt 1971:63 mentions a relief of Tiberius in the *abaton* at Philae dedicating a *sistrum*, mirrors, and breast amulet to Isis. Whereas the Greeks and Romans tend to make an offering of a single mirror, some reliefs from Egypt show pairs of mirrors being offered to the Divinity.

5. Oberländer 1967: 13, no.12, 252, 251 fig.4 – National Museum, Athens no.16508; 44, no.52, 252, 250 fig.4 – Staatliche Antikensammlung, Munich no.3644. Farnell 1896: II 427, 558 n.1 and 2 notes that Artemis was worshipped as Limnatis and Limnaia in Arcadia, Laconia and Sicyon. An uninscribed mirror-handle was also found at the Sanctuary of Artemis Limnatis on Taigetos: Oberländer 1967: 32, no.40.

6. After her wanderings following the abduction of Persephone, Demeter became nurse to Demophoon, the young son of King Keleos of Eleusis and his wife Metaneira, who had presumed her to be a mortal woman. This willingness of deities to appear in mortal guise, as witnessed by other stories, including that of Venus/Aphrodite's love affair with Anchises and the birth of the hero Aeneas, blurred the distinction between the sacred and the mundane and provided the background against which it was acceptable to make gifts of a personal and domestic nature to a goddess, as for example a loin-cloth for Demeter, or the new robe for Pallas Athene presented to her during the Great Panathenaea celebrated every four years at Athens.

7. Callimachus, *Hymn* V 'On the Bath of Pallas', 21–2: 'But Cypris took the shining bronze and often altered and again altered the same lock'. Compare the terracotta group from Myrina now in the Louvre, no. MYR 46: Pottier and Reinach 1887: 302–03, no.46, pl.VII,2.

8. I am most grateful to Dr L. Bouke van der Meer for confirmation of my own unvoiced conclusions during the conference. There are no mirrors mentioned amongst the finds described in Colonna's catalogue (Colonna 1985).

9. Oberländer obviously finds this dedication curious and suggests that it was intended for another deity, presumably feminine, who was also worshipped within the Sanctuary. The only candidate would appear to be Dione: Rose 1928/1965: 53; Parke 1967: 22.

I am most grateful to Dr Glenys Davies for her original invitation to give a paper at the Conference, and for suggesting that something on mirrors would be appropriate. It has given me the opportunity to explore one of the aspects of the use of mirrors which had been somewhat neglected since the completion of my doctoral thesis on Roman Mirrors in 1977. The facilities of the Library of the Hellenic and Roman Societies in

London, and help from friends and colleagues in the British Museum have been much appreciated during the preparation and revision of this paper. I am also most grateful to the staff of the Museum at Olympia for allowing me at very short notice to inspect some of their unpublished material held in the reserve collection (during my visit in 1969), to Dr Susan Walker of the British Museum for the gift of a copy of her forthcoming article, and to Michel Feugère of Montagnac (Hérault) for his help and information on mirrors in French collections. The active help and support of friends, colleagues and family over the years are also most gratefully acknowledged.

REFERENCES

Barratte, François (1981). *Le Trésor d'Argenterie gallo-romaine de Notre-Dame-d'Alençon (Maine et Loire)*. Gallia supplement no.40. Paris: Editions du CNRS.

Barruol, Guy (1985). Mirroirs votifs découverts en Provence et dédiés à Sélène et à Aphrodite. *Révue Archéologique de Narbonnaise* 18, 343–73.

Beazley, J. D. (1941). Bakchos Rings. *Numismatic Chronicle* ser. 6,1, 1–7.

Becatti, G. (1953). *Scavi di Ostia vol. IV: Mosaici e Pavimenti Marmorei*. Rome: Istituto Poligrafico dello Stato.

Clarke, Grahame and Stuart Piggott (1965 and 1970). *Prehistoric Societies*. London and Harmondsworth: Penguin.

Colonna, Giovanni (1985). *Santuari d'Etruria*. Catalogue of the Exhibition held at the Museo Archeologico C. Cilnio Mecenate, 19 May–20 October 1985.

Craddock, P. T. (1983). A Roman Silver Mirror 'discovered' in the British Museum: a Note on its Composition. *Antiquaries Journal* 63, 1, 131–32.

CSE = *Corpus Speculorum Etruscorum*.

Delatte, A. (1932). *La catoptromancie Grecque et ses dérivés*. Liège, Paris: Bibliothèque de la Faculté de Philosophie et Lettres de l'Université de Liège.

Downey, R. with A. King and G. Soffe (1978) The Roman Temple at Hayling Island. *Current Archaeology* 62,vi, 3 June 83–7.

— (1980) The Hayling Island Temple and Religious Connections across the Channel, in Rodwell (1980).

Dobrusky, V. (1897). Inscriptions et monuments figurés de la Thrace. Trouvailles de Saladinovo (1). *Bulletin de Correspondence Hellenique* 21, 119–40.

ES = *Etruskische Spiegel*, ed. E. Gerhard, A Klügmann and G. Körte, 1884–1897. Berlin: Georg Reimer.

Farnell, L. R. (1896). *The Cults of the Greek States* II. Oxford: Oxford University Press.

Giglioli, G. Q. (1935). *L'Arte Etrusca*. Milan: SA Fratelli Treves Editori.

Hettner, F. (1901) *Drei Tempelbezirke im Trevererlande*. Trier.

Hoddinott, R. F. (1975). *Bulgaria in Antiquity. An Archaeological Introduction*. London: Ernest Benn Ltd.

Husson, Constance (1977). *L'offrande du miroir dans les temples égyptiens de l'époque Gréco-Romaine*. Lyons: Audin.

Knocker, Group Capt. Guy (1965). Excavations in Collyweston Great Wood, Northamptonshire (TL 005 013). *Archaeological Journal* 122, 52–72.

Laur-Belart, R. (1963). *Der spätrömische Silberschatz von Kaiser Augst* (2nd. edn) Aargau.

Lilyquist, Christine (1979). *Ancient Egyptian Mirrors from the Earliest Times through the Middle Kindgom. Münchner Ägyptologischer Studien* 27.

Lloyd-Morgan, G. (1974). A Bronze Statuette from London Bridge. *Antiquaries Journal* 54, 1, 85–6.

— (1977). Mirrors in Roman Chester. *Journal of the Chester Archaeological Society* 60, 49–55.

— (1978). The Antecedents and Development of the Roman Hand Mirror. ed. H. McK. Blake, T. W. Potter and D. B. Whitehouse, *Papers in Italian Archaeology* I BAR Suppl. Series 41, 227–35.

— (1980). Roman Mirrors and Pictish Symbol. A note on Trade and Contact, ed. W. S. Hanson and L. J. F. Keppie, *Roman Frontier Studies 1979*. BAR International Series 71, 97–106.

— (1982). The Roman Mirror and its Origins. Nancy T. de Grummond (ed.), *A Guide to Etruscan Mirrors*. Tallahassee, Florida: Archaeological News Inc., 39–48.

MacCormick, A. G. and T. F. C. Blagg (1983). *Mysteries of Diana. The Antiquities from Nemi in Nottingham Museums*. Nottingham: Castle Museum, Nottingham.

Maiuri, A. (1932). *La Casa del Menandro e il suo Tesoro di Argenteria*. Rome.

Mellaart, James (1965). *Earliest Civilisations of the Near East*. London: Thames and Hudson.

Minns, Ellis H. (1913). *Scythians and Greeks*. Cambridge: Cambridge University Press.

Oberländer, Petra. (1967). Griechische Handspiegel. Unpublished doctoral dissertation, University of Hamburg.

Parke, H. W. (1967). *Greek Oracles*. London: Hutchinson University Library.

Payne, Humfry (1940/1962). *Perachora. The Sanctuaries of*

Hera Akraia and Limenia. Excavations of the British School at Athens 1930–1933 I and II. Oxford: Clarendon Press.

Pottier, E. and S. Reinach, (1887). *La Nécropole de Myrina.* École Française d'Athènes. Paris: Ernest Thorin.

Richmond, I. A. (1933). *The Roman Pavements at Rudston.* Leeds: Roman Malton and District Committee Report no.6 Rudston Excavation Committee and Yorkshire Archaeological Society.

Rodwell, Warwick ed. (1980). *Temples, Churches and Religion: Recent Research in Roman Britain.* BAR British Series 77, 289–304.

Rose, H. J. (1928/1958). *A Handbook of Greek Mythology.* London: Methuen.

Sautel, J. (1926). *Vaison dans l'Antiquité.* Lyons.

Simonett, Christoph (1941). *Tessiner Gräberfelder.* Basel.

Smetius, Johannes, pater et filius. (1678). *Antiquitates Neomagenses.* Ex Typographeia Regnem Smetii.

Waldstein, Charles (1905). *The Argive Heraeum.* II The Bronzes, Section 6: Mirrors and Mirror Handles. Boston and New York: Houghton, Mifflin and Co.

Walker, Susan (forthcoming, 1989). Two Spartan Women and the Eleusinion, ed. S. Walker and A. Cameron, *The Greek Renaissance in the Roman Empire.* Bulletin of the Institute of Classical Studies, London.

Weisshäupl, R. (1910). Pantheistische Denkmäler. *Jahreshefte des Österreichischen Archäologischen Institutes in Wien* 13, 170–99.

Witt, R. E. (1971) *Isis in the Graeco-Roman World.* London: Thames and Hudson.

HILDA ELLIS DAVIDSON

Hooded Men in Celtic and Germanic Tradition

The group of supernatural beings discussed here would presumably be included by Dumézil among the deities of the third function, those concerned with the earth, the maintenance of well-being among animals and men, fertility and health. While there are difficulties in applying Dumézil's theories about the gods of the first two functions to Germanic and Celtic religion, there are none about the third. The Scandinavians themselves realised it when they referred to the Vanir as opposed to the Æsir; while the Æsir were gods of sovereignty, magic and warfare, the Vanir were the fertility deities of the earth, with the gods Freyr and Njord and the goddesses Freyja and Frigg as the main powers, but a host of other lesser beings as well. Sometimes in the Edda poems the formula 'Æsir and Elves' is used to make the distinction. I want now to single out from this group the beings who came into close contact with men and women as protectors and helpers, and with whom a contract might be made. There is evidence for such cults among the continental Germans and the peoples of Scandinavia and Iceland in the pagan period, and I believe that we have a valuable series of actual pictures of such beings among the Celtic peoples of the British Isles during the period of Roman rule.

Some indication of the relationship between human families and supernatural guardian spirits is indicated in the records of the first settlers in Iceland before the formal acceptance of the Christian religion, about the year AD 1000. Some brief accounts are included in *Landnámabók*, the record of the settlement, which was an attempt to preserve what was remembered about the first families which took land there for the benefit of their descendants. Although these were not recorded until well after the Christian church was established, they have not been deliberately composed for entertainment or propaganda purposes, nor put to artistic use like some of the supernatural material in the Icelandic Sagas. The men who set up the remarkable Icelandic Commonwealth in the late 9th century, without king or single ruler of any kind, were immensely proud of their origins. They came mostly from western Norway, but also from other parts of Scandinavia and from settlements in the Celtic West, and only a small number were Christians, so that no early church was established in Iceland.

Their religious organisation was carefully and deliberately set up, based on the worship of the great gods Odin, Thor and Freyr, and since Iceland was an empty island when they arrived, there were no complications caused by contact with native cults. Among the supernatural beings whom they evidently felt to be important were those to whom they gave the general name of land-spirits (*land-vættir*). A wealth of folk-tales from Norway and Denmark show that these were important in Scandinavia also, and such tales continued to be told long after the coming of Christianity. It does not seem that such beings were ever visualised as coming with the settlers to Iceland; although they brought the cults of the main gods with them from their homeland, the spirits apparently belonged to the land itself. Nor can they be identified in this case with the ancestral dead, since it was some time before family graves were established in

Figure 1 Carved stone from Housesteads, 42 cm high by 49 cm
wide (drawing by Eileen Aldworth).

Iceland, and the land-spirits are sometimes represented as dwelling in wild and desolate places as well as near human habitations.

A typical tale is that of a family of brothers who soon after their arrival lost most of their livestock, painstakingly brought over in their ships, from a sudden flow of lava (*Landnámabók* S. 329, H. 284 pp. 330–31). Then one of them, Bjorn, dreamed that a spirit, here called a rock-dweller (*bergbúi*) came to him and offered to enter into partnership with him, to which he agreed. His small surviving herd of goats was joined by a strange he-goat, and from that time its numbers rapidly increased, until he was doing so well with his animals that he became known as Goat-Bjorn. It is said that those possessed of second sight could see the land-spirits following him to the Assembly, evidently to bring him good luck there, for representation in the Thing or Assembly was of primary importance to the Icelanders, and the gods were said to preside over it. The land-spirits could also be seen following his two brothers when they went out hunting or fishing. There were distinguished men among Bjorn's descendants, including bishops and lawmen, but it was evidently felt that there was nothing shameful in his relationship with the land-spirits in the period before the Conversion. It may also be worth noting that one of the few Christian settlers, a certain Asolf, who was unpopular because he refused to live with non-Christian men and finally became an anchorite, was driven out of a district more than once because he had such outstanding luck with his fishing (*Landnámabók* S. 24, H. 21, pp. 62–3). The implication appears to be that he was felt to be setting up in competition with the land-spirits whom he refused to recognise.

The link made with such supernatural beings is described as a partnership. Another settler, one Thorstein Rednose, seems to have had a similar relationship with a spirit dwelling in a waterfall, and as a result prospered with his sheep-rearing. He threw offerings of food into the waterfall, and in return he was enabled to make a wise decision as to how many sheep should be kept through the winter, so that his flock increased greatly (*Landnámabók* S. 355, H. 313, p. 328). But one autumn, when he was asked how many should be slaughtered, he replied that it did not matter; the sheep were doomed and so was he. On his death soon afterwards the flock rushed into the waterfall and was destroyed; the partnership was at an end. Another man had a guardian spirit living in a great stone near his house. This spirit is given two different names in versions of the tale in two short sagas dealing with the conversion of Iceland;[1] in one he is called *ármaðr*, meaning something like 'harvest-man', and in the other *spámaðr*, the term used for someone able to foretell the future. These two words cover the two main aspects of

Figure 2 Relief in Corinium Museum, showing hooded figures
with a seated goddess (drawing by Eileen Aldworth).

the land-spirits very well, since they are represented as aiding the
farmers and bringing good harvests, and also giving good advice
concerning the future, apparently by means of dreams. Of the spirit
in the stone the farmer declared: 'He tells me beforehand many
things that will happen in the future; he guards my cattle and gives
me warning of what to do and what to avoid, and therefore I have
faith in him, and I have worshipped him for a long while.' This spirit
and his children, sad to relate, were ruthlessly driven out by the
bishop with prayers and holy water, but the farmer clearly regretted
his departure.

We have a good deal of information about another helpful spirit,
again called a rock-dweller and also the god (*Áss*) of Snæfell, a

mountain in western Iceland. There is a whole saga about this being (*Barðar Saga Snæfellsáss*), telling how he helped the local people in various ways. He protected them from evil spirits and hostile trolls, saving one man from death at sea, assisting another in a wrestling match, and so on, and he is called *heitguð*, a god to whom vows were made. In the saga he begins as a human boy who was fostered by Dofri, a similar mountain spirit in Dovre Fjeld in Norway whom Ibsen introduced into *Peer Gynt*, but he later went out to Iceland and retired to live in the mountains away from men. However the saga is late and confused, and this would seem to be a rationalisation of local mountain folklore similar to the Norwegian tradition concerning a mountain giant. Of special interest is Bard's practice of fostering children; he would invite promising youths to spend a winter with him in his cave on Snæfell and teach them law and genealogies, while one of his nine daughters took the young visitor as her lover. One boy fostered in this way, called Odd, afterwards became a famous lawman. Bard had his human friends with whom he too seems to have entered into partnership: 'All his friends called on him if they were placed in any need', we are told (6, 15). More than once his appearance is described in detail (8; 9; 10). He wore a grey cloak and hood, with a belt of walrus-hide round his waist; he walked with a long staff like a shepherd's crook, with a two-pronged handle and a spiked tip to help him across the glacier. When the boy Odd went to visit him, he was caught in a snowstorm on the mountain and could not see his way, but suddenly a hooded figure appeared through the gloom, and Bard led him to his cave. Here such a hooded being acts as guardian and protector to men; he is called a god, but is certainly not a major one. He associates with all kinds of spirits, both helpful and destructive, and wins general respect from them for his strength and power.

Bard teaches law, and the land-spirits are represented as supporters of the established legal system. For instance in *Egils Saga* (57) when the hero Egill went to Norway to claim his wife's estate and was given a hostile reception by King Erik Bloodaxe, the king put an end to the hearing by cutting the ropes enclosing the court in a high-handed manner. This was a crime against the gods, since the court of law was a hallowed place, and Egill retaliated by raising a horse's head on a pole against the king and uttering a curse against him. This is preserved in two verses quoted in the saga which appear to be genuine early material (Almqvist 1965: 89). In one verse he appeals to Odin, Freyr and Njord against the king, two of them Vanir deities, and in the other to the Land Elf and the land-spirits dwelling in the land, declaring that they must wander restlessly up and down and not return to their homes until Erik and his queen are driven out from Norway; this in fact took place when Erik was forced to leave and move to York. It seems also that the land-spirits might protect the people of the land against enemy attack. Snorri Sturlusson has a tale about a wizard sent by the Danish king to Iceland in the form of a whale to see how strong the island defences were, and he found all the land-spirits, small and great, crowding the hills and mounds and on the alert (Almqvist 1965: 119–). Later Scandinavian folk-tales support this. A Danish story from the island of Bornholm tells how in 1645 the Swedes sent two ships to invade the island, when there was only one old soldier on guard (Thiele 1843: II, 194). There was no time to summon reinforcements, but suddenly he heard little whispering voices prompting him to 'Load and shoot!', 'Load and shoot!' and so he did. Then he saw scores of little men in red caps also shooting at the invaders, who retreated to their ships. These are the Danish Underground People, who wear red caps instead of hoods, but inhabit mounds and hillocks and are clearly linked with the land-spirits of Iceland. Although the Vanir deities stood for peace and plenty, and places sacred to them had to be kept free from bloodshed and violence, their symbols might be set on defensive weapons such as shields and helmets, since they could protect men in war as well as in times of peace. An obvious example is the boar, sacred to Freyr and Freyja.

We have only occasional hints in Icelandic literature of what such beings looked like when they appeared to men with second sight or in dreams, but there is a series of carvings from an earlier period, set up in Roman Britain, which I believe give us some indication of the way in which people pictured them. Jocelyn Toynbee made a detailed study of such figures, and published a paper on them in 1957 (Toynbee 1957) and since then a number of further carvings have been discovered. Most of the evidence comes from the two areas of the Roman Wall and the Cotswolds. Two years earlier, Waldemar Deonna had published an important article on the significance of the hooded cloak, as worn by gods, genii and demons (Deonna 1955). The hood or cowl shading the face was a practical garment in northern Europe and the Mediterranean area in Roman times, since it served as shelter against both cold and heat, and gave protection from rain and wind. It was worn by humble folk working out of doors, such as farm labourers, hunters and artisans, by those working underground, by travellers, and those of a more exalted class who desired to go unrecognised, often during the hours of darkness. The Latin name for such a garment was *cucullus*. The cloak came to have a symbolic significance, since it concealed the identity and marked off the wearer from his fellows: Deonna gives as examples the cowl of the monk, the hooded cloaks worn by mourners at funerals, and the long veil concealing the bride. In the religious iconography of south-eastern Europe the cloak is often used to indicate a being from another world, as for instance in representations of the Thracian Rider, shown on horseback with his cloak streaming behind him. The hooded cloak also suggests an unseen or disguised presence. The god Odin in the Viking Age was often said to wear a cloak as he wandered among men. In the saga literature he usually has a broad-brimmed hat instead of a hood, which would serve the same purpose of rendering him unrecognisable. It is possible however that Old Carl Hood, the evil old man in the ballad 'Earl Brand' who informs on the lovers and causes many deaths, is based on memories of Odin as a sinister hooded stranger.[2]

In Roman Britain, as in other provinces of the Empire, the Romans brought in the fashion of depicting deities in human form. Much of our knowledge of Celtic and Germanic religion is due to the attempts to portray local deities in Roman style, sometimes identifying them with a Roman god but retaining the native name or title. Among the well-known deities such as Mars or Apollo there are carvings also on small votive stones of male figures wearing hooded cloaks; some are of adult proportions and may be bearded, while others resemble children or dwarfish beings. Jocelyn Toynbee believed all these to be male, although when the cloaks go down to their feet and hoods frame their faces it is sometimes hard to be certain. The figures in Britain are usually in sets of three, while on the continent they appear as single individuals.[3] The significance of the hood is borne out by dedications on two altars from Wabelsdorf in Carinthia to the *genius cucullatus* or hooded spirit (incidentally in the masculine gender), and this is the name by which such figures are now known.

Jocelyn Toynbee's list of the examples known in 1957 consists of eleven stone carvings, mostly votive tablets; one small free-standing figure in sandstone; one pottery figurine; one carved in jet but incomplete; and some small hooded figures in a hunting scene on fragments of a beaker. Further examples have since been found on stones from Cirencester, Lower Slaughter, Bath and Daglingworth. The northern examples usually show three upright figures side by side, as on the best known carving, probably of 3rd century date, from the native settlement outside the Roman fort at Housesteads (fig. 1).[4] This seems to have come from a small domestic shrine, and there was an offering of five denarii under the stone. Another set of three, in the collection at Netherby Hall in Cumbria, shows figures in hoods and short cloaks, beneath which they are either naked or in tight-fitting hose, holding what are thought to be

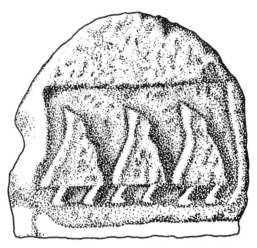

Figure 3 Stone from Cirencester (25.5 cm high, 30 cm wide).
Drawing by Eileen Aldworth.

eggs in their right hands (Toynbee 1957: 459). Two figures which
might originally have been part of a trio are shown on an incomplete
stone in the Netherhall Collection, Maryport (Toynbee 1957: 459).[5]
These northern examples are vigorously portrayed in varying styles,
and stand facing frontwards, while those from the Cotswolds are
more varied in presentation. There are several examples of three
hooded figures accompanied by a fourth being of a different type,
the finest of which is a stone found at the Police Station site at
Cirencester in 1972 (fig. 2; Toynbee 1976: 68). A similar group, less
well preserved and with the head of the seated figure missing, was
found earlier at Daglingworth and discussed in detail by Toynbee in
1959 (Toynbee 1959: 3–7). The additional figure on these stones is a
goddess; she is shown no larger than the hooded men, which implies
that they too are supernatural beings. Two of the men on the
Cirencester stone wear swords, which presumably emphasises the
protective power of the guardian spirits; Toynbee suggests also that
it signifies a victory over death (Toynbee 1976: 68). The group is
placed under a shell-canopy, and the Mother-Goddess holds what
seems to be a large cake or loaf on her lap. In the Daglingworth
group she seems to have fruit or eggs, and the foremost figure is
making an offering to her of a basket of fruit or a bunch of grapes.
Another group of four, with the seated figure on the left, was found
in 1972 with several Roman altars at Price's Row in Cirencester
(Toynbee 1976: 68; Wilson 1973: 307), while yet another possible

example is a stone put up for sale at Christies in 1981, said to come from the Gloucestershire region, although the heads of the standing figures are uncovered.[6] Among some stones recovered from a well at Lower Slaughter, suggesting deliberate destruction of the monuments, is one on which instead of a goddess a figure resembling a warrior in a kilt stands beside the three hooded men; possibly this is a war-god, or represents a donor or a worshipper (Toynbee 1958: 53; 1976: 90).

A particularly impressive carving, to my mind, is a simple one from Cirencester, undoubtedly native work, showing three hooded figures striding purposefully towards the right (fig. 3; Toynbee 1957: 461–62). They leave an impression of inevitability and supernatural power, perhaps because no details can be made out. Toynbee thought that the central figure carried a dish, but this may be part of the surface of the stone. On another stone recovered from the well at Lower Slaughter the outline of three hooded figures has been blocked out but never completed. Jocelyn Toynbee thought that the donor might have bought it before it was finished (Toynbee 1958: 53). Miriam Green takes it as an example of the schematic style preferred by the Celtic peoples (Green 1986: 200), and perhaps the buyer preferred it to more realistic representations.

Single examples of hooded men are rare in Britain, and some on incomplete stones may have formed part of an original trio, as in the case of a figure from Daglingworth (Toynbee 1959: 4) and another from Cirencester, on which a hooded figure stands beside a goddess (Toynbee 1957: 462). A roughly-carved figure on a chalk slab from a Romano-British settlement at Rushall Down in Wiltshire (Toynbee 1957: 466) is a possible example of popular art, as is also the little cloaked figurine from Birdoswald (Toynbee 1957: 461). Two stones in Cheltenham Museum from Wycomb near Andoversford show a hooded man with two bare-headed companions, who hold what might be baskets or bunches of grapes, and are perhaps similar beings with hoods thrown back. Jocelyn Toynbee comments on these stones: 'We could not find a clearer illustration than that afforded by these Wycomb carvings of the completely native background of the cult of *genii cucullati* in this region' (Toynbee 1957: 466). Deonna's examples from the continent, on the other hand, consist almost exclusively of single figures in the form of amulets or figurines, some associated with lamps. One particular group, an example of which was found in a rubbish pit at Reculver, consists of pottery dwarves about 18 cm high, with hoods hanging down their backs, and holding rolls of parchment (Jenkins 1953: 86–91). They come from the region between the Rhine and the Moselle, and might be placed in both inhumation and cremation

Figure 4 Dwarf figurine from Lenus sanctuary, Trier (10 cm high)
Drawing by Eileen Aldworth.

graves, or used as votive offerings in temples, such as that of Mars
Lenus in Trier from which the figure in the illustration came (fig. 4).
The roll is thought to symbolise the power to foretell the future, and
is sometimes placed in the hand of a Mother Goddess. We may
perhaps see in these dwarf figures the ancestors of our modern
garden gnomes; these first emerged as stone figures in Germany in
the early 19th century, and reached the garden of Lamport Hall in
Northamptonshire about 1879.[7] Some pleasant examples were
imported into England before the last war, but the standard has now
sadly deteriorated.

     Deonna concluded that the little hooded figures were derived
from popular tradition, and that they were minor spirits connected
with the earth and agriculture. They promoted fertility, and some
were shown with a large phallus, their cloaks opening to make this
visible. They had a connection with healing, and one small hooded
figure is the child Telesphorus, found in company with Aesculapius,
who first appears in Galatia about the end of the first century BC,
and may be of Celtic origin. Lanterns sometimes carried by these
beings associate them with the night, as does the fact that they are
sometimes shown sleeping; this last point might be associated with

the mantic sleep that led to healing in temples where incubation was practised, and perhaps with death. The figures are found in and around tombs, and Deonna notes their appearance on Roman sarcophagi and on Etruscan urns; the alabaster urns from Volterra go back to the 1st century BC, and on these, small hooded figures help to conduct the dead in their covered wagon, the *carpentum* of Celtic type. The dead man himself might also be portrayed as a hooded figure on horseback (Deonna 1955: 115–).[8] Parchment rolls carried by some figures seem to indicate knowledge of the future, and it seems that like the Mothers they were concerned with the destiny of infants. Their link with fertility is also emphasised by the eggs and fruit which they carry, and the Cotswold stones show them making offerings to the Mother-Goddess. They may have been linked with hunting, like the Icelandic spirits; fragments of a beaker from Colchester show little hooded figures in a hunting scene including a bear and a hare, but it is not clear if they are protecting the animals or the hunters; the scene may possibly be a humorous one (Toynbee 1957: 468–69).

The votive tablets from Roman Britain indicate that both soldiers and civilians were interested in the hooded beings, and the style of art on many of the small carved stones implies that the cult flourished among the native Celtic population. Such votive tablets are also in keeping with the idea of a contract between the hooded beings and those who set them up in temples or household shrines to request benefits or show gratitude for help received. There is a clear link with the goddesses, reminding us that in Scandinavian mythology the female deities all belong to the Vanir group. The link with death and the underworld is also in accordance with the Vanir tradition, but it would be unwise to equate these little beings with the dead in their mounds, since this could hardly have been the case in Iceland in the first period of the settlement. The fact that they are usually depicted in threes may be due to the influence of the Mother-Goddesses appearing as a trio on many votive stones, and to the Celtic fondness for the triad.

It remains to ask what happened to such beliefs and traditions once Christianity was established. It seems likely that they lived on without a great deal of change. Some spirits, like the one in the stone in Iceland, were said to be driven out, and carvings of hooded men might be thrown down a well, but on the other hand a wealth of folk-tales and traditions about household guardian spirits continued unchallenged throughout the British Isles. In the 17th century, England was full of such tales, and beings like Robin Goodfellow, Hob, Lob, Puck and many local spirits with varying names were familiar to country people and London playwrights alike, and might be introduced into masques to amuse royal visitors. In northern England and the Scottish Lowlands there were numerous accounts of the doings of the Brownie, who might also be known as *boggart* in northern England, *urisk* or *gruagach* in the Scottish Highlands, *grogach* or *grogan* in Ulster, the *bwca* or *bwbach* in Wales, and the *fenodoree* in the Isle of Man. Some of these names seem to relate to hairy beings,[9] and the guardian spirits are often described as rough and hairy, and wholly or partly naked. Milton in his poem *L'Allegro* refers to the 'lubber' (clumsy) fiend, who 'stretched out all the chimney's length/Basks at the fire his hairy strength.' Again in a tale of a household spirit from Durham, he is said to work hard at threshing and churning, drink the milk laid out for him, and then lie down 'like a great rough *hurgin* bear', the word *hurgin* meaning with long, tangled hair (Ritson 1875: 18).

In spite of emphasis on nakedness, which Deonna also noted in his study of the hooded men, a cloak and hood was consistently associated with beings of the brownie type. A household spirit called Billy Blin appears in several Scottish ballads, and his name 'blind' seems to indicate a hood shading his face; indeed Cromek describes him as wearing a brown mantle reaching to his knee with a hood of the same colour (Cromek 1810: 330). The most widespread tale about the brownie, found in all parts of the British Isles, is of how he was driven away when the householder, often with the best intentions, provided new clothes for him. There are many verses said to have been spoken by the brownie when he left, never to return, as for instance by the Cauld Lad of Hilton in Northumberland: 'Here's a cloak and here's a hood,/The Cauld Lad o' Hilton'll dae nae mair good' (Henderson 1866/1973:266–67).

The reason for so strong a reaction to a gift of clothing, remembered so widely, is not obvious; occasionally it is suggested that the new clothes were of inferior quality, but this appears to be a rationalisation. It might be felt inappropriate for such robust earthy spirits, accustomed to nakedness, to be neatly and conventionally dressed, for instance in the little knitted suit which two ladies from Donegal carefully made for him in a recently recorded story (hEochaidh 1977: 91). But I feel that the basic reason for the taboo was that it was customary for the master to provide clothes for his servants, livery for those working in the house or smocks for farm labourers. Such a claim on his service was intolerable to the brownie who had to remain his own master; his relationship with the human family he served was in the form of a contract freely made, which could come to an end if he were not treated with proper respect. Support for this is found in a tale sent to William Henderson in a letter from a lady who declared that it went back to her great-grandfather's time, telling of what happened in the old peel house in Scotland where she was born (Henderson 1866/1973: 210–11). The family brownie had been very helpful, and to show their gratitude the servants banded together to provide him with a pair of red trousers and a shirt, such as they all wore as livery. The brownie's reaction was uncompromising: 'Red breeks and a ruffled sark!/Ye'll no' get me to do yer wark!'. Cromek also has a tale of a new laird at Leithen Hall in Dumfriesshire, who when he met the servants for the first time, noticed one in ragged garments among them, and ordered a suit of livery for him. The brownie left immediately, and took the luck of the house with him, as his recorded verse makes clear: 'Ca', cuttie, ca'!/All the luck of Leithin Ha'/Gangs wi' me to Bodsbeck Ha'!' (Cromek 1810: 332–33). A gift of clothing then may have been unacceptable because of the implications that went with it, and such a gift brought the partnership to an end. In Tudor England brownies similarly resented a gift of a homespun smock, such as field workers wore, and Reginald Scot in his *Discoverie of Witchcraft* refers to the parting words of the household spirit as: 'Hemton, hamton, here will I never more tread nor stampen' as though this were a familiar saying (Scot 1584: IV, 10, 85). This seems to stand for *Hempen, Hampen* found in a number of other rhymes, meaning a homemade smock made from hemp such as labourers wore.[10]

An important aspect of the guardian spirit was that he brought good luck to the house where he took up residence, like the guardian spirits in Iceland. Even James VI with his strict Puritan upbringing realised this when he remarked that some folk 'were so blinded as to believe that their house was all the sonsier, as they called it, that such spirits resorted there' (King James 1597: 65). This was partly due to the help said to be given by the brownie so that all went well and easily in house and farm. He performed much of the hard labour, mowing, threshing, beating flax, grinding meal, making ricks, cutting wood, and doing what Burton in the 17th century called 'any manner of drudgery work' (Burton 1955: I, 2, 169). He saw to the well-being of the animals, especially those giving milk, the cows, ewes and goats; he would make sure that the cattle were brought in safely at night, and in the Hebrides men with second sight were said to see Gunna, a local brownie, driving the animals down to the shore if they grazed too near the crops (MacGregor 1937: 46). Brownies helped with the herding of the sheep, and a very widespread tale is how on one occasion, after the flock had been brought in, the brownie told the farmer that the little grey sheep had given him more trouble than all the rest, pointing to an exhausted hare along with the rest of the flock (Binnall 1940: 220;

Rhys 1901/1980: 286–87). They gave special help in the dairy; it was still a familiar tradition in Wales in the 19th century that if the dairy-maid put the churn on the whitened hearth at night alongside the brownie's bowl of milk, she would find the bowl empty in the morning, and only a turn or two needed at the churn before the butter came (Sikes 1880/1973: 30).

The association between brownies and milk is well established, and the provision of fresh creamy milk, such as they loved, was evidently part of the contract with the farmer. In a 16th-century poem by Thomas Churchyard (Churchyard 1592), Robin Good-fellow was said to skim the bowls in the dairy: 'Rude Robin good fellow, the lowt/Would skime the milke bowls all.' In the early 19th century milk was still poured into cavities of stones as an offering to the brownie on Colonsay, on the first night that the cattle were left outside (MacGregor 1937: 45–6). On the island of Inch, the milk-maid on a certain shieling would leave warm milk in the hollow of a knocking stone every evening; otherwise she might find one of the cattle had fallen over the cliff by next morning (MacGregor 1937: 48), while in Shetland, part of the milk used for churning was sprinkled in each corner of the house (Brand 1701: 171). The importance of cleanliness in the dairy was emphasised by the tra-dition that brownies could be driven away by filth and excrement, and punished slovenly maids by slaps or pinches in the dark. In Old Icelandic the word for excrement was *álfrekr*, literally something driving the elves away. A very popular tale about the famous *bwca* of Trwyn in South Wales is of how one of the servant girls there, who had always been on good terms with the brownie, one night in a fit of mischief substituted stale urine, kept for dyeing wool, and rough barley bread for the usual fresh milk and slice from the wheaten loaf. In the morning when she came down she was soundly beaten by invisible hands, and the *bwca* transferred his allegiance to another farm. Rhys translates the outspoken verse he shouted at her as follows: 'The idea that the thick-buttocked lass/Should give barley bread and piss/To the *bwca*' (Rhys 1901/1980: 593).

The brownie worked inside as well as out, busy in the dairy and kitchen and stable, helping with the brewing, keeping the servants in order, sometimes even making beds and serving at table by rolling or throwing in food (Stewart 1851: 98; MacGregor 1937: 54). He would tidy up at night, often making a fair amount of noise, and if offended or feeling mischievous might set things awry instead or indulge in other poltergeist activities (MacGregor 1937: 53, 55; Hardwick 1872: 127). When his work was done, he liked to lie by the hearth or swing on the hook that held the kettle, and sometimes would frighten the maids by coming down the chimney. Mrs

Leather has an account of a Herefordshire brownie who would take the household keys if something provoked him; the only way to get them back was for everyone to sit round the hearth with eyes closed, after putting a little cake on the hearthstone, and in due course the bunch of keys would be hurled against the wall (Leather 1912/1973: 48).

The brownie acted as a protective spirit towards members of the family. One in Scotland used his lantern (for, like Deonna's hooded men, they often carried lanterns and led travellers astray with them) to bring the laird safely back home after a night out drinking (MacGregor 1937: 54). They cared also for the women of the household. The brownie of the Maxwells of Dalswinton was said to escort the laird's comely daughter to the trysting thorn to meet her lover and see her safely home again; later it was he who undressed her on her bridal night, and when her first child was born he rode for the midwife, beating the dilatory servant who delayed too long (Cromek 1810: 334–35). The story of riding for the midwife is another widespread tale, and there are frequent connections between the brownie and both marriage and childbirth, for instance in the part played by the guardian spirit Billy Blin in a number of Scottish Ballads.[11] The English brownies clearly promoted marriages; this is one of the main motifs in *A Midsummer Night's Dream*, where in spite of all his teasing Puck finally brings the lovers together: 'Jack shall have Jill,/Nought shall go ill;/The man shall have his mare again and all shall be well' (Act IV, sc.2). The same idea comes out even more strongly in an anonymous play of the early 17th century, *Grim the Collier of Croyden*.[12] Here the brownie saves the girl from an unwelcome suitor whom her parents try to force on her and brings the true lovers together, sharing a dish of cream with them before arranging for an immediate wedding ceremony so that they can go to bed together.

Like the land-spirits who helped the Icelandic settlers, these guardian spirits of the brownie type are mostly male. There is occasional mention of a female companion, called the wife or mother of the brownie. Of these the best known is Meg Mullach (Hairy Meg), who with Brownie Clod resided at the castle of Tullochgorm with the Grants of Strathspey. Aubrey evidently knew the legend about them (Aubrey 1972: 124), and Grant Stewart in 1823 gives the name of the male brownie as Brownie Clod, due to his unpleasant habit of flinging earth at passers-by (Stewart 1851: 97). Meg was famed for her knowledge of the future, but also helped in the house while Brownie Clod did the threshing and other outside work. Signs of another possible pair in England are to be seen in references to Robin Goodfellow and Fairy Mab. Mab is not always represented as a tiny fairy queen, as in Shakespeare's *Romeo and Juliet* (I,4) and the poetry of the Jacobean poets (Briggs 1959: 56), but also appears as a more earthy being behaving like a brownie, as Ben Jonson describes her in a masque of 1603 (Jonson 1603: VII, 122, ll. 53–6)

> This is Mab the mistris-Faerie,
> That doth nightly rob the dayrie
> And can hurt or helpe the churnin
> (As she please) without discerning.

He alludes to her pinching and scratching country wenches if they are slovenly in their cleaning, and also to dreams of lovers which she brings to young girls, in agreement with Shakespeare's picture of her as a purveyor of tempting visions in sleep. Milton in *L'Allegro* refers to Mab eating junkets in the dairy and pinching her victims, and then goes on to describe the brownie figure stretched out by the fire after his work is done. She is called a midwife more than once, and in Derbyshire 'a little fairy woman called a midwife', wearing a hood, is said to come into a house just before the birth of a child, and then be taken away again by the fairies (Addy 1895/1973: 134). To be 'mab-led' in Warwickshire was said to be the equivalent of being 'pixy-led' in the West Country (Wright 1898–1905). There may well be some confusion in later folk-lore between male brownies and female guardian spirits such as were associated with aristocratic families in Scotland and Ireland, but I cannot deal with this question here.

The evidence leaves us with a fairly consistent picture of guardian spirits closely connected with the natural world, who could attach themselves to individual farms and manor houses. They guarded the flocks and herds, helped in the stable, assisted with work on the land and with the harvesting of the crops, and promoted the well-being of the family, with a special concern for marriages and the birth and destinies of children. They gave loyal service on the farms and brought luck and prosperity to the household, but they were of an independent disposition and refused to be organised. Their link with those owning the land was in the form of a contract which had to be kept by both sides, and they could be difficult neighbours if offended, with an irresistible tendency towards practical jokes. Milk and dairy produce were specially associated with such beings, and used as offerings to them, supplemented by bread or cakes. There is some archaeological evidence for offerings of this kind in sacred places in Scandinavia in the Iron Age and the Migration Period, such as Thorsbjerg in Denmark and Skedemosse on Öland. Traces of fat in vessels and farming implements have been found, and in the 6th century Gregory of Tours refers to articles of male attire being thrown into a sacred lake, together with cheeses, woollen fleeces, thread and spices.[13] The mention of male clothing suggests at least the possibility that the giving of clothes to a brownie may be a tradition with an ancient ancestry: were such offerings attempts to get rid of troublesome spirits?

In the little hooded men of the Roman period, we have a unique opportunity to see how the Celtic people in parts of Britain imagined the household spirits of their own time, the kind of spirits which in later literature might be known as elves or land-spirits, and in folklore by a variety of names. It is suggested from time to time that such beings in popular tradition may be seen as degraded Celtic deities (eg. Jenkins 1953: 88). But perhaps there has not been so much degradation after all, and these homely beings are not very far removed from those to whom gifts were offered before the coming of Christianity. Such little guardian spirits of the farms seem to have formed an important if minor part of the religious system of both Celtic and Germanic peoples. They were tolerated by the great gods, and afforded a place in the religious framework by poets and story-tellers, while they continued to be recognised and to a large extent tolerated by the Christian church. Folklore represents belief in such beings as casual yet consistent, learned in childhood and never wholly forgotten, half mockery and half genuine, the basis of both frightening and entertaining tales, helping to keep things harmonious in the household, and evidently working well enough to continue over many centuries. In this case, folklore may well help us to understand more clearly certain aspects of the supernatural world in the pre-Christian past.[14]

NOTES

1. *Kristni Saga* 2; *þáttr þorvalds en viðfǫrla* 2.
2. Old Carl Hood appears in several versions of *Earl Brand* (Child 1957: I, 99, 443, 445): 'When they met with Old Carl Hood/He comes for ill but never for good' etc.
3. Deonna has only one possible example of a trio: Toynbee 1957: 458.
4. Toynbee 1957: 460; Heichelheim 1935: 187. Heichelheim took some of the figures to be female, but there seems no real justification for this.
5. I am grateful to Lt. Cdr. B. D. Ashmore for letting me see this stone, now in storage.

6. I owe this information to Dr Martin Henig. A photograph in the catalogue shows three figures facing frontwards, each carrying a shield. They have cloaks but are bare-headed, and are described as warrior deities; however the group of three men and a goddess resembles the pattern on other Cotswold stones.

7. I am grateful for this information from the Librarian of the Horticultural Society, obtained by Dr Hilary Belcher.

8. I am grateful to Dr L. B. van der Meer for further information about the Etruscan urns.

9. *Gruagach* is translated in the *Scot Nat Dict* as 'having much hair'; it is sometimes used of a long-haired female spirit, but in many cases the *gruagach* behaves like a brownie. *fenodoree* has been taken to mean 'one who has hairy stockings' (Rhys 1901/1980: 288). Meg Mullach, a famous female brownie of Speyside, is 'Hairy Meg' (Stewart 1851: 97).

10. See OED, *hempen*; Wright 1903: *hamp*; Atkinson 1891: 55–7; Binnall 1940: 221.

11. Billy Blin is found in some versions of Gil Brenton, Willie's Lady, Young Beichan, and The Knight and the Shepherd's Daughter (Child 1957: I, 67). He appears to be a house spirit, and is concerned either with marriage or childbirth in each case. In Willie's Lady, he outwits the evil mother-in-law who is preventing the birth by witchcraft. Billy is clearly of a different nature from Old Carl Hood (see note 2) and bears no resemblance to Odin.

12. *Dodsley's Old English Plays*, ed. W. Carew Hazlitt (London 1874) VIII, 387ff. The author is unknown; the play was printed in 1662, but may be considerably earlier. Robin Goodfellow also assists a wooer in *Wily Beguild* (1606), but here his role is confused and he supports the wrong side (this may be because his protegé is a rustic while the approved bridegroom is a scholar). I am grateful to Sandra Billington for this reference. In the tract *Life of Robin Goodfellow* (Ritson 1875: 182ff), dated 1628, Robin rescues a girl from a lecherous old man and promotes a suitable marriage for her.

13. Gregory of Tours, *Liber in gloria confessorum (Mon Germ Scrip rerum* I, 1; 479), quoted in U. E. Hagborg, *Archaeology of Skedemosse* II (Stockholm 1967): 67.

14. My thanks are due to Dr Steven Blake of the Cheltenham Museums, and to David Viner and Stephen Clews of the Corinium Museum, Cirencester, for allowing me to examine the carved stones showing the *genii cucullati*, and providing photographs. I am most grateful also to Dr Martin Henig for valuable information, and to Eileen Aldworth for her work on the illustrations.

REFERENCES

Addy, S. O. (1973). *Folk Tales and Superstitions*, republished from (1895) *Household Tales*. London: E.P. Publishing Ltd.

Almqvist, B. (1965). *Norrön Niddiktning* I. Uppsala: Almqvist and Wiksells.

Atkinson, J. C. (1891). *Forty Years in a Moorland Parish*. London: MacMillan.

Aubrey, J. (1972). *Miscellanies* in ed. J. Buchanan-Brown, *Three Prose Works*. Fontwell: Centaur Press.

Binnall, P. B. C. (1940). A Brownie Legend from Lincolnshire, *Folklore* 51, 219–22.

Brand, J. (1701). *A Brief Description of Orkney, Zetland, Portland-Firth and Caithness*. Edinburgh: G. Morman.

Briggs, K. M. (1959). *The Anatomy of Puck*. London: Routledge and Kegan Paul.

Burton, R. (1955). *Anatomy of Melancholy* 6th edn, eds F. Dell and P. Jordan-Smith. New York.

Child, F. J. (1957). ed. *English and Scottish Popular Ballads*. New York: Folklore Press.

Churchyard, T. (1592). A Handful of Gladsome Verses, Given to the Queene Majesty at Woodstocke this Prograce, in *Fugitive Tracts in Verse*. London, 1875.

Cromek, R. H. (1810). *Remains of Nithsdale and Galloway Song*. London: Cadell and Davies.

Deonna, W. M. (1955). De Télesphore au 'moine bourru'. *Collection Latomus* 21.

hEochaidh, S. O. (1977). *Fairy Legends from Donegal*. Dublin: University College.

Green, M. (1986). *The Gods of the Celts*. Gloucester: Alan Sutton.

Hardwick, C. (1872). *Traditions, Superstitions, and Folklore, chiefly Lancashire and the North of England*. Manchester.

Heichelheim, F. M. (1935). Genii Cucullati, *Archaeologia Aeliana* 12, 187–94.

Henderson, W. (1866/1973). *Folk-Lore of the Northern Counties of England and the Borders*. London: Longmans, Green and Co.

Jenkins, F. (1953). The *Genius Cucullatus* in Kent, *Archaeologia Cantabrensis* 66, 86–91.

Jonson, B. (1603). A particular entertainment of the Queen and Prince at Althorpe, performed 25 June 1603, ed. C. H. Herford and P. E. Simpson, *Works* (1941–52) 2 vols. Oxford: Clarendon Press.

King James (1597). *Demonologie*. Edinburgh.

Landnámabók (1968). ed. J. Benediktsson. Reykjavik: Hólar H-F.

Leather, E. M. (1912/1973). *Folk-Lore of Herefordshire*. Hereford: Jakeman and Carver.

MacGregor, A. A. (1937). *The Peat-Fire Flame*. Edinburgh: Moray Press.

Rhys, J. (1901/1980). *Celtic Folklore*. London: Oxford.

Ritson, J. (1875). *Fairy Tales, Legends and Romances*. London: Kerslake.

Scot, R. (1584/1886). *Discoverie of Witchcraft*, ed. B. Nicholson. London: Elliot Stock.

Sikes, W. (1880/1973). *British Goblins*. London: Sampson Low.

Stewart, W. Grant (1851). *Popular Superstitions of the Highlanders* (2nd edn) London: Aylott and Jones.

Thiele, J. M. (1843). *Danmarks Folkesagn* II. Copenhagen: University of Copenhagen.

Toynbee, J. M. C. (1957). *Genii Cucullati* in Roman Britain, *Coll. Latomus* 28, 456–69.

—(1958). with H. E. O'Neill, Sculptures from a Romano-British Well in Gloucestershire, *Journal of Roman Studies* 48, 49–55.

—(1959). Daglingworth in Roman Times, in O. M. Griffiths, *Daglingworth: the Story of a Cotswold Village*. London: Museum Press, 3–7.

—(1976). Roman Sculpture in Gloucestershire, in P. McGrath and J. Cannon (eds), *Essays in Bristol and Gloucestershire History*. Bristol: Bristol and Glos. Arch. Soc., 62–100.

Wilson, D. R. (1973). Roman Britain in 1972, *Britannia* 4, 271–328.

Wright, J. (1898–1905). *English Dialect Dictionary* (6 vols.) London: English Dialect Soc.

ALAN BRUFORD

The Twins of Macha

Anyone with a knowledge of Old Irish literature will recognise what
the title of this paper means, but for other readers I must first
outline its theme and sketch in its literary background. In what can
be reconstructed of pagan Irish mythology, deities or heroes are
often grouped in threes, but explicit pairs in the manner of Castor
and Pollux are not at all obvious: this paper is designed to draw
attention to one or two implicit pairs, with certain features pointing
to the sort of dark/light alternation noticed in Emily Lyle's paper at
the Kingship conference (Lyle 1988).

   Our knowledge of pagan Irish mythology depends on a variety of
sources. Among these, inscriptions from pagan times, mainly from
neighbouring Britain and Gaul, have very limited value, but much
more survives in the literature of Christian Ireland. In historical
tracts and hero-tales – overlapping categories – pagan gods are
generally presented as members of a particular people, the Tuatha
Dé Danann ('Tribes of the Goddess Danu') who in the monastic
scholars' scheme of history preceded the Gaels or Milesians as the
dominant race in Ireland. Their leaders have names which can
sometimes be paralleled from British or Gaulish inscriptions; in
some tales they are clearly immortal, though other tales were deliberately composed by Christian writers to make it clear that they had
died; and after the Milesian conquest they 'went into hiding' in
underground kingdoms or in an overseas otherworld or earthly
paradise. The Tuatha Dé Danann survive in recent tradition as what
we translate as 'fairies',[1] and local traditions still associate particular
fairy kings and queens with natural or man-made hills and mounds
which were entrances to the underground otherworld. In a few
cases, mortal heroes represented in tales as belonging to the Milesian race seem to be incarnations or diminished versions of older
gods; at least one Christian saint preserved the name and some
characteristics of an earlier goddess, Brigit; and very often the

genealogies of the hundreds of royal lines in Dark Age Ireland, though nominally going back to Míl Easpaine, the 'Spanish Soldier' from whom the Gaels were called Milesians, have recognisable names of gods or culture heroes in the generations just below him. There are also a very few explicit Christian references to named pagan gods.

It is almost certainly a waste of time to try and arrange Irish gods into a celestial Cabinet of Ministers with specified functions, like those over-simplified textbook lists of Olympian deities – Mars, the god of War, Minerva, the goddess of Wisdom, or worse, Apollo, the god of the Sun, and Diana, goddess of the Moon. Julius Caesar tried something of the sort with the gods of Gaul, and only suc- ceeded in confusing subsequent investigators by statements such as 'they most worship Mercury'. There is more justification for deduc- ing that a particular god was venerated by a tribe which used his name in their own, but this can tell us nothing about the character- istics that went with the name. Marie-Louise Sjoestedt, the first scholar to grasp the situation, writes, 'We must dismiss the notion of one deity that is titular, as it were, of a particular function, in favour of the notion of diverse realisations of a single religious idea, groups of deities, probably local – at least in origin – who are not identical but equivalent, having evolved among different peoples, perhaps at different times, from the same generative impulse' (Sjoestedt 1949: 25–6). I would go rather further and suggest that there was in effect a stock of divine names, any of which might be chosen for particular veneration by a tribe or dynasty and in that situation credited with competence in any field, war, fertility, or poetry alike, control over sun, sea or lightning. So although the original name may imply a particular field of competence, this does not limit the user; more- over, at times forms of the same name may be used for both a male and a female deity. A number of early Irish texts tell us that A was another name for B, and by comparing lists, genealogies, plots of stories and characteristics, modern scholars have uncovered many other possible relationships: to some extent this is what I want to do now. I shall not however be taking the technique as far as its most controversial exponent, T. F. O'Rahilly, who was ready to identify 'sun-gods' (who were fast travellers or horsemen) and 'lightning- gods' (who had remarkable weapons) but in the end reduced them all to a single figure he called 'the Otherworld deity', who was overcome by one other figure, 'the divine Hero', in a multiformed 'primitive myth' (which he hoped 'to discuss at length on another occasion' but unfortunately never got round to: O'Rahilly 1946: 60–1, 271, 277–8, etc.). O'Rahilly's insights are often useful, but nobody is going to agree with them all.

I should also introduce the background to most of the stories I shall be quoting. For this theme, the so-called Mythological Cycle of tales dealing with the Tuatha Dé Danann and their relationships with the Milesians, like the later Fenian Cycle where they also play a prominent part, is actually less relevant than the Ulster Cycle. This consists mainly of heroic tales written down from the eighth century on, set against a background of war between the provinces of Ulster and Connacht, with mortal heroes often of incredible strength and courage and the Tuatha Dé Danann always present in the background and ready to intervene in the action like the Olympian gods in the *Iliad*. It is the classic heroic prose literature of Ireland for modern readers, and to a great extent for mediaeval ones too. The setting of the tales was dated by official Irish historians about the beginning of the Christian era, but is now generally agreed to be based on the situation four hundred years later, shortly before Christianity came to Ireland.[2] About that time the Connachta from central Ireland, after a long struggle, overran the greater part of the northern province of Ulster and left its former overlords as rulers of little more than the present County Down. Since the descendants of Niall of the Nine Hostages of the Connachta, the Uí Néill kings of Tara, held on to their conquests for seven centuries, dominated the whole northern half of Ireland, and later claimed to have been High Kings of all Ireland, it is surprising that the epic cycle which dominated Irish literature at the same time clearly takes the side of the defeated Ulstermen.

It has been suggested that since St Patrick chose to found his most important church at Armagh, Ard Macha, just down the road from the Ulster capital of Emain Macha, rather than near the rival royal centre of Tara, the Ulster kings cannot have been expelled from there before he arrived and may still have looked like the dominant power in the north of Ireland (Byrne 1973: 50). On the other hand, this may be putting the cart before the horse. The abbots of Armagh somehow succeeded in making their monastery the most important in the north of Ireland, if not all Ireland, and within two centuries of his death had begun a successful propaganda campaign to make out that their founder was the first and only evangelist of all Ireland, which almost certainly he was not. The legend they created was rather hostile to the successful secular dynasty, which continued to take its name from the pagan ritual site of Tara, though they had long since embraced Christianity and abandoned Tara, according to the legend, after it was cursed by St Patrick. It seems quite reasonable that the Armagh propaganda factory also employed a few members of the poetic caste to retell – and more important from the point of view of survival, a few scribes to write down – local heroic legends which made Ulstermen defeat Connachta and had no doubt been used to hearten the troops in the last days of beleaguered Emain Macha.

The Connachta were a dynasty descended from a mythical ancestor called Conn, 'the Head'. After the time of Niall of the Nine Hostages, the dynasty split into two halves: Niall's descendants the Uí Néill, who held various kingdoms in the west of Ulster and in the area north of Dublin later known as the province of Meath, with their over-king taking his title from Tara in County Meath but not living there; and several dynasties said to be descended from Niall's three elder brothers, who took turns to be over-kings of the province called after the dynasty, Connacht. In the Ulster Cycle, and especially in its central and longest tale, *Táin Bó Cuailnge*, 'The Cattle-Raid of Cooley', usually known as the *Táin* for short, the Connachta attack Ulster from the direction of Dublin, but are represented as coming from the modern Connacht, though with allies from other provinces of Ireland helping them. In fact any sort of realistic campaign using chariots, as the warriors in the tales do, could hardly attack Ulster through the rough country where it borders on Connacht. It is quite likely that this is a way of avoiding making the powerful Tara dynasty the clear villains of the piece. It is still disputed whether the Connachta expanded from the Tara area westward (cf. O'Rahilly 1946: 173–4), or from the present Connacht eastward: on the whole the latter seems more likely, since the kings of Leinster to the south sometimes tried to lay claim to Tara, as if it had been their sanctuary until it was taken from them by force (Byrne 1973: 58, 142). In that case the situation in the *Táin* may in a way reflect the campaigns of the early fifth century as they might have been, if the Connachta had attacked centuries later.

There is no doubt that the Macha in the names of Emain Macha and Armagh was the name of a goddess, though the Royal Irish Academy's dictionary suggests (with no good reason that I can see) that the word in the place-names may be the genitive of an unattested word meaning a plain, presumably a by-form of the well-known element *magh* (genitive *maighe*).[3] At any rate, Macha appears as one of a trinity with the well-attested war-goddesses Badb ('Hoodie-Crow') and Morrígan ('Queen of Phantoms'; Sjoestedt 1949: 32): since all Gaels, mortal and immortal, need a parent's name to complete theirs, they are called daughters of Érnmas, which means 'Death in Battle' (RIA Dict. s.v. *ernbas*: literally 'death by iron') – clearly a kind of Irish Valkyries. There is a story of a mortal Macha, a red-haired princess who inherited her father's kingdom, defeated two rival claimants, and in the form of a leper with beautiful eyes, seduced the five sons of one of them – not

as in similar Loathly Lady stories in order to offer them the kingship, but to enslave them and make them build the ramparts of
Emain Macha for her. Again the characteristics of a war-goddess
stand out (Sjoestedt 1949: 28–9). Another Macha is said to have
been wife of Nemed, an early settler of Ireland in the histories, but
probably a creator god or at least culture-hero in pagan times: his
name means simply 'Holy'. He cleared a plain and gave it to his wife
that it might bear her name: Sjoestedt (1949: 29) therefore calls her
an 'agrarian deity'. Emain Macha took its name from another
avatar, or two, for there are two stories: one merely says that Macha
marked out the boundaries of the fort with her brooch, and that
emain is a word for brooch, though I cannot trace it in the dictionary
(Gantz 1981: 127). *Emain* does however mean a pair of twins (RIA
Dict.), or a twin (or occasionally a triplet), as in the story which
interests us most. Quite possibly the place-name involves a different
word: as far as I know, there is no other Emain on the map of early
Ireland, but it is often used as the name of an overseas otherworld or
earthly paradise, usually called Emain Ablach, 'Emain of the Ap-
ple-Trees', the Gaelic equivalent of Avalon. The site in Ireland with
the name, though it has earthworks round it and is now called
Navan Fort, seems like Tara to have been a sacred place rather than
a military fortification, judging from the reports of ritual structures
found in recent excavations. The basic meaning may well be something like 'sanctuary'.

Sjoestedt summarises the tale of the Twins of Macha as follows:
One day Crunnchu, a rich peasant widower [in Ulster], sees a
beautiful young woman come into his house. She says nothing
but at once sets about the duties of the house. Having gone
around the room in the ritual manner, clockwise, she goes into
his bed. She becomes pregnant by him, and from that day
everything prospers in the house. The time comes when Crunnchu must go to attend the provincial assembly of Ulster, and
Macha warns him not to mention her name there. But when he
sees the king's horses racing, Crunnchu, forgetting the prohibition, exclaims that his wife is swifter than they are. King
Conchobor accepts the challenge and orders that the woman be
brought to race against his horses. In vain Macha asks for a
delay since her time is at hand. She must accept the ordeal or
see her husband put to death. Undoing her hair, she enters the
race and reaches the post before the horses; but then she cries
out and dies, giving birth to twins, 'The Twins of Macha', in
Irish *Emain Macha*, from whom the capital of Ulster is named.
Before she dies she curses the men of Ulster and predicts that
for nine times nine generations they shall suffer the sickness of

childbirth in the height of war and in the hour of greatest danger.[4]

The point of the story is to explain the curse on the Ulstermen, and the point of the curse is to explain why in the *Táin* the hero Cú Chulainn, who as the son of the god Lug is not subject to the curse, has to defend the province single-handed against the invading Connachta. In the story as it has come down to us he does this for months, whereas Macha's curse is only said to last for nine half-days (five days and four nights or five nights and four days): but this is in accord with many other exaggerations of Cú Chulainn's prowess in the *Táin*, which is very much his story.

This has been viewed as an ancient myth, full of primitive magic: but it is so clearly manufactured for a purpose in making sense of the central tale of the Ulster cycle that I am inclined to doubt this, especially since another, less often repeated, tale gives a quite different explanation for the curse: that it was brought on by Cú Chulainn's own otherworld mistress showing herself to the Ulstermen naked (Sjoestedt 1949:27). The Macha story is adapted from a worldwide legend of the man who acquires a supernatural wife and loses her by breaking a tabu of some sort that she has imposed, often revealing a secret about her origin or ability to change her shape. She should probably disappear back to the otherworld rather than die after uttering her curse, and despite Sjoestedt's summary, only one text says that she did die. Crunnchu is made a peasant in one redaction of the tale because this fits the legend, but another version makes him a rich man of the type translated 'hospitaller', and his name appears in the genealogy of the Ulster kings well before Conchobor: since he has the same father, Agnoman, as Nemed, who also had a wife Macha, he is probably another name for the same ancestor deity, Macha's divine husband. His own name is variously given as Crunnchu, apparently meaning something like 'Round Dog', Cruinniuc, 'Dewdrop', or just Cruinn, 'Round', which O'Rahilly (1946: 290 n.4) takes to mean that he was a sun-god. The one feature in this story which probably has a genuine pagan background is the representation of Macha as able to outrun horses: she was no doubt a horse-goddess of a type well-known among the Celts, like Epona in Gaul and Rhiannon in Wales.

But what about the twins? In the existing story, they are a son and a daughter, in one version given allegorical names, Fír, 'Loyalty', and Fial, 'Modest', expressing the ideal virtues for each sex: but having served their purpose in giving the assembly-place of the Ulstermen its name Emain, they vanish from the record. But if the meaning of Emain really is 'Twins', and Macha the goddess was indeed the mother of divine twins, then they would surely be significant figures, very likely brothers and to some extent rivals like twins in other mythologies, and would have a continuing career as adult deities or heroes. This is highly speculative, but I want to explore the possibilities of who these twins might have been.

One of them, I suggest, would be Fergus mac Roich. Fergus is a central but anomalous figure in the Ulster Cycle. He is not merely a character in the *Táin* but its storyteller: a band of poets bidden to recover the lost epic roused him from his grave by fasting there until the giant figure rose and dictated the *Táin* to them. He has the strength of seven hundred men and his sexual prowess is notable – Fergus means 'virility' or at least 'manliness' (Sjoestedt 1949: 36). He has been king of Ulster but resigned the office to Conchobor in exchange for his mother's hand in marriage: nevertheless he retains an undefined authority in Ulster, until Conchobor's treacherous killing of the sons of Uisliu to regain Deirdre drives him to throw in his lot with the enemy (Kinsella 1970: 3–4, 15). In the *Táin* he is therefore on the side of the Connachta, but avoids taking an active part in the fighting, and gives good advice both to the Connachta and to their opponent, his foster-son Cú Chulainn, very much in the manner of the gods in the *Iliad*. In his exile he has two partners, Medb queen of Connacht, who dominates her husband Ailill and is generally identified as another goddess of war (or sovereignty, or drink, her name means 'the intoxicator'), and Flidais, originally apparently a nature goddess whose cattle are the deer, who fell in love with Fergus and pestered him until he killed her husband, another Ailill, and carried her off (Sjoestedt 1949: 36–7; Thurneysen 1921: 317–20). He appears in the genealogies as an ancestor of numerous dynasties mainly in outlying areas of Connacht and Munster as well as Ulster. Neither Sjoestedt nor O'Rahilly (1946: 68) had any doubt that Fergus was originally a god.

One reason for making him one of Macha's twins is that Macha, particularly in this context, has been identified as a horse-goddess, and Fergus is called mac Roich, 'Son of the Great Horse'. Grammatically the form is masculine, and O'Rahilly (1946: 480–1) may well be right in saying that this was his father's name in the earliest references, and was only interpreted as the name of his mother, as it is by some genealogists, when an alternative patronymic, mac Rosa Ruaid, was invented. Certainly he can quote genealogies where Roich is Fergus's father and Rus Ruad his grandfather, or vice versa. However it might be argued that a feminine form of *ech*, 'horse', paralleling that in the Gaulish goddess-name Epona, which also means 'great (female) horse', could have existed. The genitive form would have been a letter longer, but it could be that mac Roiche was shortened and regularised to mac Roich when in Christian times the importance of Fergus's mother was largely forgotten. One or two early Irish heroes are known by the metronymic, notably Conchobor, Fergus' successor as king of Ulster and stepson – very likely in an earlier form the god's own son – who is always mac Nesa, perhaps in the same way as Apollo is more often thought of as Leto's son than Zeus's. But this represents the beliefs of an earlier age, and historical characters in early Christian Ireland invariably have a patronymic to establish their claim to nobility: it would be natural for a masculine form to be assumed to be correct.

O'Rahilly's argument depends on the assumption that the Rus who is sometimes made Fergus's father is of no importance, and only later became confused with Rus Ruad, the father of a legendary king of Leinster called Finn Fili, 'Finn the Poet', of whom more later. 'Some Leinsterman', he says, 'invented the idea' that Cairbre Nia Fer, said to have been king of Tara at the time of the Táin, Finn Fili king of Leinster, and Ailill king of Connacht, Medb's husband – another who is normally known by what is said to be his mother's name, mac Máta – were brothers (O'Rahilly 1946: 179). I was curious about their father's name Rus, which as far as I know does not appear in historical times, though one other ancestor figure, Rus Failge, ancestor of the Uí Failge of Offaly, bears it, so I looked it up in the RIA Dictionary, which sometimes does and sometimes does not include proper names. The name was not there, but a common noun with the nominative *rús* and genitive *rósa* was noted as a contraction of the compound *ro-fhis*, 'great knowledge' (with the same first element as Roich). Early sources such as Cormac's Glossary say that the uncontracted form was used in a title for the Dagda, the father of the Irish gods, In Ruad Ro-fhessa, 'The red-haired one of great knowledge' (or 'the mighty one of great knowledge': I have mentioned the implications of colour-words in Gaelic to this society before).[5] Rús Ruad is simply a reversal of this, 'Know-all the Redhead' if you like. So Fergus, along with his rival in Connacht and two other dynastic ancestors covering four of the five provinces of Ireland, is simply being identified as the son of the main god. The Dagda (meaning 'Good God') is also called Eochaid Ollathair ('Horsey Allfather', roughly: Sjoestedt 1949: 38) and is father rather than king of the gods: he himself could be a male 'great horse', but there is no reason to deny that the 'great horse' could also have been Fergus's mother, when some early sources say just that and give him a credible father.

Who is likely to be the twin? There are a number of early Irish names ending in *-gus*, 'force' or 'essence', but the only ones which are at all common are Fergus ('manliness') and Oengus (apparently meaning 'oneness', 'unity' – we will look at the significance of this in a moment). Oengus is generally recognised as the name of a god, sometimes a king of the gods, and is frequently called the son of the Dagda. O'Rahilly (1946: 516–17) typically concertinas the two: '*Oengus* was originally a name for the Otherworld-god, and in particular for the Dagda' with whom the 'youthful Hero (Macc ind Óc)' ('the Young Lad', a synonym for the divine Oengus) was 'amalgamated into a composite personage', though the one had defeated the other and expelled him from his sacred dwelling of Brug na Bóinne, the chamber-tomb of New Grange on the Boyne. Earlier writers described Oengus as the 'Celtic God of Love': as far as I can see the only basis for this is in a comparatively late tale, 'The Dream of Oengus', in which the god himself falls in love. We can safely discount both these interpretations and concentrate on Oengus 'the Young Lad', as he is generally depicted. Certainly he is also an ancestor-figure in many genealogies, like Fergus, but young men can father sons just as much as personifications of virility.

There seems to be no account linking a mythical Oengus and Fergus, but the names were commonly used for historical characters, and Angus and Fergus are still used in Scotland today, though Gaelic-speakers now use only Angus, *Aonghus*, as a first name and know Fergus only in the surname *MacFhearghuis*, Ferguson. In Ireland they certainly died out in the later Middle Ages, and have only been revived recently as relics of the Celtic past: but they had a good innings before that. A number of other names of pagan deities seem to have been used regularly by the Gaelic aristocracy well into Christian times, though only Brigit received the ultimate accolade of being borne by a Christian saint (whose historicity has sometimes been doubted), and so surviving into modern times in Ireland. Oengus and Fergus (or what seems to be a by-form, Forggus, possibly meaning 'perfection')[6] appear as names of Gaelic noblemen and clerics in the genealogies and histories of the Dark Ages, but are not very common names after the legendary heroes and mythical ancestors of pre-Christian times – for instance, numerous legendary kings of Ulster are called Fergus, including the last to rule in Emain Macha, and at one stage three brothers all called Fergus.

The only cases I know where the two names are actually paired come from Scotland. The definitely historical one is in the king-lists of Pictland, where not one but two powerful Pictish kings, in the middle of the eighth century and the early ninth, bore the name Oengus son of Fergus, in the Pictish form Unnuist son of Uurguist. Since the earlier of the two, who may be the eponym of the county of Angus, was claimed as a kinsman by the ruling dynasty of Munster, the Eoghanachta (O'Rahilly 1946: 371), and some historians are prepared to consider that he and most of his successors may have been of partly Gaelic descent, the pairing of the names may be relevant to Irish as well as Pictish mythology. The other case is the founder of Scottish Dalriada and the ancestor of the later kings of Scotland, Fergus mac Eirc. He belongs to the late fifth century, on the borderline between myth and history, and though John Bannerman is prepared to consider him a historical figure (Bannerman 1974: 73), I feel that the choice of that name for the founder of a line which settled in Scotland from Ulster makes it more likely that he is an ancestor god. His father Erc may be a masculinised mother like Roich, since this Fergus had a niece also called Erc, whose son Muirchertach mac Erca, the last completely pagan king of Tara to die a ritual 'threefold death' in mysterious circumstances, is also one of the last kings in Ireland to be known by his mother's name rather than his father's. Francis John Byrne (1979: 102) suggests that MacErca(e), which is known as an inde- pendent name, is an attached epithet rather than a metronymic – it could perhaps mean 'Son of Heaven', the title of the Chinese emperors, though *erc* as a noun (RIA Dict.) has five other possible meanings apart from 'heaven' or 'sky', including 'salmon' and 'ad- der', both sacred creatures, and apparently one of the particularly numinous breed of cows that were white with red ears. If it were the name of Fergus's mother, the name given for Erc's father, Eochaid Munremar ('Eochaid of the thick neck'), using one of the names associated with the Dagda, could well be that of Fergus's father; the genealogy reads 'Fergus son of Erc son of Eochaid' but should read 'Fergus son of Erc (feminine) *and* son of Eochaid'. At any rate, the point is that this Fergus had a brother Oengus, whose descendants held land in Islay. Even here, unfortunately, my paradigm for the twins is spoiled by the presence of a third brother, Loarn: families in Scotland up to quite recent times have always liked to claim descent from sets of three brothers, and Bannerman (1974: 121–7) in fact suggests that both Oengus and Loarn are ancestors of unrelated lines artificially brought into the line of Fergus.

The definitely divine Oengus is son of the Dagda by Boand, the goddess of the river Boyne by which his residence stands: her name means 'white cow' rather than horse, but could easily be accounted an alias for Macha. She has been identified with the Morrígán, Macha's sister in a trinity of virtually indistinguishable war-god- desses, whose mating with the Dagda by a river is described in the story of the Battle of Moytura, a tale full of ancient mythology (Sjoestedt 1949: 41). But what is the significance of the name Oengus? If it were translated as 'unique', for instance, it would be a most unsuitable name for a twin. I think the 'oneness' described by the name is the magic singularisation of parts of the body normally occurring in pairs, which appears as a feature of magicians and supernatural beings in Gaelic tradition up to modern times. (Thus the late William MacDonald, Arisaig, describing the magical hermit or 'Man in the Cassock' whom Murchadh son of Brian meets in a well-known hero-tale, recited at high speed – 'He had only one leg, one arm, one nose, one mouth, one eye, one ear, one head!' SA 1954/37 B4). The power of the mutilation is best shown in the tale of Cú Chulainn's death, where the creation of some of his killers is thus described by Sjoestedt (1949: 78):

> Cú Chulainn had killed Calatin the Brave and his twenty-seven sons long before. But his wife had borne six posthumous children at one birth, three sons and three daughters. Queen Medb, planning the hero's death, made these children into sorcerers. For that purpose the right foot and the left hand of the sons are cut off and the left eye of each of the daughters is blinded, an initiatory mutilation of magicians of which we heard an echo in other myths. So also Odin paid with one of his eyes for his knowledge of runes.

Among Irish deities Nuadu, once ruler of the Tuatha Dé Danann, had one arm and in some tales one eye; using the pagan Irish theory that the king must be physically perfect, the storytellers make him a king deposed for these blemishes. But clearly he remained a god, and is paralleled in the Norse pantheon by the one-handed Tyr as well as the one-eyed Odin. A parallel on earth is supplied by the culture-hero of the Connachta, Cormac mac Airt, who is wounded in the eye by an Oengus who probably represents the god, and though not deposed has to leave Tara, and dies soon after (Byrne 1973: 55–6).

O'Rahilly identifies a number of other one-eyed heroes, ancestors and divinities in early Irish sources, really sun-gods according to him, since he claims that the Irish word for eye, *súil*, originally meant 'sun' and is cognate with Latin *sol* (O'Rahilly 1946: 58). He goes on to connect them with the lightning-spear, *gaí bolga* – the word may be related to Latin *fulgur* – which is wielded by Cú Chulainn in the *Táin*, but belongs properly to the lightning-god Bolg, otherwise known as Oengus Bolg, the ancestor-god of the Érainn, the race to which the Ulster dynasty belonged (O'Rahilly 1946: 51, 59ff). He had avatars called Oengus of the Bloody Spear and Oengus of the Venomous Spear, the latter being the one who wounded Cormac in the eye. The weapon, however, has also associations with Fergus, though it is perhaps significant that for him it is not a spear but a sword, with which in the *Táin* he shears off the tops of three hills to sate his battle-rage – clearly Fergus is more than human. The sword's name, Caladbolg, contains the same element,

=*bolg*, and its Welsh cognate *Caledvwlch* is the original form of
Arthur's Excalibur (O'Rahilly 1946: 68–70). However, this is a
digression: at least there is reason to associate Oengus's name with
one-eyed gods, though perhaps not with one who was the opponent
of the Tuatha Dé Danann, Balor of the Evil Eye. There is also at
least one Oengus connected with one arm (or hand – the Gaelic
word means both), an Ulster hero of some importance called Oengus mac Oenlaim Gabe, 'Angus son of One-Arm the Blacksmith'
perhaps, though the last word has been variously interpreted (Thurneysen 1921: 184–6 etc.; Kinsella 1970: 164).

By this interpretation, Oengus is the magician or priest, in Celtic
terms the druid of the pair, while Fergus, as his name 'manliness'
implies, is the warrior. In Dumézilian terms they therefore represent two of the three functions, and it is interesting that their father
the Dagda, who is most often represented as a rather uncouth
fertility-figure, seems to represent the third. (Their mother,
however, covers all three: goddesses in Celtic theology tend to be
omnicompetent.) O'Rahilly might see Oengus as the one-eyed
'Otherworld deity' and Fergus as more like the 'young hero',
though as both of them are ancestor figures, they have to be in some
sense old; we may have to accept O'Rahilly's suggestion (1946: 517)
that Oengus became Oengus Óc, 'Young Angus', by a later conflation of Oengus with a separate Young Hero god, Macc ind Óc, the
equivalent of the Gaulish boy-god Maponos, the Welsh Mabon. We
can reconcile O'Rahilly's opposition with the twin picture by using a
form of the paradigm of kingship proposed by Emily Lyle in her
paper 'Whites and Reds' (Lyle 1988), though I may be slightly
altering her case. Oengus represents the 'white', priestly function,
and is king of the dead; Fergus represents the 'red', warrior function, and is king of the living. He replaced his one-eyed predecessor
by killing him and so making him king of the dead: so – and here I
think is where I may differ from Dr Lyle – every king is Fergus while
he lives and Oengus after his death; but Oengus, perhaps in the
person of a druid, will eventually help someone else to kill Fergus
and become Fergus in his turn.

I want briefly to follow this proposition by studying a death-tale
for each of the pair, which will involve a little bit of playing the
name-substitution or 'multiform' game. First and simpler is the tale
of Fergus mac Roich's death. I am astonished that, to my knowledge, nobody has ever drawn proper attention to the striking resemblance between this story and the death of Baldur in Norse
mythology: it was this that first made me wonder whether Fergus
was really human or divine. I have already outlined the situation in
the *Táin*: Fergus is the leader of a band of Ulstermen in voluntary

exile in Connacht, and he never went back to Ulster. His hosts are Medb queen of Connacht, generally agreed to be a divine figure, and her husband Ailill, whose status is more doubtful, but who is said to be a son of Rus Ruad and therefore at least half-brother of Fergus. Ailill is another name that was used by historical Irishmen in early Christian times, but O'Rahilly (1946: 300 n.3) has no doubt that it is a god-name, which he suggests is originally the same as Welsh *ellyll*, 'a spirit, an elf': I suspect the choice of this name for the euhemerised god as king of Connacht in the *Táin* is governed by the fact that, according to the histories, the last king of Connacht who ruled in Tara after Niall of the Nine Hostages was called Ailill Molt, 'Ailill the Wether'. There is in fact some justification, apart from O'Rahilly's identification of Ailill or Aillén as the 'Otherworld God', for saying he could also be called Oengus; for Bolg, the ancestor-god of the Érainn, is sometimes called Oengus Bolg and sometimes Ailill Érann (O'Rahilly 1946: 51).

Ailill and Fergus are represented as rivals for the favours of Medb, though all three are credited with other affairs on a scale that would put American soap-opera to shame. But on one occasion, as Ailill watched Fergus and Medb swimming entwined in a loch, he was seized with sudden jealousy. He spoke to Lugaid Dalléces, Lugaid the Blind Poet – his brother, according to the Edinburgh MS. which is our only source, but never mentioned elsewhere – describing them as a hart and a doe, and Lugaid, clearly a member of the sporting gentry as well as a poet, reacted as expected: 'Why not kill them?' Though he was blind, Lugaid never missed his aim, so when Ailill pointed him in the right direction and put a spear in his hand, he killed Fergus (Medb had meanwhile come out of the water). When Lugaid heard what he had done, he lamented his blameless crime: Ailill leapt in his chariot and fled, and the dying Fergus drew the spear from his breast and threw it after him, killing a hound at the back of the chariot.[7] The main point here is certainly the blameless and unnatural killing: there is also probably an element of the Threefold or at least Twofold Death motif often associated with pagan Irish kings, since Fergus should be both wounded and drowned in the loch, though the author of the tale as it survives allows him to swim ashore and die on dry land.

In terms of the Fergus/Oengus opposition, it seems here as if Oengus in this story is split into two persons: Ailill representing the seeing eye and Lugaid the blind one. The point of this is to ritualise the killing by making it blameless, impossible and yet inevitable – as none of woman born can kill Macbeth, only the shot of a blind man can kill Fergus. But this blind man has exchanged his sight for a magical insight which enables him to hit his target every time,

though not to distinguish between a deer and man. As Gordon
Howie said, the gods themselves are subject to fate. The resemblance between this story and the killing of Baldur by his blind
brother Höðr is too close, I think, to be due to mere chance or the
borrowing in Christian times of a good story: we may well be dealing
with an Indo-European myth, clothed in very different details.[8] In
the Norse account, the impossible element has changed: Höðr
knows that he is aiming at Baldur at short range, and allows his hand
to be guided by Loki, because this is a game that all the gods play,
confident that everything in creation has sworn not to harm Baldur.
But Loki has found that the mistletoe has not sworn and gives Höðr
a spear made of it, which duly kills Baldur (Turville-Petre 1964:
106). I cannot avoid wondering if there could be something more
than coincidence in the resemblance between the names of Baldur
and Loki in the Norse myth and those of Balor and Lug in a myth
equally important in Irish tradition, whose climax is the shooting of
Balor by Lug with a sling-shot.[9]

There is no tale of great interest about the death of anyone called
Oengus, though the one-eyed Balor could be taken as a multiform
of his. For this I want to substitute the other pair of names which
could be taken to apply to divine twins, though I have so far avoided
them because Fergus and Oengus are more relevant to Macha and
the Ulster Cycle. These names are Finn, best known from the hero
Fionn mac Cumhaill, who is generally agreed to be derived from an
earlier divinity, and Donn, an ancestor-figure generally agreed to
represent an ancient god.[10] The names, meaning 'Fair-haired' and
'Brown-haired', or indeed Light and Dark, are obviously contrasted. The equivalence would be between Donn, the underworld
god, and Oengus, while Finn has connections with Fergus: Finn Fili,
'Finn the Poet', is his brother as son of Rus Ruad and an ancestor of
Leinster kings, and in later tales of Fionn mac Cumhaill his poet is
Fearghus Fionn Filidh, a conflation of the two names. But again,
Finn and Donn are not normally the names either of brothers or
even of a contrasting pair, except in the case of the Donn Cuailnge,
the Brown [Bull] of Cooley, and Finnbennach Aí, the Fair-Horned
one of Aí in Connacht, the two bulls whose rivalry for pre-eminence
is the root of the whole epic of the *Táin*. O'Rahilly (1946: 278–9)
makes much of Fionn mac Cumhaill's opponents who are one-eyed,
including his rival Goll mac Mórna, whose name means 'one-eyed',
and his own ancestor the god Nuadu. But one major conflict of his
life is with a follower who has been taken as an avatar of the god
Donn, Diarmaid, who is sometimes given the epithet Donn himself
and sometimes said to have a father, grandfather or other ancestor
called Donn. *Diarmaid* itself has been explained as meaning 'the

Armed God', *deus armatus*, though again the name was used by mortals, most significantly by Diarmait mac Cerbaill, son of Fergus of the Crooked Mouth, the last more or less pagan king of Tara. He is credited with a remarkably complex fated death, dressed in a shirt made of one flax seed (and its produce), and a cloak made of one sheep's wool, having eaten the meat of pigs that were never born and beer brewed from one grain of corn, killed by a spear-wound, but also by the roof-beam of a burning house falling on him, and drowned in an ale-vat where he had taken refuge from the flames (Byrne 1973: 97–9).

I am not sure whether we *should* look for tales of the death of the Oengus or Donn member of the pair, given that this is the king of the dead by my interpretation, and it is Fergus or Finn, the king of the living, who has to be killed by his successor. But looking at it another way, he is about to change places and names with his predecessor and become Oengus or Donn himself, and as O'Rahilly says, there are many tales of the defeat of the one-eyed 'Otherworld deity' by the 'young hero'. He was in fact puzzled by the rivalry of Diarmaid and Finn for the hand of Gráinne (perhaps a fertility goddess originally, whose name seems to mean 'grain'), because he thought that Finn had changed from the role of young hero to that of Otherworld deity here, when Gráinne deserts him for the younger Diarmaid (O'Rahilly 1946: 277 n.7). But though Finn is the older and more passive of the pair in the story as now told, Diarmaid is the one who is killed. In terms of our equivalence, it is worth noticing that Diarmaid is depicted in the late mediaeval romance as a foster-son and protégé of the god Oengus of the Brugh, who after his death misses him so much that he adopts the rather gruesome device of putting a spare soul in his body so that he can talk to him. But the wild boar that kills Diarmaid is also the reincarnation of his own half-brother, the son of Oengus's steward and Diarmaid's mother, killed as a child by Diarmaid's father Donn. Diarmaid is therefore placed under a tabu by Oengus never to hunt swine, but disobeys it. His death is naturally compared with that of Adonis, but in the version preserved in a Scottish ballad he is not killed directly by the boar, but kills it, and then Finn, who knows something he does not, asks him to measure its length by pacing along its back with his bare feet. He has to do this in both directions before a poisonous bristle goes into his foot and causes his death: apparently he is invulnerable otherwise, and this is his Achilles heel. At any rate Finn like Ailill manages to avoid directly killing his rival, but secures his death in an improbable way by use of magic or at least of another's supernatural powers.

I hope there may be some real significance in all this speculation and playing of the name-game. At any rate it has been fun for me, and I will be pleased if other members of the Society are interested in following up some of these ideas.

NOTES

1. This is most easily shown by the survival of the element *síd*, 'otherworld', from which the Tuatha Dé Danann are also known as *aes síde*, 'people of the *Síd*', in modern Irish and Scottish Gaelic words such as *sídheóg* or *sìdhiche*, 'fairy', or *sìdhean*, 'fairy hill'.

2. The classic study of the cycle remains Thurneysen 1921, but I have occasionally referred to accessible English translations of the main stories now available in Kinsella 1970 and Gantz 1981. For the historical setting see Byrne 1973, chapters 4 and 5 particularly.

3. References to RIA Dict. should always be understood to be under the word being discussed, in this case *Macha*, and this is the basic source for any translation of a single word, whether or not explicitly cited.

4. Sjoestedt 1949: 318. Gantz 1981: 128–9 and Kinsella 1970: 6–7 give different translations of another version from that summarised here; for the three recensions and their differences see Thurneysen 1921: 360–3.

5. O'Rahilly 1946: 318. See Bruford 1985, especially p. 16 for *ruad(h)*.

6. See RIA Dict. s.v. *forgu* or *forggu*, 'choice': I assume this root could be involved, though historians treat the name as simply a by-form of Fergus.

7. Thurneysen 1921: 575–6; full text and translation in Meyer 1906: 32–5.

8. It is generally assumed that borrowing of this sort is from Irish to Norse, but it seems unlikely from Christian Irish to pagan Norse; on the other hand the Irish tale is well naturalised and though the existing MS is later than Snorri's Edda it is difficult to imagine the latter or the verse sources it uses being taken to Ireland, and in any case the tale judging by the language is much older than Snorri.

9. The Battle of Moytura, see Sjoestedt 43–4: note that although Lug's opponent is the one-eyed Balor, Lug himself exhorts the army 'on one foot and with one eye'.

10. See Mac Cana 1970: 42–4, 110, 113 and O'Rahilly 483–4; but for a caveat about the roles of the rivals and the whole method indulged in in this paper, see also Bruford 1987: 29–30.

REFERENCES

Bannerman, John (1974). *Studies in the History of Dalriada*. Edinburgh: Scottish Academic Press.

Bruford, Alan (1985). Colour Epithets for Gaelic Chiefs. *Shadow* 2, 14–23.

—(1987). Oral and Literary Fenian Tales, in *The Heroic Process*, ed. Bo Almquist, Séamus Ó Catháin and Pádraig Ó Héalai. Dublin: The Glendale Press.

Byrne, Francis John (1973). *Irish Kings and High-Kings*. London: B. T. Batsford.

Gantz, Jeffrey (1981). *Early Irish Myths and Sagas*. Harmondsworth: Penguin Classics.

Kinsella, Thomas (1970). *The Táin*. Oxford: Oxford University Press.

Lyle, Emily (1988). Whites and Reds: The Roman Circus and Alternate Succession. *Cosmos* 2, 148–63.

Mac Cana, Proinsias (1970). *Celtic Mythology*. London: Hamlyn.

Meyer, Kuno (1906). *Death-Tales of the Ulster Heroes*. Dublin: Royal Irish Academy Todd Lecture Series 14.

O'Rahilly, Thomas F. (1946) *Early Irish History and Mythology*. Dublin: Dublin Institute for Advanced Studies.

RIA Dict. *Dictionary of the Irish Language* (and *Contributions to a Dictionary of the Irish Language*), based mainly on Old and Middle Irish Materials. Dublin: Royal Irish Academy, 1913–76. See note 3.

SA. Recorded tapes (main chronological series) in the School of Scottish Studies, University of Edinburgh.

Sjoestedt, Marie-Louise (1949). *Gods and Heroes of the Celts*, translated by Myles Dillon. London: Methuen.

Thurneysen, Rudolf (1921). *Die irische Helden- und Königsage bis zum siebzehnten Jahrhundert*. Teil I und II. Halle (Saale): Max Niemeyer.

Turville-Petre, E. O. G. (1964). *Myth and Religion of the North*. London: Weidenfeld and Nicolson.

EMILY LYLE

Old Myth and New Morality: A Theogonic Interpretation of the Fourth Branch of the *Mabinogi*

The set of Middle Welsh prose narratives known as the *Four Branches of the Mabinogi* (*Pedeir Keinc y Mabinogi*) seems to have been first set down in writing in or about the twelfth century AD, but, despite this relatively late date, it is reckoned to be one of the principal repositories of reminiscences of pre-Christian Celtic religion in Welsh tradition, and I suggest that we can tentatively trace in the Fourth Branch the entire Indo-European pantheon of major gods, ordered as a theogony. The *Mabinogi* as a whole is a distinctive and remarkable piece of writing, which is held to be the work of a single redactor, to whom I shall refer in this study as 'the author'.

Recent sensitive studies of the *Mabinogi* (Bollard 1974–5, 1985; Mac Cana 1977: 21–61; Lloyd-Morgan 1988) have given insight into the characteristics of the author and his modes of composition, and this allows us, I suggest, to disentangle the threads of old myth from those of the new morality congenial to him. Of course, the disentangling is not relevant to the study of the work as artistic composition, except in so far as understanding the process of creation may highlight certain features of it, but, when it comes to the exploration of the mythic level, it is essential to attempt the task of distinguishing the mythic narrative from later accretions. This is not, as might be supposed, a matter of identifying all the fantastic elements as mythic, and stretches of sober narrative as the author's individual contribution. Understanding of the author has reached the point where it is possible to be more subtle and allow for the possibility that fantastic features may stem from his imaginative handling of narrative motifs rather than from a mythic source.

The author values highly the virtues of restraint and moderation; he has a keen sense of right and wrong and is an upholder of law (cf. Mac Cana 1977: 46–9, 60). The 'wrong' in his narrative may be actual crime or may be some departure from a code of social conduct, but in any case it is striking how often the wrong has a consequence in the following action in terms of guilt, shame, reparation, retribution, or punishment. It is not simply that we can identify a cast of mind of the author, but that we can distinguish a means by which the author weaves his narrative. A wrong has its consequences in inner feelings and outer manifestations. The opening episode of the First Branch may be taken as an illustration of the point. When Pwyll sees a strange pack of hounds kill a deer, he drives these hounds from the carcase and feeds his own hounds on it. This is immediately shown up as a wrong action when the huntsman whose hounds had killed the deer comes up and drives off Pwyll's hounds. Pwyll acknowledges his discourtesy and asks to be allowed to redeem himself in the stranger's eyes, and this request motivates his visit to Annwn which forms the rest of this sequence of action. An event is judged in moral and legal terms, and action flows from that judgement. This is quite different from myth. Although myth may receive a moral gloss, it is not fundamentally moral, and is frequently either amoral or actually immoral in terms of normal social conduct. In the case of a theogony, the only essential is the coming into being of the gods. The births in the Fourth Branch stem from rape followed by condemnation and punishment, and from illicit intercourse, and stripping away the moral overtones typical of this author seems to enable us to see more clearly the mythic pattern of the conception and birth of the young gods. It should be noted that the Fourth Branch does not deal with the initial stages of creation. People of two generations are already adult when the story opens, and, assuming that this is indeed a theogony, these people correspond to the old gods, and we only witness the birth of the young gods who are their children. Before examining their birth stories in more detail, it is necessary to look at the current state of scholarship on the question of Indo-European theogony.

I differ from C. Scott Littleton and Jaan Puhvel in my placing of what has been called the 'kingship in heaven' theme (Littleton 1970; 1982: 85–6, 161), which, as Puhvel states in his recent book (1987: 23), is characterised by 'a certain dynastic depth, as if the "current" layer of ruling divinity resulted from generations of succession'. For these scholars, this is emphatically not an Indo-European theme and its occurrence in Indo-European contexts, as in the *Theogony* of Hesiod, is the result of 'ancient Near Eastern diffusionism' (Puhvel 1987: 31) from non-Indo-European sources. While I am quite prepared to grant that there may have been a specifically Near Eastern development of the theme, I find that a narrative of the succession of three generations of kings is one way – and a most important way – of expressing the Indo-European cosmogony, which in my view forms a continuum with other cosmogonies in the archaic old world and is not to be sharply distinguished from them. The birth of the final king in the succession and the completion of the creation of the cosmos are one event. Bruce Lincoln (1986: 159–62) has studied the Irish story of Lugaid Red Stripes (*Lugaid Riab ndearg*) exclusively as a regiogony – the creation of a king – but I do not think it necessary to have the concept of a regiogony as distinct from a cosmogony here, or perhaps elsewhere either.

Nor do I think it desirable to distinguish anthropogony from cosmogony in a key story that Lincoln and Puhvel have done much to elucidate, that of 'twin and man' (Lincoln 1975; Puhvel 1975; 1987: 284–90). They treat this as anthropogony, Puhvel speaking of a 'reconstructed Indo-European creation myth of man and society' that rests on the triple foundation of Yama and Manu in India, Tuisto and Mannus in Germania, and Remus and Romulus in Rome (1987: 289–90). I have shown elsewhere that this story of the hostile twins can be treated as cosmogony, the Romulus figure being the last in the succession of three kings while the Remus figure is king of the dead (Lyle 1985: 3–5; 1986: 154–7). Some earlier scholars have been inhibited from using the full evidence on the hostile twins because the story is found outside the Indo-European tradition as well as inside it and so could not be regarded as uniquely Indo-European, but this does not create any difficulty when one sees Indo-European and other old world cosmogonies as a continuum instead of hypothesising a complete break between them.

My approach gives a more integrated result than that arrived at by former scholars, without separate king-creating and man-creating stories, but simply with a total cosmogony which deals at once with the creation of the cosmos, kings, and mankind. In so far as it deals with personalised beings, it can be studied as a theogony. In the final stage of creation, we are looking for the birth of a) a series of children, each one of whom takes after a specific parent (see Lyle 1982: 36–9; 1985: 88–9), and b) the birth of a Yama and Manu pair. Both parts of this pattern are in evidence in the Fourth Branch.

It is a further aspect of the general cosmological hypothesis that the Manu or Romulus figure, the young king of the living, corresponds to Lugaid Red Stripes, and combines the attributes of three fathers. This is explicit in the Lugaid case, where Lugaid is said to have the head of one father, Nar, the upper body of a second, Bres, and the lower body of a third, Lothar. Although this story is of great value, it does not set the birth in the context of the birth of siblings, and, for a useful model here, we have to go to the parallel account of a birth from three fathers in Plutarch's *Of Isis and Osiris* (see Lyle 1985: 7). In this cosmological story, Rhea (Nut) lies with three gods and gives birth to five gods by all three of them, of whom Seth and Horus correspond to Yama and Manu. Taking some elements from this theogony and some from the theogony of Hesiod in the light of other parallels, I have proposed a model with four old gods consisting of earth (female) and sky (male) and their two sons, and six young gods including the Yama and Manu pair. It is largely on the strength of the Indian Mādhavi story which was compared by Dumézil with that of Lugaid Red Stripes that I have also postulated that each of the four young gods (apart from the separate pair) takes after a specific parent and that ideally there are three males and one female (Dumézil 1973: 70–107; Lyle 1982: 36–9).

This total pattern is shown in Figure 1, with males indicated by triangles and females by circles. I have distinguished the Yama twin associated with death by showing this figure as a black triangle. I have also distinguished one of the fathers by shading the appropriate triangle and have shown the corresponding young god in the same way. This father is the one who claims exclusive rights over the female, as illustrated in the Plutarch story where one god is regarded as the husband and the others as lovers, that is, he is in a separate and exclusive category whereas the other two old gods belong to the same non-exclusive category. This god is opposed to the conception or birth of the young gods, or a particular one of them, and has the role of preventer. This role is clearly present in the Fourth Branch but is treated unusually, and at this point in the discussion it will be useful to recount the first of the two birth stories in the Fourth Branch.

Math, the king, 'might not live save while his two feet were in the fold of a maiden's lap, unless the turmoil of war prevented him' (*ny bydei uyw, namyn tra uei y deudroet ymlyc croth morwyn, onyt*

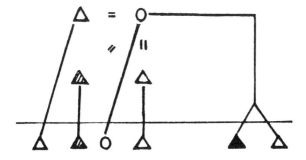

Figure 1

kynwryf ryuel a'y llesteirei).[1] When the story opens, the maiden who serves as Math's foot-holder is Goewin. Math has two nephews, Gwydion and Gilfaethwy, the sons of his sister, Dôn, and Gilfaethwy falls sick out of desire for Goewin. Gwydion, to enable his brother to satisfy his desire, creates a war through the use of his magic powers and Math leaves Goewin at home and goes off to fight. In his absence, Gwydion and Gilfaethwy return, and Gilfaethwy spends a night with Goewin against her will. When Math returns from the war, Goewin tells him of her rape, and Math marries Goewin to make reparation to her, and punishes his nephews by turning them into pairs of wild animals over a period of three years. In the first year, Gwydion is a stag (*carw*) and Gilfaethwy a hind and they return to court with a male fawn, in the second year Gilfaethwy is a boar (*baed*) and Gwydion a sow and they return with a male piglet, and in the third year Gwydion is a wolf (*bleid*) and Gilfaethwy a she-wolf and they return with a male wolf-cub. In each case, Math changes the offspring into human form and the three are called Hyddwn, Hychdwn, and Bleiddwn, their names referring to their animal form and perhaps being translatable as Fawn, Piglet, and Wolf-Cub.[2]

There is one woman in this pattern, Goewin. There is a preventer, Math, who does not allow other males to approach her sexually. He is, however, circumvented by Gwydion and Gilfaethwy working in combination against him and Gilfaethwy lies with Goewin. It can be said that as a result of this rape three sons are born, but clearly the relationship between intercourse and birth is quite exceptional. A story of a sexual encounter is generally a conception story (the category *compert* in Irish tradition) and the encounter is followed in due course by a birth. Here, I suggest, this straightforward link is displaced by a more elaborate tale where the intercourse is treated as the crime of rape which is followed by punishment, the manner of the punishment being to some degree dictated by the ending of the original story, so that the sequence comes to a close with the births. As the crime and punishment sequence is in keeping with the narrative method of the *Mabinogi* author, it can be said that it is likely that a natural conception plus birth story underlay this intricate treatment and that, in terms of the basic story pattern, Goewin is 'really' the mother of the three sons.

Let us look now at the three males who relate to Goewin. The preventer in other narratives may be a usurper and a tyrant, as in the case of Cronus, but here the preventer is sympathetically handled, and he is shown as having an established and respected authority over the other two men both as their senior and as their king. Whereas it is quite possible to show the tricking of the preventer in a positive light, here the act of intercourse is treated both by the author and by Math within the narrative as a crime. Similarly, in the Irish story of Lugaid Red Stripes, the intercourse of the three young men with Clothru is treated negatively, so that we have some justification for positing a specific narrative adaptation in a strain of Celtic tradition which has the effect of allowing Math to be given a positive role in the Fourth Branch.[3] However, despite the sympathetic handling of Math, he is identifiable through his role as preventer as the 'second king' who deposed his father. I have argued elsewhere (Lyle 1985: 153) that the second king is associated with Dumézil's second function, and, accordingly, would place Math as a second function figure, and the pair who oppose him as first and third function figures. The three functions have already been adduced in connection with this narrative by Brinley Rees and Ceridwen Lloyd-Morgan (Rees 1975: 21, 41; Lloyd-Morgan 1988: 5, 10), who relate the transformations to stag and hind, wolf and she-wolf, and boar and sow, to the first, second, and third function respectively. This relationship also seems probable to me, and I think we may be able to work backwards from this series to identify the slots appropriate to Gwydion and Gilfaethwy. Supposing that Goewin is 'really' the mother in the sense defined above, then there seems some likelihood that it is when each of the two brothers is in his male role that he is 'really' the parent of a son. In that case, in the first transformation, Gwydion, who is the stag, would be the father of Hyddwn (Fawn) and first function, and in the second transformation Gilfaethwy, who is the boar, would be the father of Hychdwn (Piglet) and third function. This seems to make good sense of the order of species. The odd one left till last is the second function one appropriate to Math, and, reading at this inner level, we can say that Math is 'really' the father of Bleiddwn (Wolf-Cub), although Gwydion is again the male animal in this transformation.

A second birth story commences when Math seeks another maiden to serve as his foot-holder. The sister of Gwydion and Gilfaethwy, Aranrhod, is proposed for the office, but when Math tests whether or not she is a maiden by causing her to step over his magic wand, she gives birth to a son, Dylan, and also drops a 'small something' (*ryw bethan*) which is kept for a time in a chest by Gwydion and eventually grows into the boy later called Lleu Llaw Gyffes. Gwydion keeps the boy and there is some suggestion in the story that he is his father, though this is never made explicit. Certainly, the shame exhibited by Aranrhod indicates that her sons result from an illicit union. Dylan slips away into the sea shortly after his birth and is not heard of again, and the narrative concentrates on Lleu. In terms of the theogonic model, the covert member

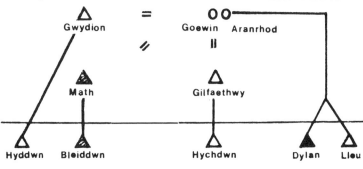

Figure 2

of the twin pair, Dylan, corresponds to the Yama figure and relates to death, while the overt member who lives on earth corresponds to Manu or, in other traditions, Romulus or Horus. The Irish figure that it seems worth while to posit as a possible equivalent to Dylan is Donn, god of death. The Irish equivalent to Lleu has often been identified as Lug, who is one of the principal gods, and the one whom I have already placed as 'third king' in the succession (Lyle 1986: 154–5).

We can now return to the theogonic model and illustrate the roles of the characters in the Fourth Branch in its terms (Figure 2). It will be noticed that there are two females involved at the level of the old gods, where the model calls for only one, and that no female appears at the level of the children, and this superabundance at one point and lack at another suggests that the name of the second woman to be included in the narrative, Aranrhod, may have been borne by a young goddess at the same generational level as Lleu, and that the first of the women named, Goewin, is the representative of the mother goddess who gives birth to all the children.[4] The name Goewin itself may be a substitution for a much more famous one which is mentioned in the narrative, that of Dôn, who is stated to be the mother of Gwydion, Gilfaethwy, and Aranrhod, but who is not introduced as a character. Dôn is thought to correspond to the Irish Danu, the mother of the gods known as the Tuatha Dé Danann, and would be perfectly cast as the single mother goddess in the theogonic model. The failure to give her a role in the narrative could be accounted for by avoidance of the mythic theme of mother-son incest.

A theogony, of course, displays a structure of relationships, and it is through relationships that the gods can be defined. The Fourth Branch provides a particularly rich cluster and supplies a set of names for the total pattern of ten that I have hypothesised. It should

The Fourth Branch of the Mabinogi 149

now be possible to move cautiously from this set to examine possible counterparts in other Celtic narratives, with a view to enriching the contexts and to testing the validity of each of the initial identifications.

Finally, I should make the point that I do not think we are exploring a free system of gods as anthropomorphic deities or of the men or women who stand in for them, but instead that we have to do with a total structure which operates in other areas as well, such as, for instance, divisions of space or of the colour spectrum as well as divisions of the body, as in the story of Lugaid Red Stripes. Each god can be apprehended on a variety of levels, and it is the heavy redundancy of the system, as well as its broad spread throughout the archaic old world, that gives us a good chance of recovering it and comprehending its function. There is no reason why the total system (supposing, as I do, that it once existed) should have been conveyed in every society into the written record on which we are dependent. I take the Fourth Branch of the *Mabinogi* as an indication that it may well be possible to outline the total system in the Celtic instance.

NOTES

1. The Welsh quotations are taken from Williams 1930 and the English translations from Jones and Jones 1949.
2. W. J. Gruffydd discusses the etymology and suggests 'stag-born', 'wolf-born', and 'swine-born' (1928: 319–20); Patrick K. Ford translates 'little stag', '(wolf) cub', and 'piglet' (1977: 189, 192).
3. The adaptation did not affect Celtic tradition as a whole. The preventer figure is shown negatively in the story of Balor and the birth of Lug (see, e.g. Gruffydd 1928: 72–4).
4. The sense that there is one mother at the back of the story as found in the Fourth Branch is conveyed by W. J. Gruffydd (1928: 172–3): 'It will be recollected that it was Goewin who 'was slept with in her despite,' but that it was Arianrhod who gave birth to Llew; that is to say, the *compert* or conception-story of Llew has been divided between two women, one conceiving him, and the other giving birth to him. In other words, his mother is divided into two persons, Goewin . . . and Arianrhod.'

REFERENCES

Bollard, J. K. (1974–5). The Structure of the Four Branches of the Mabinogi. *The Transactions of the Honourable Society of Cymmrodorion*, 250–76.

— (1983). The Role of Myth and Tradition in *The Four Branches of the Mabinogi. Cambridge Medieval Celtic Studies*, No. 5, 67–86.

Dumézil, Georges (1973). *The Destiny of a King*. Chicago and London: Chicago University Press.

Ford, Patrick K., ed. (1977). *The Mabinogi and other Medieval Welsh Tales*. Berkeley, Los Angeles and London: University of California Press.

Gruffydd, W. J. (1928). *Math vab Mathonwy*. Cardiff: University of Wales Press.

Jones, Gwyn and Thomas Jones, tr. (1949). *The Mabinogion*. London: J. M. Dent.

Lincoln, Bruce (1975). The Indo-European Myth of Creation. *History of Religions* 15, 121–45.

— (1986). *Myth, Cosmos, and Society: Indo-European Themes of Creation and Destruction*. Cambridge (Mass.) and London: Harvard University Press.

Littleton, C. Scott (1970). The 'Kingship in Heaven' Theme, in *Myth and Law Among the Indo-Europeans*, ed. Jaan Puhvel (Berkeley, Los Angeles, and London: University of California Press), pp. 83–121.

— (1982). *The New Comparative Mythology: An Anthropological Assessment of the Theories of Georges Dumézil*. 3rd ed. Berkeley, Los Angeles, and London: University of California Press.

Lloyd-Morgan, Ceridwen (1988). Triadic Structures in the Four Branches of the *Mabinogi. Shadow* 5, 3–11.

Lyle, Emily (1982). Dumézil's Three Functions and Indo-European Cosmic Structure. *History of Religions* 22, 25–44.

— (1985). The Place of the Hostile Twins in a Proposed Theogonic Structure. *Cosmos* 1, 1–14.

— (1986). Whites and Reds: The Roman Circus and Alternate Succession. *Cosmos* 2, 148–63.

Mac Cana, Proinsias (1977). *The Mabinogi*. Cardiff: University of Wales Press.

Puhvel, Jaan (1975). *Remus et frater. History of Religions*, 15, 146–57.

— (1987). *Comparative Mythology*. Baltimore and London: Johns Hopkins University Press.

Rees, Brinley (1975). *Ceinciau'r Mabinogi*. Bangor: the author.

Williams, Ifor, ed. (1930). *Pedeir Keinc y Mabinogi*. Cardiff: University of Wales Press.

ANTHONY SHELTON

Preliminary Notes on Some Structural Parallels in the Symbolic and Relational Classifications of Nahuatl and Huichol Deities

Before the Conquest, partition by four was a common principle underlying the symbolic classifications of many Mesoamerican peoples. Historically, the system has deep roots, while geographically, it has been reported from groups in the north-west and Central Mexico to Maya communities in the south and the neighbouring countries of Guatemala and Belize. This paper is concerned with sketching the similarities in the internal and external relations between deities in two linguistically and culturally related Uto-Aztecan groups: the historical Nahuatl communities which occupied the valley of Mexico between the 14th and 16th century, and the contemporary Huichol who inhabit the isolated mountainous terrain in the northern tip of Jalisco and adjacent states.

I. PROBLEMS AND ISSUES IN THE STUDY OF NAHUATL THEOLOGY

The religious and ritual organisation that the Spanish encountered during their first campaigns in México was unlike anything they had previously seen. Its rituals carefully orchestrated by a specific calendar,[1] its doctrine organised into distinct and coherent schools, with a body of sophisticated metaphysical and theological thought to support them, and its integration into the heart of the social, political and economic organisation of the civilisation, was quite unlike that practised by the Caribs, whom the Spanish had already subjected, and called for more sophisticated models to be developed to aid them in understanding its nature and help devise means of undermining it.

Confronted by this strange and bewildering complexity, the Spanish first applied Biblical analogies in an attempt to understand it but later, towards the end of the 16th century, comparisons were increasingly drawn from classical antiquity (King 1972: 25–7). The ideological legacies of these early descriptions of the religious traditions and practices of the new world included lists of deities, formulated as discrete beings with specific powers, like those of the

Old World; deities conceived anthropomorphically; the description of religon and ritual as fields of action distinct from other institutions of the society; and often, in the case of deities, the loss of the internal relations between them which organised them into classes and distinct categories.

Figure 1 *Codex Fejérváry-Mayer* Folio 1, illustrating the pairing of the Lords of the Night and their distribution between the four cardinal points and the centre. Note also the four solar birds and the four sacred trees also associated with the four cardinal precincts of space.

The nature of the Spanish documents and manuscripts has continued to haunt more recent studies: the relationship between the personifications of deities and their internal relationship to more general and encompassing godheads, the nature of the association between godhead and the powers, forces or authority attributed to it, and the external relationship between godheads in their hierarchical and non-hierarchical organisation. Such problems have occasioned two principal schools of thought, which we shall call the abstractionist, and the materialist, approaches. The first, proposed by Alfredo Chavero (Chavero: 1887) considered Nahuatl religion to be focused on the worship of nature, while others identified a spiritualistic pantheon loosely connected to natural phenomena. Chavero conceived deity as creative energy, such as fire, which engendered other phenomena of the world including, by its action on earth, the creation of man. Although León-Portilla is critical of Chavero for denying the spiritual nature of Nahuatl religion (1963: 207) the dynamic creative aspect of deity and its conception as abstract force or energy is similar to the view sometimes held among the Huichol (Shelton 1989). The materialist school includes various interpretive currents which can be summarised as contending sub-themes in their general argument.

1. *The polytheistic and monotheistic interpretations.*

The Spanish chronicler Francisco Lopez de Gómara claimed the number of Aztec gods exceeded two thousand. Early chronicles and native texts supported this view with long lists of different deities which frequently named more than one god with identical powers and jurisdiction. Early studies, most notably by Eduard Seler (1849–1922) on the Sahagún manuscripts and the Borgia group of codexes, and by his student Walter Lehmann, disclosed some of the principles underlying this apparently luxurious and quixotic pantheon.

Against this position, Hermann Beyer, a contemporary of Lehmann and a fellow member of the German School, favoured a view of Aztec religion as monotheistic. In his essay (Beyer 1910) he argued that if:

> . . . we penetrate further into the symbolic language of the myths and the images portrayed in the illustrated manuscripts, we shall note that the blatant polytheism which appears to be characteristic of ancient Mexico is simply a symbolic reference to natural phenomena. The thought of the priests had conceived philosophico-religious ideas of much greater scope. The two thousand gods of that great multitude of which Gómara speaks were for the learned priests and the priestly initiates only so many manifestations of the one. In the figure of the god Tonacatecuhtli we find a substitute for monotheism . . . In order to express the idea that the cosmic forces were emanations of the divine principle, the gods of nature were called children of Tonacatecuhtli.
>
> (Quoted in León-Portilla 1963: 212).

Figure 2 *Codex Borgia* Folio 27. The five aspects of Tlaloc, the
god of rain: top left, the western Tlaloque; top right, the northern
Tlaloque; bottom left, the southern Tlaloque; bottom right, the
eastern Tlaloque. In the middle of the folio, the centre Tlaloque,
also associated with the heavens.

The argument between a polytheistic or monotheistic interpretation of Aztec religion was mediated by Alfonso Caso, who further
developed and focused some of Beyer's insights. In particular, in *La
Religión de los Aztecas* (1936) Caso distinguished three views held
about religion by different sections of the population. He suggests
that the mass of the people endorsed polytheism, anthropomorphis-
ing many natural phenomena including not only elemental forces
but the features of topography which surrounded their dwellings.
The gods more closely connected with agriculture assumed a special

significance and were the subject of exceptional veneration. The priestly class held an intellectual view of these dieties, seeing some as aspects of others and classified them into discrete sets, while working at the same time to extend this intellectual work by integrating the gods of conquered nations and subsuming them under the aspects of already existing categories (Caso 1936: 16–17). Caso also identifies a third religious view inherited from ancient times and held by an élite few, which attributed the origin of the world to a single dual principle, sometimes anthropomorphised and worshipped as a single invisible god (Caso 1936: 8).

Subsequent scholars have accepted the effect of social stratification and occupational specialisation on determining different foci and points of elaboration in Nahuatl religion.

2. *Quadripartite classification as a means of clustering deities and as expressing the relationship between the aspects of a deity and the total godhead*

It is important to distinguish between the pictographic records which illustrate the different spatial aspects of one composite deity or godhead, such as that of the Tlaloques on folio 27 of *Codex Borgia*, and those which depict distinct godheads distributed between the four or five partitions of space, such as the earth deities on leaves 49–52. Nicholson (1971: 403) has proposed a classification of Aztec deities around certain cult themes which sometimes accords well with indigenous depictions, which associate distinct qualities with particular godheads and order them by spatial principles. Within such themes he places complexes of deities which express particular sub-themes subsumed under a general category. The importance of this distinction will become germane when we compare and discuss Huichol concepts of deity.

3. *The relationship between godheads, aspects and their associated powers and jurisdictions*

The Spanish conquerors were quick to testify to the extreme and pervasive religious sentiments of the inhabitants of México. Cortés in a letter to Charles V observed: 'if . . . these people were to be introduced to and instructed in our very holy Catholic faith and were to exchange the devotion, faith and hope they have in their idols for that in the divine power of God . . . it is certain that if they were to serve God with such faith, furor, and diligence, they would accomplish many miracles' (quoted in Nicholson 1971: 395).

The Nahuatl creation stories attribute particular actions and associations with natural phenomena to specific deities. Surviving Aztec narratives describe how the gods sacrificed themselves and became transformed into the phenomena which composed the Nahuatl world. According to one version in the *Histoyre du Mechique* (1905: 28–9), Tezcatlipoca and Quetzalcoatl looked down on the earth monster, Cipactli, swimming in the primordial waters. They transformed themselves into huge serpents which grasped the earth monster and tore her into two halves. From one they formed the earth while the other they raised to become the sky. The other gods, angered by the violence inflicted on Cipactli, decreed that all the food necessary for man's sustenance would grow from her body; trees, flowers and herbs from her hair; grass and small flowers from her skin; wells, springs and small caverns from her eyes; rivers and caves from her mouth; mountains and valleys from her nose and shoulders. The same source (1905: 31–2) describes how Piltzintecuhtli and his wife Xochiquetzal allowed their son Centeotl to be buried so that cotton sprang from his hair, two plants from his ears, chia from his nose, sweet potatoes from his fingers, maize from his nails and other cultigens from the remainder of his body. The Huichol preserve similar myths, attributing the origin of wild plants to the disembodiment of the senior earth deity and mistress of growth, Nakawé.

The theme of the creation of the present world by the sacrifice of the gods underlies many other myths. According to the Aztec, the Sun was formed by Nanahuatl who threw himself on to a huge fire. He was followed by Tecciztecatl, who became the moon. Then the assembled gods appointed Xolotl to be their executioner and sacrificed themselves to feed the sun. Again, similar myths persist today among the Huichol. This shared mythology attests not to the deification of natural phenomena but to the naturalisation of deity among these two Uto-Aztecan groups. The taxonomy of the segmentation of sky, earth or water was expressed through the language of religion, and the relationship of the resulting category to the set which it subsumed incorporated both supernatural and natural precepts.

4. *Hierarchical and non-hierarchical classification of godheads*

Not all Nahuatl deities were directly related to natural phenomena. Some were associated with certain political offices, crafts and industries. Others, such as Quetzalcoatl Ehecatl or Xiuhtecuhtli, combined stewardship over certain natural forces, in these cases wind and fire, with technological or political crafts and arts. This latter tendency may have been more pervasive than so far recognised. Huitzilopochtli, an aspect of the Sun god, was also the patron deity of the Aztec state; Tezcatlipoca, the nocturnal aspect of the sun, was connected with royal descent; and Tlaloc, the rain god, also represented the succession from the Toltec dynasty claimed by all Aztec emperors. Certain deities were associated as patrons or patronesses of particular mercantile and craft groups within Aztec society. It is possible that the position of any such social group within the total hierarchical arrangement of the society closely coincided with the position of their patron deity arranged in a parallel hierarchy of divine beings (Zantwijk 1985). At the peak of this hierarchy was the fire god Xiuhticuhtli, the master of space and time, and closely associated if not identified with the supreme being, Ometeotl. He was recognised as the archetypal ruler and directly affiliated with the emperor or Tlatuani. The close relationship between Xiuhticuhtli and the office of emperor was expressed through the use of turquoise, a highly priced luxury import, over which the emperor had a virtual monopoly (Shelton 1988: 23–5).

Thus in the Aztec pantheon godheads obeyed a quadripartite or quinquepartite partition impregnated by dual natures.[2] It was organised hierarchically to encode and express a political discourse which shadowed the social arrangement within the society.

II. CLASSIFICATORY PRINCIPLES IN NAHUATL RELIGION

A quadripartite principle, often in association with five-fold and binary divisions, ordered the cosmology, cosmogony and part of the social organisation of the Aztec civilisation.[3] By periodising history into five eras and arranging geographical and cosmological space into the four cardinal points complemented by the centre, the Aztec deities and their associated qualities were given definite and well-ordered positions within a highly structured cosmogony.

Quadripartite systems are sometimes transposable to dyadic pairs, but even outside of such higher denominational classifications, binary principles are common in Nahuatl thought (León-Portilla 1963: 99; Nicholson 1971: 409). Such dyadic classifications are characterised not so much as oppositions but as complementary pairs and often signify 'wholeness'. Two examples, the first taken from cosmogony, the second expressing a more pervasive characteristic of cosmology, will serve to illustrate this tendency. In Nahuatl cosmogony, Tonacatecuhtli and his spouse Tonacacihuatl were conceived as the creators of the world who partook and shared the name of Ometeotl. The couple were conceived as an hermaphrodite and together, as aspects of Ometeotl, were used to express the most general, abstract and pervasive force of nature encompassing both spatial and temporal divisions within their unity (León-Portilla 1963: 33–4).

The dyadic principle is also recognisable in the Nahuatl tendency to pair male deities with female consorts, each characterised by similar powers and affiliations. So important is this tendency that León-Portilla contends that paired deities represent a fundamental principle of Nahuatl divinity, juxtaposing an active masculine aspect with a passive or conceiving female counterpart (León-Portilla 1963: 99). Examples include the pairing of the male rain deity, Tlaloc, with Chalchiuhtlicue and the male lord of the underworld, Mictlantecuhtli with his consort Mictecacihuatl.[4]

This section will describe these principles, and their operation, as fundamental vectors for ordering Aztec religious classifications among the five classes of deities, including fire, sky-bearer, earth, rain and wind divinities. These principles will also be seen to be active in defining the association of different godheads with particular cults.

The quadripartite system has its origin in the dual deity Tonacatecuhtli-Tonacacihuatl, Ometeotl, who engendered four sons each associated with a particular colour. The first of these was the Red Tezcatlipoca (Mixcoatl-Camaxtli or Xipe); the second the Black Tezcatlipoca; third, Quetzalcoatl, probably associated with the colour white; and fourth Huitzilopochtli whose diagnostic colour was blue (Nicholson 1971: 398; Olmos 1883: 617). It is Nicholson's opinion that these four deities are aspects of the composite godhead Tezcatlipoca, expressed as a multiplicity to suggest omnipresence.

Two aspects of this godhead, Quetzalcoatl and Huitzilopochtli, created the common people, the Macehualtin, and engendered the fire to warm them and the first only partly luminous Sun which gave but a dull light (Olmos 1883 617–18). This was the first of five creations each of which succeeded the former which ended in a divinely sent cataclysm.[5]

(a) *Fire gods*

Seler (1963) understood the Aztec fire deity, Huehueteotl as having a quadripartite nature. According to Seler, the illustrations of four seated beings in the bottom right-hand corners of leaves 49–52 of the *Codex Borgia* indicate the spatial distribution of fire deities: the direction with which each is associated is the opposite of that of the earth deities, illustrated on the same leaves. Thompson declined to confirm Seler's identification of these deities (or their priestly impersonators) and add his support to the notion of their four-fold nature. Among the older class of Aztec deities, only Quetzalcoatl Ehecatl was thought to have a four-part nature. Furthermore, some of the qualities attributed to Huehueteotl were also shared by Tonacatecuhtli-Tonacacihuatl and might indicate a certain correspondence between them. Because of the indivisible nature of the creator god, any four-fold division would be highly unlikely.

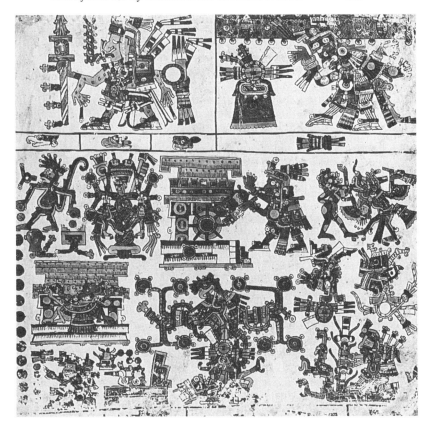

Figure 3 *Codex Borgia* Folio 49. The West. In the top left-hand
corner, Xipe-Totec, an earth-related deity; in the top right-hand
corner, sky-bearer with the heavens resting on his shoulders. The
eastern priest of the fire deity is illustrated in the bottom right-
hand corner. All these deities are associated with the west,
Cihuatlampa, the land of women.

Tatewari, the Huichol equivalent of the Aztec fire god, is attributed a similarly senior status within his respective pantheon and
identified as one of the original creator deities. While regarded for
most purposes as an indivisible being, narratives nevertheless record that he created the world by emitting sparks which fell in each
of the four world directions. Huehueteotl and Tatewari appear to
share many common characteristics and occupy analogous positions
in their respective pantheons.

(b) *Sky bearers*

The quadripartite principle is most clearly evidenced in the account of the fifth creation narrated in the *Historia de los Mexicanos por sus pinturas*:

> And when the four gods had seen that the heaven had fallen upon the earth (after the flood) . . . they ordained that all four should make through the centre of the earth four roads by which to enter it in order to raise the heaven, to assist in which task they created four men. One they called Cotemuc, another Yzcoaclt, another Yzmali, and the fourth Tenesuchi. These four men having been created, the two gods, Tezcatlipuca and Quizalcoatl, then formed themselves into enormous trees, Tezcatlipuca becoming the one known as Tazcaquavilt, meaning the tree of the mirror, and Quizalcoatl the Quezalhuesuch, and gods and men and trees together raised on high the heavens and the stars, just as they are today, and as recompense for having raised them, Tonacatecti (Tonacatecuhtli), the father, made them lords of the heavens and the stars and, when the heaven was raised, Tezcatlipuca and Quizalcoatl walked through it, and made the road that we now see there and met in it, and remained there in it, and held their abode there. After that the heaven was lifted up, the gods renewed life to the earth which had expired when the heaven fell on it, and in the second year after the deluge which was Acatl, Tezcatlipuca altered his name and changed himself into Mixcoatl. (Olmos 1883: 621).

The four sky-bearers are illustrated and given their directional associations on the top right-hand leaves (49–52) of the *Codex Borgia*. Seler in his commentary identifies them as Tlahuizcalpantecuhtli, god of the planet Venus, in the west; Huitzilopochtli, god of fire, in the south; Quetzalcoatl, god of wind, in the east; and Mictlantecuhtli, god of death, in the north. Seler's identification of these deities is not consistent with the account in the *Historia*. Furthermore, Thompson (1934: 217) suggested that Seler misidentified the southern sky-bearer as Huitzilopochtli and argued that the iconography more accurately reflected the Otomie diety Otontecuhtli, a male version of Itzpapalotl, the obsidian butterfly goddess. The sky-bearers are shown in another series of illustrations in *Codex Vaticanus* 3773, folios 19–22, which Seler claims are identical to those shown in the *Codex Borgia*. Thompson confirms this view with the exception of the case already mentioned (Thompson 1934: 218).

The belief that the sky bearers formed a discrete set of four deities is therefore confirmed by all three sources, while the latter two codexes agree on their individual identities and directional associations.

(c) *Earth-related deities*

The top left-hand figures shown on folios 49–52 of the *Codex Borgia* and 19–22 of the *Vaticanus* 3773 have been recognised as earth-associated deities, again arranged by a four-fold principle. The class is identifiable by the rattles which they hold in front of their bodies. Seler named them as Xipe Totec, god of spring and vegetation, in the west; Mictlantecuhtli, god of death and the underworld, in the south; Xochipilli, god of flowers, in the east; and Centeotl, the maize god, in the north.

Thompson proposed that Seler's identification of Xochipilli with the east be amended to Xochipilli-Piltzintecuhtli the young sun-god and hunter. He also pointed out that the earth deities, although clearly directional deities, do not correspond to the same directions as the sky bearers. The day signs below each of the earth deities suggests that they represent the contrary direction to that of the sky bearer (Thompson 1934: 223) as tabulated below.

Quadripartite and quinquepartite classification is also apparent among the important class of rain deities associated with Tlaloc and the wind deities closely related to Quetzalcoatl Ehecatl (Nicholson 1971: 414).

(d) *Rain deities*

The Tlaloques, described as the four helpers of Tlaloc, but better considered as four aspects of that godhead, were each associated

Table 1. The distribution of sky and earth associated deities between the cardinal directions
(Adapted from Thompson 1934: 223)

Codex Borgia	Vaticanus 3773	Spatial Affiliation	Associated Deity	Class Affiliations
Leaf 49	Page 19	East	Tlauizcalpantecutli	Sky
		West	Xipe Totec	Earth
Leaf 50	Page 20	North	Otontecutli	Sky
		South	Mictlantecuhtli	Earth
Leaf 51	Page 21	West	Quetzalcoatl-Ehecatl	Sky
		East	Xochipilli-Piltzintecuhtli	Earth
Leaf 52	Page 22	South	Mictlantecuhtli	Sky
		North	Centeotl	Earth

with a particular quadrant of space. Folio 27 of the *Codex Borgia* illustrates their various manifestations, which Seler 1963: 258–61 has been able to correlate with the four cardinal points by the various colours in which the gods are painted. The Tlaloque associ- ated with the east is painted black and appears in the bottom right-hand corner of the manuscript. His head looks upwards to a dark sky full of clouds while he walks above Cipactli, representing the earth, from which strong ears of maize are sprouting. Illustrated above the Black Tlaloc is the Yellow Tlaloc associated with the north. The sky above him is bright with rays of light, while the earth below him is dry. The ears of maize that grew from the earth are consumed by locusts, and those that fall from the vessels of water that he empties on the earth are already devoured. In the upper left-hand corner of the manuscript, a Blue Tlaloc is shown corre- sponding to the west, below a dark sky obscured by clouds. The ears of maize beneath him, while well formed and abundant, are inun- dated by water, indicating his association with excessive rainfall. Below this section is the Red Tlaloc, related to the south. He stands beneath a clear sky with rays of light shooting down towards the sky. The earth is arid and the maize, unable to sprout through its surface, is consumed by animals with skeletal jaws.

According to the *Historia de los Mexicanos por sus pinturas*, Tlaloc lived in a mansion with many rooms, occupied by the Tla- loque. Each had a vessel containing water and a pole with which to bang it to bring the rains. The account confirms the illustrations on folio 27 of the *Borgia Codex* and describes the water of one Tla- loque as good, causing the plants to germinate, while the water of another is excessive, and inundates the fields, another brings ice and sleet, and the fourth is ineffective in causing germination of the maize (Olmos 1883: 618). Other authors claim that there were many Tlaloques and each took his name from the mountain which he was believed to inhabit (Durán 1971: 156). Sahagún names several such mountains – Tepetzinco, Tepepulco, Quauchtepetl, Yoaltecatl Poiauhtla, Cocotl, Yauhquene – and a whirlpool in lake Tezcoco called Pantitlan (Sahagún 1976: 72–73), but Seler believes these need not be oriented to the cardinal directions (1941: 8). With one exception, these do not correspond with the names of the Tlaloques given in the *Primeros Memoriales*:[6] Opuchtli, Yauhqueme, To- miyauhtecuhtli, Atlahua, and Napatecuhtli (León-Portilla 1958: 130–41). It has not been possible, with the exception of the associ- ation of Opuchtli with the south, to relate these last-named deities to the quadrants of space occupied by the figures on leaf 27 of the *Codex Borgia*.

(e) *Wind gods*

Closely connected with the Tlaloques were the wind gods, who 'swept a path' in anticipation of the rains. Again they were considered to be four in number, arranged between the cardinal directions under the godhead of Quetzalcoatl Ehecatl. From the east blew Tlalocayotl, a gentle, warm and beneficial wind; from the north blew Mictlampa Ehecatl, a cold and violent wind that caused the canoes in the lake around Tenochtitlan to capsize. Ciuatlampa Ehecatl issued from the west, a fresh but humid wind that had its origins in the house of women. The fourth wind, Uitztlampa Ehecatl, was associated with the south and was also considered violent (Soustelle 1959: 78).

(f) *Cult themes*

Besides the Nahuatl tendency to impute a four-fold nature to their secondary divinities (secondary in the sense that most were created by the four sons of the supreme god), godheads were themselves clustered together and organised according to a quadripartite or quinquepartite principle according to the cults with which they were connected (Nicholson 1971: 408). One such example identified by Seler (1963: 258–61) and Thompson (1934: 224) centres on the deities connected with the vicissitudes of the maize, and is illustrated on leaves 49–52 of the *Codex Borgia*, leaves 12 and 13 of the *Codex Bologna* and sheets 33 and 34 of the *Codex Fejérváry-Mayer*. The deities which all three illustrate are Tonatiuh, the sun deity, associated with the east; Itztlacoliuhqui (or Itztlacoliuhqui-Tezcatlipoca in the codexes Bologna and Fejérváry-Mayer), a god of cold and penitence connected with the north; Centéotl, the maize god, associated with the west; and Mictlantecuhtli, god of death and the underworld, related to the south. The earth deities previously discussed may be another example of this tendency.[7] A similar tendency is also observable in Huichol religion and will be described in the next section.

Clearly quadripartite classification was an important principle underlying the concept of deity in Aztec Mexico. Since the distinct aspects were related to spatial partitions, deities were sometimes expressed as being composed of five aspects by the inclusion of the centre, a precept which Thompson believes was more commonly used when describing terrestrial deities rather than those of the sky (Thompson 1934: 224). Similar principles may have extended as far south as the Maya, where Thompson has argued that the Bacabs, Chacs and Pauahtuns – sky bearers, rain gods and wind gods respectively – also shared in a quadripartite nature (Thompson 1934): it is also probable that the supreme deity Itzamna similarly had a

four-fold being (Thompson 1939: 160). Although Thompson identified twenty general elements shared by both México and Maya
religious thought and practices, and nine particular similarities
between their conceptions of sky bearers (1934: 239–40), many may
have been exported from central México and took root within a
conceptual system already responsive and amenable to incorporating ideas from a classificatory system arranged along similar
principles as itself (Thompson 1934: 238).

III. CLASSIFICATORY PRINCIPLES IN HUICHOL RELIGION

The complexity and the political integrations of Nahuatl religion
would not have been possible without the existence of a specialised class of priests. The intellectual achievements of the Aztec
civilisation, with its elaborate division of labour and specialisation
organised by a complex state apparatus, are perhaps what
distinguishes the structure of its ideological system most from
that of the Huichol and other contemporary Uto-Aztecan
societies.

    I have written on Huichol cosmology elsewhere (Shelton 1989).
What I now propose to do is to develop certain themes discussed
there which will permit comparison between Huichol religion and
that of the historical Aztec described above.

    Huichol thought is strongly structured by dualism and quadripar-
tite, quinquepartite and seven-fold classificatory principles.

    Huichol dualism is most importantly manifested in the division
between male and female deities. Each category is associated with
control over particular elements: female deities affiliated to the
earth, water and maize, and male deities affiliated to light, heat and
wind. However, although the principal deities with jurisdiction over
these elements follow this strict division, lesser deities subsumed
under them may not always correspond to such gender distri-
butions, as will be seen later. Male deities were created first, followed by female deities. Each category was created by the
paramount deity representing each category. The fire deity Tatewari created the male deities from flames and arranged their spatial
distribution, while Nakawé, the principal earth deity associated
with growth, brought the female deities forth from the primeval
waters. The birth of the male and female deities is recounted by
myth:

    Nakawé then seated the great gods of the world around her,
    and blessed them in their order, men on one side and women
    on the other. Thus were the gods dedicated, as well as the
    arrows and votive bowls belonging to each.
    Then Nakawé said, 'I wish to see whether this new world is

not better than the old one made by the Sun. I will fix and determine the work of all you gods.'

To the male gods who had not been drowned in the flood she assigned the seas and waters. They passed through the seas to the other side. Nakawé saw that this was well. Then she assigned to each god the thing that corresponded to him. She also caused the female gods to bathe in the sea. They went into the water and walked to the other side.

To another woman she said, 'You were the water, but I shall change you into foam. You will be called *Ereno* (foam).' Nakawé sent Ereno to the end of the sea where the sun rises. Here Ereno sat like air (or wind). After five days Ereno, the Huichol goddess of love, became a beautiful woman. She sat on the topmost of five mesas. Nakawé made her fields fixing them with her *bordon* (staff).

Nakawé then found a suitable cave for Ereno, to which Ereno could climb in five flights (jumps). Water in a spring, as well as implements, were also provided by Nakawé. Ereno was well content with the cave. Here she placed her arrows and votive bowls.

Keamukame, another goddess, was also assigned a cave (near Jesus Maria, in the Cora country) because there were too many goddesses in the sea. It was a pretty place and it pleased her.

Nakawé took *Kokolumali*, another goddess, to a cave near that of Keamukame. Similarly *Hautsikupuli* was given a cave nearby. Another uínu was likewise provided for not far from Hauttsikupuli. *Rapawieme* chose a great rock, since she was very delicate. Nakawé brought her some blessed (or sacred) water, so she became a spring of water.

Another goddess was placed at a second point of the sea where there is a cave. Aisulita was sent to a cave in this quarter of the world. *Noitcikatci*, too, was given a cave. Here water was placed and blown through the air by Nakawé. The water fell on the floor of the cave resulting in a beautiful round spring.

Then from her belt Nakawé took the things needed by these goddesses. When they were thrown near the springs, beautiful flowers sprang up, each side showing flowers of different colours (Zingg MS 188–90).

As with the Aztec, the Huichol evidence a tendency to pair female deities with male deities, but it appears to be more weakly developed. The only instance where deities of identical form and associated with similar powers are paired is found among the five male deer deities assigned to the five partitions of the earth which

Figure 4 *Codex Borgia* Folio 50. The South. In the top left-hand
corner Mictlantecuhtlī, the underworld god connected with the
earth class of deities. The sky-bearer illustrated in the top right-
hand corner is Huitzilopochtlī. In the bottom right-hand corner is
the northern priest of the fire god.

share their presence with five female deer deities. León-Portilla's
contention that Nahuatl thought embodies a fundamental duality in
combining an active male principle and a passive fecunding female
principle, already discussed, also applies to the Huichol. It is most
clearly evidenced in the myth recounting the birth of the earth,
Tatei Yurianaka. Kauyumarie, a male deer helper of the fire god
Tatewari, and a powerful shaman, had sexual intercourse with Tatei
Yurianaka and caused her womb to grow until finally it was large
enough to provide the land mass of the earth.

In another version (Negrin 1977: 84), similar to the creation story recounted in the *Historia de los Mexicanos*, the male deities, Tatewari, Tau, the Sun, and Kauyumarie emerge from their original home in the underworld Watetuapa and create the earth by journeying down a river on rocks which smash against the contours of the topography to form the present landscape. Then they lift up the sky and elevate the rains to their position in each of the cardinal directions. As has already been indicated by the Huichol narratives recounting the birth and distribution of the gods, a five-fold classification of space incorporating the four cardinal directions and the centre is always adhered to, over and above the quadripartite discriminations that we have so far discussed in the Borgia and Vaticanus codexes. Quinquepartite divisions of space are, however, also much evidenced in central Mexico, as in the illustration of the nine lords of the night paired in each cardinal direction and one in the centre space of the first sheet of *Codex Fejérváry-Mayer* (Burland 1950) or the representation of the Tlaloque on folios 27 and 28 of the *Codex Borgia*.

The quadripartite organisation of Huichol space is described in the narrative retelling the story of the flood. The land mass of the earth was circumscribed and surveyed by Watakamé after the great flood, caused by Nakawé, which destroyed the previous creation. Safe in a canoe that the goddess had instructed him to build, the tide took Watakamé to four rocks which marked the farthest points of the earth. First he sailed to Reunar in the east, then to Rauramanaka in the north and Washao in the west. When Watakamé reached the rock Mahakate in the south, which lies by present day Lake Chapala, the waters began to subside and he disembarked to make his home. The narrative describes the limits of terrestrial space marked by the four rocks which lie at each of the cardinal points. These rocks are believed to be the home of certain deities:
– Reunar in the east is the birth place of the sun, surrounded by the original home of the ancestral deities, the emergence point where they left the underground world to establish the earth. The Sun is believed to rise anew each morning from this mountain which also marks the exit from the underworld.
– Washao, the westernmost rock, stands just off the coast of the state of Nayarit near the small Mexican town of San Blas. It is believed to be the dwelling of the sea goddess Tatei Haramara.
– Mahakate is situated in the south by Lake Chapala, and is associated with an important rain and fertility deity Tatei Rapaviyeme.
– Rauramanaka, in the northern part of Nayarit, is usually associated with the underworld lord Tukakame.
It should be emphasised that the conjunction of these deities repre-

Figure 5 *Codex Borgia* Folio 51. The East. Xochipillī, god of
flowers, associated with the earth class of deities occupies the top
left-hand corner. To his right is pictured Quetzalcoatl Ehecatl, the
eastern sky-bearer. In the bottom right-hand corner is the western
priest of the fire deity.

sents a cluster of different godheads. Generally, they may be con
sidered as part of the cult themes surrounding the propagation and
maturation of the maize, and their similarity with the Nahuatl
version in the *Codex Borgia* is striking.

Both the Huichol and the Nahuatl associate their respective sun
deities with the east. The Nahuatl associate Centéotl, the maize
god, with the west, while the Huichol identify it with Tatei Haramara, the mother of the maize goddesses and the place of their home.
Itztlacoliuhqui, a god of cold and punishment, is assigned by the

Borgia to the north, while the Huichol identify it as the region of cold winds, frost and ice ruled over by Tukakame. Although the Nahuatl god Mictlantecuhtli is usually identified as the underworld deity, death is intimately associated with growth and regeneration (Furst 1982, Baquedano in this volume). Elsewhere, on leaf 50 of the *Codex Borgia*, he is illustrated holding a rattle associating him with the earth and fertility deities. In this guise, his affiliation to the south may correspond to the Huichol version which relates Tatei Rapaviyeme to the same region. Therefore there is a concordance between Nahuatl and Huichol godheads which constitutes a cult theme, although divergences exist on the distribution of their aspects.

Turning now to the composite nature of godheads and their spatial distribution, we may note that the Huichol also preserve the tradition that the heavens are supported by four sky bearers, which like the Nahuatl versions, are distributed between the four cardinal directions. However, unlike the Nahuatl versions, where the sky bearers are distinguished from the trees which Quetzalcoatl and Tezcatlipoca transformed themselves into to raise the sky, the Huichol collude them together. The four trees which uphold the sky were erected by Tatewari in creation times to support the weight of the sun.

(a) *Rain deities*

Perhaps because of their immediate and fundamental importance, the Huichol have greatly elaborated the class of water deities connected with rain and fertility. Lumholtz (1900, 1903), Zingg (1938) and Benitez (1968), previous investigators who have focused on the religion and cosmology of the Huichol, have all enumerated long lists of rain and fertility deities. They have been identified as representing stretches of water (Lumholtz 1900: 13–14) and attributed to particular spatial partitions in the four-fold classification.

Tate Naaliwa'mi	east (red serpent)	Mother	East Water.
Tate Kyewimo'ka	west (white)	Mother	West Water
Tate Rapawiye'me	(blue)	Mother	South Water
Tate Hau'tse Kúpuri		Mother	North Water

Elsewhere they have been described as clouds (Lumholtz 1903: 199 and Negrin 1977: 82, 110) and identified with the four quadrants of space (Shelton 1989).

In most accounts these deities are identified as feminine, are often conceptualised as serpents, and are intimately connected with the rain. In all cases they bear the prefix *tatei* and are closely associated with Nakawé, as their creator, and the wet season ceremonies.

Elsewhere (Shelton Ms) it has been argued that an important characteristic of this set of deities is their transformative capacities. A consideration of Huichol cosmology demonstrates a complex cycle of transformations that such deities undergo in order to bring the rains and renew the fertility of the soil. According to this interpretation, as the wet season draws near the fertility goddesses in the form of serpents ascend the trees – these may be the four trees that support the sky in each of the cardinal directions – and take up their places in the appropriate quadrant of space associated with them. There they become cloud serpents, attracted to the centre world over the Huichol sierra by the ceremonies organised for their propitiation. The cloud serpents, each moving from the direction associated with them, meet in the centre, where they become entangled and fight, sometimes momentarily becoming visible as streaks of lightning crossing the sky. They descend as rain, eventually joining the rivers where they are changed into fish which then return to their original homes, and begin the cycle over again. The belief may have been widely held at one time in Mesoamerica. Although it has little in common with the Nahuatl beliefs that the rain was sent by the Tlaloques pouring their gourds of water down on the earth from each of the cardinal directions, it does suggest that many of the names formerly thought to represent distinct deities may refer only to different manifestations of the four rain deities distributed between the four cardinal directions, themselves, perhaps, only aspects of one central godhead.

(b) *Sea deities*

Fresh water and salt-water deities are clearly distinguished in Huichol thought, and are the subject of distinct classifications. The Huichol conceive of the earth as surrounded by five sea deities, each having her residence in a ridge identified by a particular colour and affiliated to one of the cardinal directions.

1. Tatei Haramara	Muyuavi	clear water	East
2. Tatei Haramara	Mutuza	white water	South
3. Tatei Haramara	Mutazaiya	yellow water	West
4. Tatei Haramara	Mumeriayuve	black water	North
5. Tatei Haramara	Shure	red water	(?)

All five deities share the same prefix *tatei*, indicative of her kin relationship – mother (or aunt) – and an identical principal name. The repetition of the name and the different characteristics of colour and direction assigned each of the appellations strongly suggests that these terms express the omnipresence of the goddess. Different aspects of her being incorporate different characteristics, which taken as a whole represent the complete nature of this serpent being (Shelton MS).

(c) *Wind deities*

A similar principle underlies the assignation of the deer deities, associated with the winds, to the four quadrants of space.

Kauyumarie was placed in the east
Ushikuikame was given guardianship over the south,

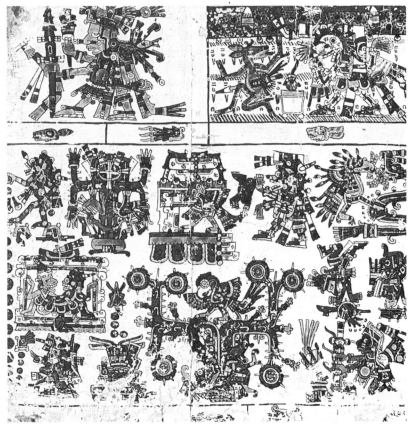

Figure 6 *Codex Borgia* Folio 52. The North. Centeotl, the maize god associated with the earth-related class of deities, stands in the top left-hand corner. To her right is the northern sky-bearer, Mictlantecuhtlī (?). In the bottom right-hand corner is the southern priest of the fire god.

Watemukame was placed in the west and
Nariuame assigned to the north.
Each one of these deer was made ruler over that section of the earth
apportioned to him, while Tatewari, the fire deity and source of
shamanic power, was placed in the centre.

Lumholtz, who worked among the Huichol in the late 19th century, produced another list of deer deities which is unlike the above.
He fails, however, to record the directional association of all but
two of the male deities. By comparing his orthography with that
used by Benitez (1968) and correlating the colour associations of the
deer to that of the five eagle deities which reign in the sky and which
will be discussed next, it has been possible to suggest the directional
distribution of all ten male and female deer (Shelton MS). The deer
deities are distinguished by the length and width of their antlers, the
degree of branching, and their colour.

Deer antlers and the feathers of certain birds are believed to be
the instruments which enable communication between the gods and
between men and the gods to take place: the *mara'akame*, shaman-
priest, uses a prayer stick to which are attached bird feathers to
carry his words to the deities, while Kauyumarie, the deer deity
closely linked to the solar deities and representing the archetypal
shaman, uses his antlers to communicate with both humans and
gods. The colours of the antlers and the plumage of the birds are the
same, and that allows us to suggest the following directional attri-
butions to the set of deer deities listed by Lumholtz (1900: 21–2):

Male deer deities
    Tomat's Wawatsa'li   South (Lumholtz)
    Tomat's O'tota 'Wi   North (Lumholtz)
    Wélika Moye'li Toma'ts   Centre
    Kwir Moye'li Toma'ts   East (?)
    Teola'li Moye'li Toma'ts   West (?)
Female deer deities
    Piwa'mi Moye'li Tate Tako'tsi   North
    Suli'kwai Moye'li Tate Tako'tsi South
    Túra Moye'li Tate Tako'tsi   Centre
    Hapo'li Moye'li Tate Tako'tsi   East
    Totowi' Moye'li Tata Tako'tsi   West

The male deities related to the winds, the five lords with jurisdiction
over terrestrial space, are coupled with five principal eagles or
hawks which the Sun appointed as governors of the sky realm,
Tajeima. They are distributed according to the quinquepartite
classification already discussed, and related to the deer deities by
the colours attributed to their plumage. Japuri reigns over the east,

Kuishutasha, the west, Shurikwe, the south and Piwame the north, while Werika (Tatei Werika Wimari) oversees the central region. As the senior and most important eagle deity, she is sometimes said to be flanked by two smaller birds, Tusha and Ralu. All these bird deities, although appointed by and associated with the Sun, bear the kin term *tatei*, mother/aunt, and may, in fact, be thought of as the solar equivalents of the water deities.

(d) *Maize deities*

The final example to be presented from the Huichol of a quinque-partite deity is that of the maize. The maize is anthropomorphised as the daughters of Tatei Haramara and, in one account, the Sun. Five daughters are recognised, each corresponding to a particular colour of the cultagen: red maize, Taulawime; white maize, Tuzame; yellow maize, Tuzawime; mottled maize, Chiwime; while Yoawime, blue maize, is the elder sister of the others. There is not, as far as I am aware, any attempt to associate each maize daughter with a particular division of space.

A characteristic of the Huichol quinquepartite classification of deities is that the aspect assigned to the centre region is often more important than the four other aspects which surround it. Thus Tatewari has greater seniority than the four deer which inhabit the four terrestrial cardinal points.

Tatei Werika, Wimari, the solar eagle which inhabits the central region of the sky, is better known and more greatly venerated than the four birds which surround her. If we were to consider Nakawé as part of the set of fertility deities associated with rain, making their number up to five, then because her shrine is in the centre of the Huichol world, and because of the seniority accorded to her in this role, she could also be thought of as confirming this principle of ascribing seniority to the centre.

Among other sets, including those of the sea and maize deities, seniority is asymmetrically attributed to one divinity above the remaining four. Among the maize deities it is Yoawime who assumes this importance, because she sacrificed herself to bring the plant to the Huichol. This asymmetry suggests that the god at the centre of each set arranged by the five-fold partition of space may represent the composite identity of all its four associated aspects. This would then leave us with five principal godheads among the Huichol, which between them control the agricultural cycle and the cycle of human fertility and reproduction enshrined in a contract of mutual self sacrifice for divine and human well-being. The much reduced pantheon would then consist of five godheads, repre-senting;

Table 2 Summary comparison of the internal relationships, affiliations and class relationships of Nahuatl and Huichol deities

Nahuatl deity	Spatial affiliation	Class relationship	Huichol deity	Spatial affiliation	Class relationship
Tezcatlopoca		Sky bearer			
Red Tezcatlipoca (Mixcoatl)					
Black Tezcatlopoca					
Quetzalcoatl	East				
Huitzilopochtli	South				
Xipe Totec	West	Earth deities			
Mictlantecuhtli	South				
Xochipilli-Piltzintecuhtli	East				
Centeotl	North				
Tlaloc		Rain deities	Nakawé		
Blue Tlaloque	West		Tate Kyew'mo'ka	West	Rain deities
Red Tlaloque	South		Tate Rapawiye'me (Tatei Rapawiye'me)	South	
Black Tlaloque	East		Tate Naal'wa'mi (Tatei Nariuame)	East	
Yellow Tlaloque	North		Tate Hau'tse kupuri	North	
			Tatei Haramara		Sea deities

Nahuatl	Direction	Category	Huichol	Direction	Category
Quetzalcoatl Ehecatl		Wind deities	Tatei Haramara Mutazaiya	West	Wind deities
Ciuatlampa Ehecatl	West		Tatei Haramara Mutuza	South	
Uitzlampa Ehecatl	South		Tatei Haramara Muyuavi	East	
Tlalocayotl	East		Tatei Haramara Mumeriayuve	North	
Mictlampa Ehecatl	North		Tatei Haramara Shure(?)		
			Tatewari		Maize deities
			Watemukame	West	
			Ushkuikame	South	
			Kauyumarie	East	
			Nariuame	North	
			Yoawime	?	
			Taulawime		
			Tuzame		
			Tuzawime		
			Chiwime		
			Yoawime		
			Tatei Werika Wimari		Solar guardians
			Kuishutasha	West	
			Shurikwe	South	
			Japuri	East	
			Piwame	North	

1. rain and fertility under the tutelage of Nakawé;
2. light under the tutelage of Tatei Werika who might also be seen
   as a female manifestation of the sun;
3. fire, wind and shamanistic authority represented by Tatewari
   and Kauyumarie;
4. the seas under the authority of Tatei Haramara;
5. the maize represented by Yoawime.

This might leave certain important deities such as Tatei Yurianaka, the earth, and Tukakame, the lord of the dead and the underworld, as undifferentiated, but as among the Nahuatl these deities represent special problems that we can only come to terms with in the context of the general ideology of these peoples.

Further, both Nahuatl-speaking peoples and the Huichol show a tendency to cluster deity complexes around particular cult themes, following the same classificatory principles as are used to internally organise aspects of their godheads. We have described a similar complex clustered around the conditions related to the growth of maize among the Huichol, as Thompson described from the *Codex Borgia*. Although Nicholson has discussed this same tendency among Nahuatl speakers, and it may also exist among the Mayo (Crumrine 1981), it still cannot be said how important or pervasive this was and is, or whether such classifications were more fundamental than the more elementary systems that this paper has discussed. At the structural level, we have argued that the classificatory systems of the Nahuatl and Huichol share similar and fundamental principles which organise what at first appear a plethora of deities into a small number of categories constructed by certain precepts which are remarkably alike and which may form basic criteria for defining a common Uto-Aztecan ideology.

IV. STRUCTURAL   GENERALISATIONS   CONCERNING   A
COMMON UTO-AZTECAN IDEOLOGY

The history of ethnographic work on the Huichol and the neighbouring Uto-Aztecan groups, the Cora and Tepehuan, has consistently noted cultural similarities between them and the post-classic civilisations of central Mexico, since its instigation in the 19th century.

Mauss (1901), reviewing Lumholtz (1900), commented on the many parallels between the Huichol and the Aztec and the Zunis, and Seler (1939), in a notable article based largely on the same ethnography, opined that further research on such marginal groups which conserved substantial amounts of their pre-Columbian religious ideology could significantly contribute to the understanding of the Aztec and other post-classic Mesoamerican peoples. This line of thought influenced the Berlin ethnographer, Konrad Preuss, to devote a substantial period of fieldwork to collecting the mythology and oral literature of the Cora, Huichol and the isolated Nahuatl community in the southern tip of Durango. Only part of Preuss's total work was ever published. Both the Huichol manuscript and his ethnographic collection housed in the Hamburg Museum was destroyed during the Second World War.[8] However, Preuss laid the foundations for the development of a comparative Uto-Aztecan literature from his surviving Cora and Nahuatl texts.

Zingg's work in the 1930s focused on the eastern area of the Huichol sierra, and resulted in the collection of an impressive corpus of oral narratives. Previous fieldwork conducted among the Tarahamara with Bennet (Bennet and Zingg 1934) sharpened Zingg's appreciation of the close similarities between Uto-Aztecan systems and later resulted in an attempt to reconstruct Uto-Aztecan history. In recent years, Peter Furst (1973, 1975) has used Huichol material to construct ethnographic models which he has used in the interpretation of the pre-classic shaft-tomb cultures which inhabitated central western Mexico.

None of these accounts have isolated consistent fundamental and pervasive complexes which can be said to underline the thought or practices of Uto-Aztecan societies. They have compared isolated cultural traits, represented by behavioural patterns, material culture, ritual practices or mythology, and no coherent comparative conceptual system has been constructed which could persuasively demonstrate deep structural similarities between such societies.

Other researchers, including Underhill (1948), Spicer (1964) and Crumrine (1981), working from the perspective of neighbouring Uto-Aztecan groups, have tried to define the underlying tenets of a central (Sonoran) proto-Uto-Aztecan religious system by comparing ritual complexes and ceremonial organisation. Spicer focused on a comparison of the ceremonial organisation of the Huichol and Yaqui who inhabit the north of Sonora, although recognising that a more definite comparative approach must take into consideration the Tarahumara, the Tepehuan, Pima and Nahuatl communities, as well as the Cora and the Mayo which he considered variations on the Huichol and Yaqui systems respectively.

He argued that: – the most marked shared characteristic consisted of a division of the ritual calendar between the dry and wet season, each of which has distinctive themes and is associated with particular sets of deities;
– the deities associated with the wet season are female, while those connected with the dry season are male;
– deities are organised among themselves by kinship terms;

– ceremonial work is organised by groups who make heavy personal sacrifices to fulfil their responsibilities;
– ceremonial activities are effected to harmonise social relations;
– dance and song are the most important elements of ritual, performed on a special patio reserved for ceremonial occasions;
– blood and flowers are important offerings, linking the mutual obligations and responsibilities between the world of men and the world of gods (Spicer 1964: 36–7).

Crumrine (1981: 123) has offered corroboratory evidence to sustain this typology from the Mayo, a people closely related to the Yaqui. He argues, however, that the ecological conditions and the historical contingencies particular to any one society are also an important source which may modify these proto-Uto-Aztecan tendencies (Crumrine 1981: 113–14) and account for variations in the Mayo case.

The structure of ritual actions enumerated by Spicer and Crumrine corresponds to some of the classificatory principles that have been isolated as fundamental to Huichol and Nahuatl thought, including the binary division of the seasons, the different affiliations of male and female deities, and the concern of dualism with reconciliating and harmonising relations rather than with perpetrating opposition. These characteristics derive directly from the principles underlying the ideology that we have discussed. However, other traits isolated by Spicer appear to be of less importance, only surface manifestations generated by more fundamental conceptions of which they are the effect: organisation of ritual by group activity, song and dance as the most expressive actions of ritual activities.

Spicer's list of traits includes fundamental ideographic structures and behavioural complexes which are no more than secondary phenomena based on precepts of the former type. By confusing these two distinct levels, Spicer's attempt to define the fundamental characteristics of Uto-Aztecan systems loses some of its coherence.

In this paper we have tentatively suggested the existence of a core of structuring principles which govern the conceptions, and influence the ritual prescriptives, of two Uto-Aztecan groups which have long been considered to share many characteristics. By situating the study at the structural level, we have tried to identify an immutable core at the basis of a classificatory current[9] which, although it undisputably discloses variations among different Uto-Aztecan groups as a result of the contingencies of ecology and history, may nevertheless be considered a fundamental locus of this type of ideology. Much more comparative work is required to confirm this classificatory system as a fundamental denominator of Uto-Aztecan ideology, and ethnographic enquiry should also include the mapping of the degrees of variation between communities and correlating them with the historical and ecological vicissitudes of individual societies.

NOTES

1. Quinquepartite divisions of space together with their associated deities were articulated into the Tonalpohualli, a ritual calendar of 260 days divided into 20 periods of 13 days duration. This was the basis of a complex divinatory system in Mesoamerica. Consideration of the Tonalpohualli is superfluous to the present discussion since it is not shared by the Huichol. Comparison is thus made at a more elementary level.

2. With the notable exception of Quetzalcoatl in the guise of the wind deity, the four sons of Tonacatecuhtli-Tonacacihuatl are usually presented as unified and indivisible godheads. The second generation of deities that they engendered such as the rain and earth divinities appear to be more often conceived as quadripartite godheads.

3. For the much discussed importance of four-fold classifications for cosmology, see Soustelle 1959, Caso 1953, Burland 1950, León-Partilla 1963 and Martí 1960. Its importance as a classification after social organisation is commented on in Durán's *Historia de los Indias de Nueva Espana* vol II: 50 and in Fernando Alvarado Tezozomac, *Crónica Mexicayatl* (trans. by Adrian León, Mexico, *UNAM* 1949, p.74). Huitzilopochtli commanded the priests to 'divide the men, each with his relations, friends and relatives, into four principal wards, placing at the centre the house you have built for my rest' (trans. and quoted by W. Elzey, 1976: 319).

4. Examples of paired deities in the codexes are numerous. Page one of the *Codex Fejévaŕy-Mayer* illustrates the Nine Lords of the Night distributed in pairs around the four world directions with one, Xiuhtecuhtli, occupying the centre. The *Codex Borgia* illustrates fifty deities on folios 58–60 paired to form twenty-five couples. Folios 56 and 73 of the same codex show Mictlantecuhtli, the god of death, paired with his apothesis Quetzalcoatl, the god of wind and creator of men, in a manner not unlike that found in Huastec sculptural traditions.

5. The Huichol also preserve an account of successive eras each destroyed by a cataclysm which, like the narrative concerning the creation of the present world, bears many similarities to that described for the Nahuatl communities (Shelton 1986: 362–3). For a description and analysis of the different Nahuatl versions of this myth, see Moreno de los Arcos, 1968.

6. *The Primeros Memoriales* constitutes the oldest part of the *Codex Matritense del Real Palacio* whose texts were collected by Sahagún in the area around Texcocana de Tepepulco. I am grateful to Dr M. León-Portilla for kindly lending me his time to discuss the nature of the Tlaloques with me, and referring me to the descriptions contained in the above-mentioned source.

7. The Aztec earth deities represent a particularly problematic set, composed of beings with widely different attributes whose iconography and internal relationships can only be understood in the context of indigenous ideas of life, death and rebirth. These will not be discussed here and readers should compare the Huichol earth deities described later in this text with Baquedano's paper (in this volume) which deals specifically with their Aztec counterparts. I have come increasingly to believe that a polytheistic principle underlies the classification of not only earth deities, but also those associated with the sea, rain and wind. Thus Mictlantecuhlti-Mictacacihuatl share some of their characteristics with Coatlicue-Cihuacoatl who in turn overlap with the more purely regenerative and fertilising qualities of the earth goddesses Toci. Deified women connected with the earth cult, *cihuatateo*, were also described as clouds, causing a further overlap with the Tlaloques. In Huichol thought, the sea deity Tatei Haramara is also considered one of the rain deities which, as a class, are synonymous with fertility goddesses which again overlap with Tatei Yurianaka, the earth womb and Nakawé, associated with growth and regeneration.

8. The larger part of the material culture collections which Preuss made from the north-west remain deposited in the Berlin Museum für Volkekunde. His planned volume dealing with the significance of this material was never realised.

9. The idea of a general Uto-Aztecan ideology is implicit in the definition of the Greater North-west as a distinct culture area. The approach taken in the present paper, however has been influenced most by the work of Georges Dumézil on Indo-European ideology.

REFERENCES

Baquedano, E. Aztec Earth Deities. In this volume.
Benitez, F. (1968). *Los Indios de Mexico*. Mexico: Biblioteca ERA II.
Bennet, W. C. and R. M. Zingg (1934). *The Tarahumara: An Indian Tribe of Northern Mexico*. University of Chicago Press.

Beyer, H. (1910). Das aztekische Götterbild Alexander von Humbolt, in *Wissenschaftliche Festschrifte zu Enthüllung des von Seiten S. M. Kaiser Wilhelm II, dem Mexicanischen Volke zum Jubiläum, seiner Unabhängigkeit Gestifteten Humboldt-Denkmals. Von . . . Müller Haas.* Mexico.

Burland, C. A. (1950). *The Four Directions of Time: An Account of Page One of Codex Fejéváry Mayer.* Santa Fe: Museum of Navajo Ceremonial Art.

Caso, A. (1936). La Religion de los Aztecas. *Enciclopedia Illustrada Mexicana.* Mexico.

— (1953). *El Peublo del Sol.* Mexico: Fondo de Cultura economica.

Castile, G. P. and G. Kushner, eds. (1981). *Persistent Peoples: Cultural Enclaves in Perspective.* Tucson: University of Arizona Press.

Chavero, A. (1887). *Historia Antiqua y de la Conquista.* Mexico Traves de los Siglos I. Barcelona: Espasa y Cia.

Codex Borgia, with commentary by E. Seler (1963). Mexico: Fondo de Cultura Economica.

Codex Fejérváry Mayer (1901). Paris: Le Duc de Loubat.

Codex Vaticanus 3773 (1972). Graz: Akademische Druc.

Crumrine, R. (1981). The Ritual of the Cultural Enclave Process: the Dramatisation of Oppositions among the Mayo Indians of Northwest Mexico, in Castile and Kushner 1981 (above).

Durán, D. (1971). *Book of the Gods and Rites and the Ancient Calendar.* Trans. by D. Heyden and F. Horcasitas. Norman: University of Oklahoma Press.

Elzey, W. (1976). Some Remarks on Space and Time of the 'Centre' in Aztec Religion. *Estudios de Cultura Nahuatl* 12, 315–34. Mexico: UNAM.

Furst J. L. (1982). Skeletonization in Mixtec Art: a Re-evaluation, in ed. E. H. Boone, *The Art and Iconography of Late Post-Classic Central Mexico.* Washington D.C.: Dumbarton Oaks.

Furst P. (1973). West Mexican Art: Secular or Sacred. *The Iconography of Middle American Sculpture.* 98–133. New York: The Metropolitan Museum of Art.

— (1975). House of Darkness and House of Light: Sacred Functions of West Mexican Funerary Art, in E. Benson ed., *Death and the Afterlife in Pre-Columbian America.* Washington: Dumbarton Oaks.

Gomara, F. L. (1966). *Cortez. The Life of the Conqueror by his Secretary.* Ed. and trans. by L. B. Simpson. Berkeley: University of California Press.

Histoyre du Mechique (1905). (Ms. of Thevet). *Journal de la Société des Americanistes de Paris.* II, 1–41.

Jonghe, E. de (1905). Histoire du Mechique, *Journal de la Société des Americanistes de Paris* II, 1–41.

King, J. L. (1972). La Introduction posthispanica de elementos à las religiones prehispanicas: Un Problema de aculturacion retroactiva. in J. L. King and N. C. Tejerov (eds), *Religion en Mesoamerica*. Mesa Rodonda XII Mexico: Sociedad Mexicana de Antropologia.

León Portilla, M. (1958). *Ritos, Sacerdotes y Atavíos de los Dioses* (Informantes de Sahagún 1) Mexico: UNAM.

— (1963). *Aztec Thought and Culture. A Study of the Ancient Nahuatl Mind*, trans. J. E. Davis. Norman: University of Oklahoma Press.

Lumholtz, C. (1900). Symbolism of the Huichol Indians. *Memoirs of the American Museum of Natural History*. 3,1.

— (1903). *Unknown Mexico* II. London: Macmillan.

Martí, S. (1960). Symbolismo de los Colores, Deidades, Numeros y Rumbos. *Estudios de Cultura Nahuatl* II, 93–128. Mexico: UNAM.

Mauss, M. (1901). Review of C. Lumholtz, The Symbolism of the Huichol Indians. *L'Année Sociologique* VI, 247–53.

Moreno de los Arcos, R. (1968). Los cinco soles cosmogénicos. *Estuidos de Cultura Nahuatl*. VII, 183–210.

Negrin, J. (1977). *El Arte Contemporaneo de los Huicholes*. Guadalajara: Universidad de Guadalajara/INAH.

Nicholson, H. B. (1971). Religion in Pre-Hispanic Central Mexico, in ed. R. Wauchope, *Handbook of Middle American Indians* 10,1, 398–446. Austin and London: University of Texas Press.

Olmos, A. (1883). Historia de los Mexicanos por sus pinturas. trans. H. Phillips. *Proceedings of the American Philosophical Society* XXI, 616–51.

Preuss, T. K. (1912). *Die Religion der Cora. Der Nayarit Expedition* I. Leipzig: B. G. Teubner.

— (1968–1973). *Nahua Texte aus San Pedro Jicora in Durango* (3 vols.) ed. E. Ziehm. Berlin: Veröffentlichungen des Ibero-Amerikanischen Instituts Preussischer Kultur besitz.

Robelo, C. A. (1951). *Dicionario de Mitologia Nahuatl*. Mexico: Ediciones Fuente Cultural, Libreria Navarro.

Sahagún, B. de (1976). *A History of Ancient Mexico: The Religion and Ceremonies of the Aztec Indians*, trans. F. R. Bandelier. Glorieta: Rio Grande Press.

Seler, E. (1939). *The Huichol Indians of the State of Jalisco in Mexico*. trans. A. M. Parker, 3. Washington: Carnegie Institute, Gesammelte Abhandlungen zur Amerikanischen Sprach und Altertumskunde.

— (1941). *The Pictorial Representations of the Annual Feasts of the Mexicans*, trans. E. S. Thompson. Ms. in Museum of Mankind, London.

— (1963). See *Codex Borgia*, above.

Shelton, A. (1986). The recollection of times past: Memory and event in Huichol narrative. *History and Anthropology 2*, 355–78.

— (1988). In the Realm of the Fire Serpent. *British Museum Society Bulletin* 58, 20–25.

— (1989). Huichol Natural Philosophy. *Canadian Journal of Native Studies/Cosmos* 4 (forthcoming).

— Ms. *The Huichol: A Highland People of Northwest Mexico.*

Spicer, E. H. (1964). Apuntes sobre el tipo del religión de los yuto-Aztecas centrales. *Actas y Memorias del XXV Congresso International de Americanistas.* 27–38: Mexico D.F.

Soustelle, J. (1947). Observations sur le symbolisme du Nombre Cinq chez les Anciens Mexicains. *XXVIII Congrès International des Americanistes.* Paris.

— (1959). *Pensamento Cosmologico de los Antiguos Mexicanos.* Puebla: Libreria Hermann y Cia.

Sullivan, T. D. (1972). Tlaloc: A new etymological interpretation of the God's name and what it reveals about his essence and nature. *XL Congresso Internazionale degli Americanisti* 2, 213–19. Rome-Geneva.

Thompson E. S. (1934). *Sky bearers, colours and directions in Maya and Mexican religions.* Contributions 10. Washington: Carnegie Institute.

— (1939). *The Moon Goddess in Middle America with notes on related deities.* Contributions 29. Washington: Carnegie Institute.

Underhill, R. M. (1948). *Ceremonial Patterns in the Greater Southwest.* Monograph of the American Ethnological Society 13. New York.

Zantwijk van R. (1985). *The Aztec Arrangement: The Social History of Pre-Spanish Mexico.* Norman: University of Oklahoma Press.

Zingg, R. M. (1938). *The Huichols: Primitive Artists.* New York: G. H. Stechert and Co. Reprinted 1977: Millwood, New York: Kraus Reprint Co.

— (not dated) *Reconstruction of Uto-Aztecan History.* Private edition: distributed by the University of Chicago.

— Ms. *Huichol Mythology.* Santa Fe, New Mexico: Laboratory of Anthropology.

ELIZABETH BAQUEDANO[1]

Aztec Earth Deities

All of the post-classic earth goddesses seem to have embodied the idea of fertility, more specifically agricultural fertility. The earth was perceived as the generatrix of all living things, linked to natural phenomena such as rain. Water allowed for the staple foods such as maize to grow, and the earth, the Great Mother, made them germinate and sprout.

The sixteenth-century written records, however, mention specific domains and functions for each deity, for instance weaving or spinning in the case of Tlazolteotl, while some deities – like Cihuacoatl – seem to emphasize political aspects. Some rituals also have political overtones, but masked, as if the major concern was that of agriculture, as in the maize rituals such as those associated with Ilamatecuhtli. Some earth deities seem to be connected with war, for instance Itzpapalotl, and, in fact, most earth deities seem to have this aspect in common. Some earth deities seem to express through their activities – spinning and weaving in the case of Tlazolteotl – a cosmological aspect. Mircea Eliade (1975: 45–6) has stated that these two activities are 'raised to the rank of a principle explaining the world'. Finally, certain cults such as that of Cihuacoatl are important for propagandistic purposes (symbols of victory for the Mexica state and for the ruling class).

I shall begin by examining the origins and different names that earth deities have, and then I shall mention some differences and similarities between them. The reason for doing this is that most earth deities seem to have performed the same role: the promotion of the fertility of the earth, with regional variants and functions, under different names.

According to Nicholson (1971: 420), the two regions where the earth-mother goddess cult appears to have been most vigorously developed were the Gulf Coast (Cuextlan [Huaxteca], Totonacapan, Cuetlaxtlan, Coatzacoalco [land of the Olmeca Huixtotin Mixtecal) and the chinampa zone of the Valley of Mexico (especially Colhuacan and Xochimilco).

Tlazolteotl belongs to the first region. Both Sullivan (1982: 7–8) and Nicholson (1971: 420) favour the idea that her cult may have originated in the Huaxteca. In the region of the Basin of Mexico a group of goddesses were clearly identified with their Gulf Coast counterparts, although they may have had distinct origins: Teteoinnan-Toci, Cihuacoatl-Quilaztli-Ilamatecuhtli-Tonan(tzin), Coatlicue-Chimalman. A closely related goddess, Itzpapalotl-Itzcueye seems to have been particularly identified with the earlier 'Chichimec era' (Nicholson 1971: 420). Another important goddess with whom all these appear to have eventually merged was Xochiquetzal, who represented the youthful side of the mother-goddess. The earth-mother goddesses seem to have been associated with the moon. 'Noteworthy also was the highly martial aspect of the earth-mother goddesses, especially Cihuacoatl and Tlazolteotl-Ixcuina. Itzpapolotl was considered to be the first to die in war. This was directly connected with the institution of war to feed the earth – together with the pre-eminent sun' (Nicholson 1971: 421–2).

CIHUACOATL

The name means 'Snake Woman', though Sahagún (1950–1982: Bk. 2, 31) gives other names for Cihuacoatl which obviously have different meanings. These names are: Ilamatecuhtli (goddess of old age, and noble woman), Tonan and Tonantzin (our mother), Cozcamiauh (necklace of spikes) and Chantico (wolf's head). Durán (1971: 210) mentions also Quilaztli (mother goddess of mankind).

Cecilia Klein, in her thorough study 'Rethinking Cihuacoatl: Aztec Political Imagery of the Conquered Woman' (1988), analyses the different processes of change of this deity. The following are some of the points raised by Klein which I summarize, but I extend some of the quotations given by the Chroniclers. I have also added some quotations for the sake of clarity.

According to Clavijero (1987: 105), the cult of Cihuacoatl entered the Mexica capital of Tenochtitlan shortly after the successful conquest of Cuitlahuac, obviously before Itzcoatl's death in 1436, according to Clavijero's date. In the words of Clavijero: [Itzcoatl] 'construyó después de la conquista de Cuitlahuac, un templo a la diosa Cihuacoatl y otro algún tiempo después a Huitzilopochtli'.

'Cihuacoatl, better known in other places as Chantico, had long been the patron deity of several of the southern cities including Colhuacan, Xochimilco and Cuitlahuac. Almost certainly the Mexica derived this cult from those cities' (Klein 1988: 238).

The *Historia de los Mexicanos* describes 'a very fine temple in which the people of Culuacan celebrated a feast to Ciguacoatl, the wife of the god of the infernal regions, whom the people of Culuacan reverenced as their especial god'. A hymn sung to Cihuacoatl (Sahagún 1950–82: Bk 2, 211) also indicates that the Mexica took her cult from Colhuacan, and Klein (1988: 239) rightly calls Colhuacan 'a city of pivotal importance to the Mexica ruling class because of its alleged residue of Toltec nobility'. Durán (1971: 210), on the other hand, says that 'Cihuacoatl was a deity of the people of Xochimilco; and though she was the special goddess of Xochimilco, she was revered and greatly exalted in Mexico, Teztcoco and all the land'. Klein says that Durán implies from the former quotation that the Mexica almost certainly took her cult from Xochimilco (Klein 1988: 239). From the quotation I would say that perhaps the Mexica took her cult from Xochimilco. Klein goes on to say that, according to the *Historia de los Mexicanos* (1883: 625), Quilaztli was carried from Tollan to Xochimilco during the Aztec migration. According to Klein (1988: 239), 'The *Historia's* association of Quilaztli with the original Aztec migrants and Tollan is not unique. Several sources put one or another of Cihuacoatl's "avatars" at the scene of the migration from Aztlan. According to some of these, the migration involved a stopover at the Hill of Coatepec, which is said to be near Tollan.' This stopover was preceded by a woman (Tezozomoc 1980: 23). This woman, whose name was Malinalxochitl (Flower of the Malinalli Plant), was the sister of the tribal god of the Aztec, Huitzilopochtli; she was said to be 'an eater of hearts . . . an enchanter of people' (Tezozomoc 1980: 23–4). Huitzilopochtli abandoned his sister, who with her supporters moved south of Malinalco near present-day Chalma.

> La hechicera hermana de su Dios quando amaneció, y vió la burla que le habían hecho comenzó a lamentar y quejarse a su hermano Huitzilopochtli, y al fin no sabiendo a que parte había encaminado su Real, determinó quedarse por allí, y pobló un pueblo que se dice Malinalco, pusiéronle este nombre porque lo pobló esta hechicera que se dezía Malinalxochi, y deste nombre y desta partícula componen Malinalco, que quiere dezir lugar de Malinalxochi. Y assí a la gente deste pueblo han tenido y tienen por grandes hechiceros como hijos de tal madre, y esta fue la segunda división del real de los Mexicanos, porque como queda referido la primera fue en Michhuacan (Tezozomoc 1980: 23–4).

Klein (1988: 239) states that 'Malinalco, like Xochimilco and Cuitlahuac, became famed as the centre of the magic arts'. The implication of the foregoing is that Cihuacoatl's affiliation with sorcery may have had a basis in Mexica political history. Tezozomoc's

(1975: 34–5) version of events at Coatepec, which designates Huit-zilopochtli's antagonist Coyolxauhcihuatl 'as the god's mother in-stead of as his sister, thereby assigning her the role assigned to Coatlicue in Sahagún's rendition (1950–1982: Bk. 3, 1–5), suggests that Coyolxauhqui and Coatlicue were interchangeable'.

The political importance of Cihuacoatl

Klein (1988: 245) states that Cihuacoatl and her cult were not simply adopted at the time of the Mexica conquest of the southern cities, but were forcibly appropriated as a sign of victory. This is important because the individual who became the first Mexica high priest of Cihuacoatl's cult, and who first adopted her title and dress, was the very individual who had led the attacks upon the Chinampaneca and who had effected the triumph at Cuitlahuac (Klein 1988: 245–6). This man was the Mexica war captain Tlacaelel I, half-brother of the then reigning *tlatoani*, Itzcoatl (Durán 1967: v. 2, 105–23).

According to Klein (1988: 248), the power gained by Cihuacoatl is also evident in the iconography that symbolised her, and Klein mentions two different types of Cihuacoatl depictions:

1. more cruedly carved, non-official images that lack many, if not most, of the negative features (Figure 1).
2. images with the protruding stone tongue and monstrous joints (e.g. the representations that display the dorsal pose), noxious insects and skeletal costume elements: these appear largely on the courtly images (Figure 2).

Klein thinks that the first group was produced for *macehuales* (commoners) as 'they did not consider her an altogether evil being'. I think that whether the *macehualtin* did or did not consider her an evil being is irrelevant. What is true is that unofficial or non-state-sponsored art was always less intricate, while state sculpture was always more complex iconographically – for instance, the monu-mental Coatlicue as opposed to a maize goddess holding ears of corn.

Most sixteenth-century sources associated Cihuacoatl with lasciv-iousness and forbidden sex (similar to what was believed about Tlazolteotl). In her aspect of Chimalma, she died in childbirth (*Leyenda de los Soles* 1975: 4). Both pregnant women and young children were regularly threatened by her and by her vengeful followers, the *Cihuateteo*, the souls of women also dead in child-birth. According to Sahagún (1950–1982: Bk. 6, 161–64) the *Mo-ciuaquetzque* were also feared:

> They believed in them as they did in the *Ciuateteo*. And they
> took from them their hair or some part of their bodies; they

Figure 1 Cihuacoatl stone sculpture. Museum of the American
Indian, 15/5597. Photograph courtesy of Emily Umberger.

believed in these as relics. And they took [these relics] from
them before they buried them. And it is necessary that the
priests should make known to themselves the different things
regarding those who died in childbirth. They named them
Mociuaquetzque. And the place where the sun set, it is said,
they named *ciuatlampa*, after them . . . And as it became night
they bore this little woman to bury her there before the images

of their devils whom they named *Ciuapipiltin*, celestial princesses. And when they had borne her, then they buried her, they placed her in the earth. But her husband and still others helped to guard her for four nights, that no one might steal her. Her parents and the husband rejoiced therefore even more, for it was said she went not to the land of the dead; she went there to the heavens, to the house of the sun.

It was they, in turn, who accompanied the sun from the zenith to its setting place in the west. They were the female counterparts of the male.

The brave warriors, the eagle-ocelot warriors, those who died in war, went there to the house of the sun. And they lived there in the east, where the sun arose . . . And these little women who thus had died in childbirth, those said to have become *Mociuaquetzque*, when they died, they said became goddesses (Sahagún 1950–1982: Bk. 6, 164).

Sahagún (1950–1982: Bk. 2, 236) recorded a song of Cihuacoatl that describes the different roles of Cihuacoatl very well:

Figure 2 Underside of a stone vessel: relief representing
Tlaltecuhtli with the face of the earth goddess, and Cihuacoatl.
National Museum of Anthropology, Mexico City.

The eagle
The eagle quilaztli
With blood of serpents
Is her face circled
Corncob of the godly field

Our mother
War Woman

She is a mother-goddess, related to agriculture ('corncob of the godly field'). The serpents are symbols of fertility *par excellence*, but she is also associated with war, a war woman. Moreover, Durán (1971: 217) says that Cihuacoatl was the sister of Huitzcilopochtli, the Aztec's god of war, and she was the female equivalent, the 'eagle quilaztli'. Sahagún further states that Cihuacoatl embodied the concept of the earth[2] as 'she gave men the digging stick'. There is no doubt that the *coa* or digging stick was the most important farmer's tool, thus linking her with the earth and agriculture in her role as an earth deity.

CIHUATETEO (GODDESSES) OR CIHUAPIPILTIN OR IXCUINAME (CELESTIAL PRINCESSES): SINGULAR, CIHUATEOTL.

According to Sahagún (1950–1982: Bk. 1, 19),

There were five devils, whose images were of stone. Of them it was supposed and men said: They hate people; they mock them. When one was under their spell, possessed, one's mouth was twisted, one's face was contorted; one lacked use of a hand; one's feet were misshapen – one's feet were deadened; one's hand trembled; one foamed at the mouth. Whence it was said, one had met and contended with the Ciuapipiltin . . .

They were women who had died in childbirth, who were compared to warriors and who descended at the crossroads on the days 1 Deer, 1 Rain, 1 Monkey, 1 House, and 1 Eagle. They were greatly feared (Sahagún 1950–1982: Bk. 4, 9; 41–2; 81; 93; 107–8). The days on which they descended at the crossroads were at intervals of 52 days, which divided the 260 divinatory cycle (*tonalpohualli*) into fifths.

Nicholson (1983: 68) describes one Cihuateotl image as follows:

the face of the goddess is a skull, with large, staring round eyes and an open mouth with a set of prominent teeth. Her hair is twisted, a characteristic of the mortuary aspects of the earth deities . . . Cihuateotl images are fairly common and they display on the tops of their heads the dates that initiated the 13-day periods assigned to the West (only 1 Quiahuitl [Rain] is missing).

Figure 1 shows a Cihuateotl sculpture with the day sign 1 Eagle carved on the top of her head. This piece was found with three other nearly identical sculptures in the present-day avenues of 16 de Septiembre and Isabel la Católica.

Some iconographic descriptions given by Sahagún (1950–1982: Bk. 1, 19) correspond to some of the features of Itzpapalotl: 'Their paper garments were covered over with the obsidian point design. They had sandals decked with feathers'. This is an example of the overlapping of features between two supposedly different deities of a different origin.

TLAZOLTEOTL

(also known as Ixcuina-Tlaelquani, Sahagún, 1950–1982: Bk. 1, 23–27.)

Sullivan (1982: 7) says that 'Tlazolteotl means "God" or "Goddess of Filth".' Tlazolli, 'filth, rubbish, garbage', is a metaphor for licentiousness. It is a word derived from the prefix *tlah-*, 'thing', and *zolli*, a pejorative suffix meaning 'old, worn, dirty, deteriorated', which in turn is related to *zolin*, 'quail', a bird associated with the earth and the night. *Teotl* is the generic term for 'deity'; thus Tlazolteotl can be both a male and a female name.

Tlazolteotl's cult seems to have originated in the Huaxtec area in the north-east. The Huaxtecs were people of Maya linguistic affiliation. According to *Codex Chimalpopoca* (1975: 13), the infiltration of the Tlazolteotl cult, and the sacrifice of shooting captives with arrows, into the Central Plateau began during the reign of the Toltec ruler called Huemac (whose son-in-law was Huaxtec). According to Sullivan (1982: 8) 'It must be recalled, however, that Quetzalcoatl, the Toltec culture-hero and predecessor of Huemac, also seems to have come from the Huaxtec region, so that it is possible that the Tlazolteotl-Ixcuina cult may have been introduced at an earlier date. In fact, Tlazolteotl-Ixcuina is sometimes depicted with an occipital adornment of Quetzalcoatl, called *coxoliyo huey itepol*.' In the *Codex Borbonicus* depiction (1981: 13) the goddess wears the conical hat of the Huaxtec region. Sullivan (1982: 7–35) in her study of Tlazolteotl-Ixcuina states that the word Ixcuina is indeed a Huaxtec word and that its meaning is 'Lady Cotton' or 'Goddess of Cotton'. Sullivan (1982: 13) rightly says that cotton was a principal import item in the Central Plateau of Mexico. She goes on to say that it is not known how early it was introduced, since climactic conditions do not permit the preservation of perishable materials over an extended period of time. This is of course a poor generalisation, but even if it was indeed possible to know the dates, there are other areas where cotton could have been obtained, not necessarily all from the Gulf Coast region, for example, the area of

Morelos. In any case cotton weaving is only one type, although she mentions maguey (agave) weaving in Central Mexico as an alternative. Tlazolteotl's array consisted of spindles which indicate her association with spinning and weaving, and in fact she was the goddess of these crafts. Spinning and weaving were, of course, women's activities. However, Sahagún (1950–1982: Bk. 1, 23–7) states that her realm, her domain, was that of evil and perversion, lustful and debauched living. So she presided over carnal love and could bring about disease, and if one wanted to be cured the person at fault had to be purified at the *temazcalli* (steam-bath), where 'she cleansed one, washed one. And thus she pardoned' (Sahagún 1950–1982: 23–4). Tlazolteotl was also a goddess of forgiveness through confession: 'before Tlazolteotl, one recited, one told one's sins'. Then the penitent kissed the earth and cast incense upon the fire (Sahagún 1950–1982: 25). As a penitence the sinner had to fast for four days in the feast of the Ciuapipiltin or the Ixcuiname (Sahagún 1950–1982: 26). Tlazolteotl therefore, is linked to the Ciuapipiltin. It is interesting that Sahagún calls them Ciuapipiltin or Ixcuiname, another name for Tlazolteotl. As confession involved everybody, I suggest that Tlazolteotl's cult was both a popular and an élitist cult. On the other hand, Tlazolteotl-Tlaelquani was the Great Parturient, the creative Earth Mother, in the words of Sullivan (1982: 15):

> the goddess of the fertile earth, and symbolised, too, the earth that receives all organic wastes – human and animal excrement, vegetable and fruit remains, fish, fowl, and animal bones, and so forth – which when decomposed are transformed into humus. Humus in Nahuatl is called *tlazollalli* – from *tlazolli*, 'filth, garbage', and *tlalli*, 'earth' (Sahagún 1950–1982: Bk. 11, 251). In the same way that Tlazolteotl caused the symbolic rebirth of the transgressor by eating the ordure of his wickedness, she also symbolized the transformation of waste into humus, that is, the revitalization of the soil.

Sullivan (1982: 17) mentions that Tlazolteotl-Ixcuina, in her aspect as goddess of spinning and weaving, appears to have eventually merged with Xochiquetzal, 'Flowery Quetzal Feather', considered by the Aztecs as the inventor of spinning and weaving. She, like Tlazolteotl-Ixcuina, was associated with licentiousness, and according to Durán (1971: 239) she was the goddess of pregnant women. Tlazolteotl is also closely associated with maguey gods, especially with Mayahuel, goddess of the agave (maguey): Sullivan (1982: 25) states 'she was the poor man's Tlazolteotl'.

According to Thompson (1970: 207, 242–9), Tlazolteotl-Ixcuina was originally the Huaxtec moon goddess, although in post-classic

Mexico the moon was almost always considered as male. In all probability the moon was both male and female as in the case of many other deities, for instance Tlaltecuhtli. Tlazolteotl was also the patroness of the 14th day-sign, *ocelotl*, 'jaguar'. 'Associated with the earth and the night, the jaguar was the antagonist of the sun and was identified with Tlazolteotl-Ixcuina in her role of the ferocious, hungry earth that devours the sun at nightfall, and who is also the regenerating earth from the depths of whose womb the reborn sun emerges at dawn' (Sullivan 1982: 29). This earth-related aspect was later identified by the Aztecs as Tlaltecuhtli, whose cult in turn was closely linked to human sacrifice.

ITZPAPALOTL

The name means 'obsidian butterfly'. Also known as Tlazolteotl, Toci, Tonan, Coatlicue, Teteo Innan, Cihuacoatl-Quilaztli.

Itzpapalotl is a deity of Chichimec origins, a manifestation of the mother-goddess. On conquering new towns, the Mexica incorporated into their pantheon the deities of the dominated towns. This same system was also practised by former groups. In this way, Itzpapalotl (Chichimec) and Tlazolteotl (Huaxtec) were identified with other figures of the great Mother-Earth-Moon (Heyden 1974: 3). Obsidian Butterfly (Itzpapalotl) also represented the west, and, like Cihuacoatl-Quilaztli, she is the patroness of the *Cihuateteo*. In Codices she is sometimes represented with a skull characteristic of the deities of death, and as such she is depicted with a fleshless jaw (for example, in the *Codices Borbonicus* 1981: plate 11, *Telleriano-Remensis* 1964: plate 2 and *Borgia* 1980: plate 11). According to Heyden (1974: 35), the goddess's attire is that of a butterfly (figure 3), and she has eagle claws instead of hands and feet. The eagle claws, the eagle-feathered headdress and the loin-cloth are all traits associated with eagle warriors; they are also part of Itzpapalotl's iconography as she had a warrior-like nature, as represented by the *Mociuaquetzque* or *Cihuateteo*, the spirits of women who had died in childbirth, already mentioned.

Itzpapalotl also carries sacrificial knives, and it should be recalled that obsidian or flint knives were used for human sacrifice. The *Cihuateteo* were the female counterparts of the male warriors slain in battle or on the sacrificial stone. Garibay (in Heyden 1974: 7) states that 'Itzpapalotl is associated with the four quadrants of the earth in personified maternity'. According to the *Annales de Cuahtitlan* (1975: 3), Mixcoatl, a powerful hunting god, killed her with arrows: 'Itzpapalotl arremetió contra la biznaga; salió de prisa Mixcoatl, luego la flechó repetidas veces y evocó a los cuatrocientos mixcoas que habían muerto y aparecieron en seguida la flecharon

una y otra vez. Así que murió . . .'³ Xipe Totec's victims were
dedicated to Mixcoatl during the month *Tlacaxipeualiztli* and these
victims were transfixed with arrows so that their blood should drop
on the earth like rain. This ritual is obviously associated with the
fertility of the earth and with Xipe who was above all a fertility
deity, the fertility of the spring rain being connected with the
renewal of nature and the fresh growth. In this way Itzpapalotl is a
symbol of death and rebirth. Furthermore, in highland Maya
thought obsidian was associated with creation and represented the
heart of the earth (*Anales de los Cakchiqueles* 1950: 49). Among the
Aztecs, *tlalli yiollo* (heart of the earth) was one of the names of the
mother-goddess. As Neumann (1974: 191) has pointed out:

> Itzpapalotl changed from a goddess of the hunt, of blood, and
> the night, to an earth goddess. According to myth, the son of
> her fertility became the corn – which was identical with the
> obsidian knife – and she herself became the fertility goddess of

Figure 3 Underside of a stone relief representing Itzpapalotl.
National Museum of Anthropology, Mexico City.

the corn. But her old terrible nature persisted, for fertility, death and sacrifice belong together, and the husking of the corn is identical with the tearing out of the heart of a victim with the help of the obsidian knife. The earth goddess Itzpapalotl bears life, agriculture, and she also bears death, the obsidian knife. This twofold aspect, in which life becomes death and death life, and in which one depends on the other, recurs again and again in Aztec myth and ritual.

The concept involved in all of the above-mentioned deities is mainly that of agricultural fertility, but war, human sacrifice and politics were important constituents. The Aztec earth deity Tlaltecuhtli (figure 2) summarizes this statement very well. His sex was both male and female, he was related to the earth and agricultural deities such as Mayahuel and Tlaloc, but his cult revolved around warfare and human sacrifice. In other words he was related to life and death, but the emphasis was on regeneration and life, and he represents agricultural fertility despite his death imagery. Tlaltecuhtli is an aspect of the mother-goddess and there is a dual character to this earth deity, typical of the nature of most Mesoamerican deities. Likewise there is a constant overlapping of functions and features among earth deities, which indicates that they are all variations on a theme.

Earth deities were associated with the rebirth of the forces of nature and of growth after they had apparently died in the dry season. Or, as Soustelle (1976: 105) has expressed it: 'the whole of ancient Mexican thought, and their vision of the world, turned about this central idea, whether it concerned man or nature', and I would add that the State used this notion for its own benefit. After all, rituals and human sacrifices offered some reward here on earth or in the afterlife to the sacrificial victims themselves, whilst keeping the gods satisfied, maintaining the population's productivity and also keeping their enemies terrified. The earthly reward for those who were to die by beheading or flaying, for instance the female impersonators of Toci, Teteo Innan, Ilamatecuhtli and others, was the 'honour' of sleeping with the *Tlatoani* (Ruler). Sahagún (1950–1982: Bk. 2, 119) wrote in respect of this: 'much did the women physicians console her. They said unto her: my dear daughter, now at last the ruler Moctezuma will sleep with thee. Be happy.' Another justification for Moctezuma to dispose of human lives was to kill undesirable members of society, such as thieves and evil-doers. Sahagún (1950–1982 Bk. 4, 42) recorded that 'by them his fate was strengthened; by them he was exalted, and on them he placed the burden. So it was as if through them once more he became famous, achieved honour, and became brave, thereby making himself terrifying.' With the blood of the victims the Ruler was strengthened, and also with blood the earth was rejuvenated and fed.

NOTES

1. I would like to thank the Mexican Embassy in Britain for financing my travelling expenses to Edinburgh to read this paper. I am especially grateful to Ambassador Eduardo Navarrete and to Margo Glantz. I am also very thankful to Warwick Bray and Nicholas James for reading this manuscript and for their valuable comments and suggestions.
2. For present-day beliefs about earth goddesses, see A. Shelton in this volume.
3. Itzpapalotl was killed with arrows and, according to *Codex Chimalpopoca* (1975: 13), Tlazolteotl-Ixcuiname introduced the killing with arrows to Tollan. This is again another similarity between two different deities of different origins.

REFERENCES

Anales de Cuauhtitlan (1975). In *Códice Chimalpopoca: Anales de Cuauhtitlan y Leyenda de los Soles*, translated from Nahuatl by Primo Feliciano Velázquez. México: UNAM, 3–68.

Anales de los Cakchiqueles: Título de los Señores de Totonicapan (1950). Mexico: A. Recinos.

Baquedano, Elizabeth (1987). *Los Aztecas: historia, arte, arqueología y religión*. México: Panorama.

Clavijero, Francisco Javier (1987). *Historia Antigua de México*. Mexico: Porrúa.

Codex Borbonicus (1981). Commentary by E. T. Hamy. Mexico: Siglo Veintiuno.

Codex Borgia (1980). México: Fondo de Cultura Económica.

Codex Telleriano-Remensis (1964). In *Antiguedades de México basadas en la recopilación de Lord Kingsborough*, commentary by José Corona Núñez I, 152–337. México: Secretaría de Hacienda y Crédito Público.

Durán, Fray Diego (1971). *Book of the Gods and Rites and the Ancient Calendar*, trans. and ed. Fernando Horcasitas and Doris Heyden. Norman: University of Oklahoma Press.

Eliade, Mircea (1975). *Rites and Symbols of Initiation: The*

Mysteries of Birth and Rebirth, trans. Willard R. Trask. New York: Harper and Row.

Heyden, Doris (1974). La Diosa Madre Itzpapalotl, *INAH Boletin* 11, December, 3–14.

Historia de los Mexicanos por sus pinturas or *Codex Ramírez* (1884), trans. H. Phillips Jr. *Proceedings of the American Philosophical Society* vol. 21, no. 116, 616–51.

Klein, Cecilia F. (1988). Rethinking Cihuacoatl: Aztec Political Imagery of the Conquered Woman, in J. Kathryn Josserand and Karen Dakin (eds), *Smoke and Mist. Mesoamerican Studies in Memory of Thelma Sullivan*. BAR International Series 402, Oxford, 237–77.

Leyenda de los Soles (1975), in *Códice Chimalpopoca: Anales de Cuauhtitlan y Leyenda de los Soles*, trans. from Nahuatl by Primo Feliciano Velázquez. México: UNAM, 119–28.

Neumann, Erich (1974). *The Great Mother: An Analysis of the Archetype*, trans. Ralph Manheim. Princeton, N.J.: Princeton University Press.

Nicholson, Henry B. (1971). Religion in Pre-Hispanic Central Mexico, *Handbook of Middle American Indians* 10, ed. Robert Wauchope. Austin: University of Texas Press, 395–446.

—with Eloise Quiñones Keber (1983). *Art of Aztec Mexico. Treasures of Tenochtitlan*. Washington D.C.: National Gallery of Art.

Sahagún, Fray Bernardino de (1950–1982). *The Florentine Codex: A General History of the Things of New Spain*, trans. Arthur J. O. Anderson and Charles E. Dibble. 11 vols (12 Books). *Monographs of the School of American Research* 14. Santa Fe, New Mexico: The School of American Research and the University of Utah.

Soustelle, Jacques (1976). *Daily Life of the Aztecs*, trans. Patrick O'Brien. Stanford, California: Stanford University Press.

Sullivan, Thelma (1982). Tlazolteotl-Ixcuina: The Great Spinner and Weaver, in Elizabeth H. Boone (ed.), *The Art and Iconography of Late Post-Classic Central Mexico*. Washington D.C.: Dumbarton Oaks.

Tezozomoc, Hernando Alvaredo (1971). The Finding and Founding of Mexica. Selection from the *Cronica Mexicayotl*, trans. Thelma D. Sullivan. *Tlalocan* 6 (4), 312–36.

—(1975). Crónica Mexicana, in Manuel Orozco y Berra (ed.), *Crónica Mexicana/Códice Ramírez* (2nd edn) Porrúa, Mexico: Biblioteca Porrúa 61, 223–701.

—(1980). *Crónica Mexica*, annotated by Orozco y Berra. México: Porrúa.

Thompson, J. Eric S. (1960). *Maya Hieroglyphic Writing: An*

Introduction (2nd edn). Norman: University of Oklahoma Press.
Umberger, Emily (1981). Aztec Sculptures. Hieroglyphs and History. PhD dissertation, Columbia University.

CAROLINE KARSLAKE

Images of Otomi Deities: A Review of the Literature

And the Toltecs knew
that there are many heavens.
They said there are twelve superimposed divisions.
There dwells the true god and his consort.
The celestial god is called the Lord of Duality.
And his Lady is called the Lady of Duality; the Celestial Lady.
Which means He is King, he is Lord above the twelve heavens.

The traditional religion of the Otomi shares many of the concepts
prevalent among the natives of pre-Columbian Mesoamerica. This
extract of Toltec poetry displays the ambiguity which pervades
native philosophy. All forms of life and existence derive from the
supreme creative force, but the complexities of the universe are
infinite and its deepest meanings are ultimately obscured from man.
It is through an attempt to understand the prosaic things in life,
however, that man comes to terms with his destiny. The contemporary Otomi ethnographic material illustrates the way that this particular ethnic group defines and represents the elements of its
universe. In conformity with traditional Mesoamerican philoso-
phies, the Otomi perceive their universe as a complex of interrelated forces or spirits, which can affect the fate of human beings. It is
the role of the shaman or ritual specialist to avert disaster in the
human realm, by propitiating the gods appropriately and also by
maintaining the balance between forces in the universe. Shamans
are recognised as having a superior understanding of the interrela-
tionships both in the human and spiritual world and concerning all
levels of life. In pre-Columbian religion, worship was more to do
with identifying with the attribute or function of a deity, in order
that it could be venerated with the appropriate ritual and associated
paraphernalia, than with defining a moral relationship with the gods
(Brenner 1929).

When the Aztec kingdom was at its height, the Otomi people remained a peripheral ethnic group. Like many of their neighbours their culture was influenced by the Aztecs, and inherited many of the cultural traits that had been passed down over the centuries throughout Middle America. The Otomi are thought to have entered the Central Plateau area after the decline of the Olmec kingdom. Pimentel, Genet and Wolf state that from the 12th century to the 14th century Otomi was the dominant language in the Central Plateau. In 1370 the Aztecs destroyed the Otomi kingdom and the Otomi were forced to move out into the peripheral areas of Meztitlan to the north and Tlaxcala to the south. Many Otomi have continued to occupy the desert areas of the valley of Mezquital and isolated groups also live today in the Sierra de Puebla, which has long remained inaccessible. Although the separation and isolation of pockets of Otomi people has caused a diversification of culture, the evidence from the ethnographic literature suggests there are still many common elements, which makes an overall assessment of the literature worthwhile.

An indication of the extent to which the Otomi share a common cultural inheritance with the Aztecs is provided by Fernando Benitez, writing about the religion of the Olmecs of the valley of Mezquital. A version of the myth of how Nanahuatzin, the pock-marked deity, threw himself into the fire to become the sun, while Tecuciztecatl became the moon, is also recounted by the Otomi. The brilliance of Tecuciztecatl was partly obliterated by a rabbit covering his face. In the desert, where the maguey cactus was the source of life and pulque the source of joyfulness, the myth of the moon and the rabbit had particular connotations. In myth the rabbit was condemned to unremitting drunkenness, and was associated with pulque, the alcoholic beverage made from the fermented sap of the maguey. Pulque is also a ritual intoxicant, given as a sacrificial offering to the gods. The four hundred rabbits of the creation myth become the four hundred faces of drunkenness. Mayahuel, the moon, was the principal goddess of the maguey. She also represented fertility and fecundity and was thought of as a mother bearing the milk of the cactus. It was also her role to eat dirt and rubbish and the sins of man. She was the prostitute goddess of the earth, from whose breast life was born again from death in springtime, and from whom the rivers flowed and the menstrual cycle of women originated. The moon had a special role for the Otomi. Whereas the Aztec stressed the importance of Tonatiuh, the sun, depicted as a resplendent and beautiful eagle in the ascendant, the Otomi looked to the moon. The moon waxes and wanes, mirroring the universal law of becoming; of birth and of death (Benitez 1972). Thus the

Otomi celebrated the moon at harvest time as the patron of the living fruit who gave life to the apparently dead seed. The moon was also associated with movement or the Aztec term *Ollin*, which was the symbol of change and variation.

Galinier writes about metaphors of castration among the Otomi of the Valley of Mezquital. Among the people studied by Galinier, ideas about sexuality reveal a dualist cosmology, which parallels that of the pre-Columbian peoples. In myth the qualities of male and female may become merged and every deity has its alter ego. Women may become men, or take on their qualities. The moon is associated with women who are the castrators of men, but the moon herself is also castrated and thus she wanes. The waning of the moon is thought to be analogous to women's menstruation. The sacrifice of male power, which is thought to take place in the castrating act of intercourse, is described in the same terms as the death of the sun at night when it is displaced by the moon. This struggle for supremacy at a cosmic level is also reflected in colour imagery or described as an ongoing fight between animal spirits.

The Otomi still slit open or 'castrate' the maguey two days after the full moon. The act is conceived of as a sacrifice: the farmer cuts to the heart of the cactus, as the priests of old cut to the heart of the sacrificial victim. Paul Guerrero, an anthropologist who has lived in the Valley of Mezquital all his life, also writes about the plurality of deities with maguey associations. The different deities embody the diverse aspects and qualities of the plant and are thought to be the offspring of the parent god Tezcatzonlatl. There appear to be an infinite number of words with sacred or godly connotations associated with the plant. This suggests that what might be termed a polytheistic religion is more accurately understood as a rather precise science of nature and human existence.

Benitez suggests that the numerous gods of the Mesoamerican pantheon represent aspects of the human dilemma. His description of Otomi deities would seem to bear out this theory. Alongside the deities with counterparts in the Aztec pantheon, the Otomi worship certain gods with specific relevance to their culture. Sahagún mentions Yocippa as being an important Otomi deity. He was a snake of the clouds and the god of hunting. Yocippa appears to have been the local manifestation of Quetzalcoatl, but has an obvious similarity to the god worshipped by more northerly desert tribes. Another deity who has a counterpart among North American Indians such as the Navajo and Hopi is 'Coyote Viejo'. The Otomi describe him as a kind of 'Adam'; the one who is taken in, or allows himself to be taken in. He also starts wars and introduces discord into the world. But although Coyote represents negative aspects of man's character, he also has a positive side, as it is he who brings the joyfulness of singing and dancing into the community. Another interesting Otomi deity who illustrates the tendency for gods to represent human dilemmas is the so-called 'Dios de la Curiosidad', whose role it is to question human destiny.

In contemporary ceremonies in the Valley of Mezquital, it is most often saints' images which are revered in ceremony. Cristo lo Sagrado is one of the most commonly found images. He is a doleful figure, crowned with cactus thorns, portrayed as a suffering Otomi. Among his devotees he excites extreme emotions of terror and love. His presence is considered sanctifying. The Virgen de Remedios, another important local saint, is portrayed as a comforting figure, whose serene countenance shows pity towards suffering humanity. Interestingly, in areas where the goddess Mayahuel is no longer worshipped, she has been substituted by the Virgen de Gaudalupe, who has become the contemporary Senora de los Magueys. Community patron saints also play their role in the articulation of human relations. These divine entities are exchanged between communities, conferring mutual honour and trust.

León Portilla, among other Mesoamericanists, has pointed out the redundancy of the concepts of the developed western world for the analysis of Middle American cosmologies. In Amerindian culture there is not the same distinction between the sacred and the profane which lies at the basis of Western philosophy. A quotation from the famous Aztec poet Nezahualcoyotl indicates a sophisticated understanding of the way the supreme deity can be understood through the metaphors of nature. He says, 'In truth no one is intimate with you, Oh giver of Life: only as among the flowers, we might seek someone, thus we seek you, we who live on earth, we are at your side.'

The following descriptions of Otomi ritual illustrate how symbols of the forces of life are articulated to convey a similar understanding of existence. Much of the material in the section which follows has been documented from groups living in the Sierra de Puebla. This is a remote and inaccessible area, where many groups continue to practise their traditional religion. Icons or material symbols of deities and cosmic forces continue to feature as an important element in ritual. These symbolic elements can be manipulated to effect an interchange or transformation. In order to understand the attitudes and beliefs which accrue to religious icons, it is essential to understand their role as the bearers of metaphorical statements, which reflect upon or elucidate the human role in the universe. It is evident that many of the isolated Otomi groups interpret their contemporary world with reference to traditional pre-Columbian concepts. The Otomi continue to cut images of the spirits from bark paper, or, in more recent times, commercial tissue paper. In the pre-Columbian world, paper had certain connotations. Not only was paper the medium on which all knowledge could be recorded, but it was also used as an adornment to confer status. Sahagún's version of the Aztec description of the fifth sun indicates this. 'And when midnight had come, thereupon (the gods) gave them their adornment, they arrayed them and readied them . . . For Nanauat-zin they bound his head-dress of mere paper and tied on his hair, called his paper hair. And (they gave him) his paper stole and his paper breech clout.' Similarly, Frederick Starr writes that in pre-Columbian times 'the temple, idols, victims, priests and performers were decked with paper: great sheets of paper were carried in processions; paper streamers were attached to rods and staves to be carried or set up at designated spots, bones were wrapped about with paper and special pieces of paper were supplied with the dead as passports.' The sacred associations of paper thus made it an appropriate material from which to create images of supernatural forces. It appears that this practice may once have been widespread, but is now confined to the remote ethnic groups of the Sierra de Puebla.

James Dow describes the Otomi of the Sierra, whose contempo-rary rituals continue this ancient tradition (Dow 1984). What at first appears to be a simple manipulation of two-dimensional paper images reveals itself as a metaphorical statement about the relation-ship between the spirit, natural and human worlds. The papercuts are lacking in detail because they represent only the 'zaki' or life-force of the being. The shaman aims to attract the person's 'zaki' to the paper representation, and by the use of appropriate ritual he may be able to realign forces that have been displaced. In his songs the shaman refers to the feelings and emotional problems of the patient and attempts to restructure his experience (Dow 1984). In the words of Nancy Munn, 'Ritual symbols release the relevant shared meanings embedded in the cultural code into the ongoing social processes, through this objectification they can come to work on the individual imagination with the authority of external reality' (Munn 1973).

Sandstrom has documented paper-cult rituals for the Sierra region and compiled data from Otomi, Nahua and Tepehua Indian groups (Sandstrom 1986). Although there are many similarities in the cult practices of these different ethnic groups, it is interesting that the Otomi shamans are particularly revered for their strength and knowledge and are often called in to assist at rituals. A general pattern emerges concerning the sequence and form of rituals with different objectives. Firstly the altar which is set up is made to represent a microcosm of the universe. For example, the palm-leaf strips which are curved above the altar are decorated with marigolds called guardian stars. A paper sun may be attached to the centre of the firmament. Beneath this arch are erected the paper images of the spirits participating in the ritual. The earth is symbolised in displays below the altar. The earth is the basis of life and its importance is so obviously recognised that it does not have to be emphasised in ritual. The altar is always decorated with a number of symbolic papercuts which are designed to keep away malevolent spirits or 'malas aires'. The altar is thus set up like a stage, defining the arena of action within which the characters play out their discrepancies according to the direction of the shaman.

A major concern of paper-cult rituals is fertility and health for both crops and humans. One of the most important elements of any ritual is the cleansing ceremony, intended to rid the area of the malevolent spirits which could bring harm to these domains. Although the aim of this part of the ritual is ostensibly to drive the harmful spirits from the place of ceremony, it is notable that the shaman is careful not to offend the 'malas aires'. Instead they must be appeased with a variety of offerings, which usually include items that appeal to human tastes, such as rum, coca-cola, coffee, eggs, bread and cigarettes. The one exception is the offering of fresh blood, usually acquired by cutting the throats of sacrificial birds, a custom which no doubt throws back to much earlier traditions. Once they have been satiated with offerings, the winds or harmful spirits are requested to depart. Their departure is usually symbolised by the removal and disposal of their paper images.

The main part of the ritual can now begin, and the paper images of the spirits to be propitiated and manipulated must be assembled. Apart from the 'malas aires', there are six other categories of spirits: gods, saints, animal companions, human beings, plants and animals. Spirits are usually associated with one of the four domains of the sky, the earth, the underworld or water. The papercut images of the earth, water, fire and Christian cross are found in nearly all ceremonies. Interestingly, Otomi shaman often opine that the ancient god was once more powerful, but that Jesus Christ has since usurped his superior position. The papercut image of the Christian cross symbolises the syncretised power of the sun and Jesus Christ. In the symbolic shorthand of the papercut medium, two crosses or flowers are often cut into so-called beds which are provided for the spirits during rituals. This design also points to the four sacred directions. The earth mother once ruled alongside the Ancient Lord and she still has to be appeased in ritual. It is the evil alter ego of the earth mother who brings disease to both crops and humans. The fire god, Maka Xita Sibi, is also commonly represented in ritual. The association of fire with the hearth of the household is emphasised and the metaphor is extended to symbolise the family or kin group.

James Dow has taken a particular interest in the metaphysical forces affecting health and has collected data from a number of different Otomi communities in the Sierra Norte de Puebla (Dow 1984). In a recent article, he attempts to analyse the meaning of 'superhuman animal images' in Otomi traditional culture. His approach to the subject of healing takes a therapeutic perspective, and inevitably touches on the psychological aspects of the shaman's work. Other writers such as Lévi-Strauss (1962) and Reichel-Dolmatoff (1971) have explored healing rituals from a structural point of view. The work of James Dow helps to further elucidate the theme. The Otomi have a word, 'rogi', which roughly translates as superhuman animal protector. When translating the word into Spanish, the Otomi use the word 'tona', as opposed to the over-used term 'nagual', which for the Otomi refers to a variety of evil beings. To avoid confusing the Otomi conception of animal spirits with that of other Mesoamerican ethnic groups, it is thus probably easiest to keep to their own term 'rogi'. The shaman stresses that the most important criteria for defining the qualities of a supernatural deity are those which come to them in dreams, and these have to be most carefully analysed. The kind of animal, its colouration and attributes are all important. The animal will also define itself by its behaviour and certain tests may be set up by the shaman, who then observes its reactions. For example, an evil spirit will be stunned and dispersed by tobacco. A basic concept of animism is that the essence of life is action and where there is action there must be a life force. Sometimes the force behind the action is invisible and what we see is the outcome. Only shamans and specialists are able to understand the way the unseen forces work; they are able to predict happenings and avoid disasters because of their capacity to re-arrange certain elements of the natural and supernatural.

At the beginning of a healing ritual, the shaman works to cut a paper figure, which is a portrait of the patient's 'zaki' or life force. The patient's 'zaki' should then be attracted to the papercut during the ceremony. The shaman may also cut images of the 'zaki' of other humans or spirits deemed to have a role in the situation. During the ritual, he intends to re-order the relations between these 'zaki' for the benefit of the patient. By comparison with other living forces, the 'zaki' of the human is weak. However, as every being lives without consciousness of his 'zaki', the shaman is able to influence their actions and have feedback at a conscious level. The Otomi believe that every person is born with one or more 'rogi', or companion animals, whose destinies mirror that of the human. If one of a person's 'rogis' dies, he will weaken; if they all die, he will die too. A 'rogi' can be either good or bad, depending on the character of the person whom they are protecting. In healing ceremonies the shaman calls on the 'rogi' of the patient and also his own. The papercut figure of the patient's 'zaki' is depicted as being surrounded by the 'zaki' of the patient's and shaman's companion animals, who help to protect the patient during the potentially dangerous curing ceremony. A particular papercut of a patient in a ceremony witnessed by Dow was shown surrounded by companion birds and dogs. The shaman teacher expressed the situation as follows:

> so these animals that are attached to the cutting of the 'zaki' watch out for the patient. For example if he were to fall the doves would lift him up with the wind. So you dream that you're flying over the troubles below and that they can't touch you, and it's the doves who are carrying you. Whenever those on the ground are about to get you, quickly the doves carry you away. High in the sky nothing can touch you. You go up and come down on another hill; for example, from here you would fly to that other hill over there. There you would be set down. This is the defense of these little animals. They're doves. They're the 'rogi'. The dogs go with you on the land. We say in Otomi, 'They're for another day.' . . .
>
> This next song is to call your shaman's great dogs to help you, but they're really pumas, great large pumas that defend you. When they arrive they control your enemy. They're called 'ra zate'. One does not see pumas normally. They're there but well hidden. To counter sorcery you use these songs. So your spirit helper, which is a great white dove that flies with the wind, swoops down low where your patient lies and looks at him. Then your pumas arrive and fight with the other animals that were attacking your patient. They get into a tangle with each other. They circle each other and fight; therefore they forget about your patient. Meanwhile the dove circles above, rising higher and higher. When it sees that the animals have moved off and forgotten about the patient, it dives down and picks him up and takes him to the curer's house. They must arrive at his altar. So after this, all is well.

Only the shaman knows the form and number of the person's 'rogi'. These animals may be beneficial or detrimental, depending on the person's 'zaki', which defines his motivation, desire and other emotions. Sorcerers have bad 'rogi', for example owls or foxes. As Dow says, 'The Mesoamerican world view seems to be based on the premise that reality has multiple appearances. Persons such as shamans, who can perceive a greater variety of appearances, have a better idea of what lies behind them.' Thus the average person is unable to understand how it is that 'rogis' can protect a person. If a person looses his 'rogi', he will be open to attack from the supernatural realm, which, according to the Otomi, also includes disease and psychological disorders. Dow thus concludes that a person's 'rogi' represents the feelings of caring that people have for themselves and for each other. It may be true that what people are really saying when they say that a person is protected by 'rogi', is that they are protected by god. 'Rogi' are the symbols by which people and particularly shamans articulate and understand forces emanating from the divine realm. The manipulation of papercuts in ritual by the shaman attempts to restructure the client's experience of life. Unlike Western psychology, it is the shaman who becomes emotional and undergoes 'catharsis' and not the patient. The patient has to accept the power of the shaman to undergo the transaction for him.

Rituals to ensure crop fertility often require offerings to mother earth, or the moon, whose ambivalent reputation associates her with both fertility and the dangers of the night. Interestingly, the bark used in the paper-making process should be cut from the tree when the moon is young (Christensen 1942). In ceremonies for fertility, the seed spirits to be propitiated are represented in papercut form. Their 'zakis' are thought to reside in sacred caves in the mountains. The paper images of the seed spirits are usually kept in locked cabinets. They wear tiny outfits which mimic those worn by the young girls of the community. During fertility rituals there are two main objectives: to appease the spirits with offerings, in order to oblige them to reciprocate appropriately; and to demonstrate to the spirits what it is they should do. Thus in the ceremony to bring rain to crops, small forked sticks are erected symbolising the growing plants and these are sprinkled with water. The young girls, who are described in a way analogous to seedlings, shake rattles to imitate the sound of rain. These acts are a form of sympathetic magic, with an easily deciphered message.

During such ceremonies, musical symbolism is important. Boiles, writing in 1969, maintains that the melodies inherent in the music represent beings and places, whereas the rhythm is representative of action. Although the music is essentially repetitive, the combinations of rhythm and melody are varied and can thus express many different messages. The ritual participants are required to dance or play out the actions indicated by the musicians.

Although it can be dangerous to try and draw parallels between contemporary native concepts and those of pre-Columbian cultures, certain similarities are evident. The pattern of ritual and its motives exhibits obvious similarities. The depiction of papercut images is also revealing. Firstly, images often have a female or alter ego, which might be called a dual aspect. Secondly, images are usually cut 'en face'. Sandstrom suggests that the reason for this is that traditionally, in the pre-Columbian codices, it was only the earth and fertility deities which were depicted in this way. Profile views are much more common in the codices. This theme has been investigated by Klein, who adds that these face-front reproductions in their pre-Columbian context are usually associated with westerly, southerly or central directions. These are the directions of femaleness, the earth, fertility, death and darkness. The head shape is also important for defining the identity of papercuts. Harmful spirits usually have head-dresses decorated with animal horns or crescent moons. Bodil Christensen, who investigated the paper-making practices of the Otomi of San Pablito, Puebla in the 1930s, says, 'To distinguish the women from the men he cuts a tuft of hair on top of the head' (Christensen 1942). The heads of spirit beings are usually rounded going to a point, which gives them an other-worldly aspect. Sandstrom suggests that this shape originally evolved because of the practice of occipital deformation, but this idea would seem difficult to prove. Christensen mentions several other defining features. He says some paper dolls have four arms and two faces in profile. Perhaps these are spirits cut with their alter egos. Bad people – that is, those killed in fights or accidents, women who die in childbirth and people who do not respect their parents – are all represented by dolls with shoes. Contrastingly, paper dolls cut with toes represent the good people who died from an illness or old age. Christensen states that the people with shoes are thought to be Ladinos, whereas those who go bare-foot are Otomi.

The colour of paper images is also symbolically important. Generally, the darker the papercut, the more likely it is to represent an evil spirit. Seed spirits are often cut in the colour of the fruit they bear. Nowadays shamans use commercial tissue paper, which offers a wide range of colours. In the past, the bark of four different trees produced a variety of colours of paper. Marti comments on the moral connotations of colour (Marti 1971): 'The colour black and dark coloured paper is associated with black magic, priests and wizards. Black is the colour of the west, where the flaming sun endures self-sacrifice and is swallowed by the Earth monster in order to become the sun of the night and be reborn the next day.'

Dyckeroff, who also worked in an Otomi community, that of San

Pablito in the Sierra de Puebla, cites certain parallels between the structures of pre-Columbian and contemporary rituals (Dyckeroff 1984). He describes a typical curing ritual, in which the number symbolism of papercuts is of paramount importance. Offerings and papercuts are usually arranged into lots of four and laid out according to a square design. Qualities are also indicated according to the directional orientation of the items. The order of ritual and pre-occupations of the curer also appear to be similar to those described by the first missionaries, such as Sahagún (Sahagún 1950–69).

Maria Cervantes, in her article on Otomi household shrines, comments on the tendency for the identity of pre-Columbian deities to become syncretised with their Catholic counterparts. Soustelle described household cults in a paper written in 1935. He believes that saints' cults became popular in the 18th century, after centuries of missionary effort. The cult of the household shrine represents the private, individual aspect of ritual and ceremonialism. It provides some kind of unity to the disparate elements which make up Otomi religion. Although Cervantes does not attempt to analyse the form of household altars, where saints are venerated or the rituals for propitiation are carried out, it is evident that there is a great similarity with the pagan rituals already discussed. Both pagan spirits and saints must be propitiated before the shrine is erected or consecrated, and the traditional deities must be satisfied before they can be removed. Spirits of the dead, owners of the mountains and the supernaturals associated with the stars and heavenly bodies are represented by clay figurines called Tzaguas. These have to be taken to rest in a special cave, where they are left with offerings of flowers, sweetbreads and liquor. Some of the Tzaguas may later be placed on the consecrated altar. Before consecrating the household shrine, a cleansing ritual must take place to exorcise the devil. The saints and advocations of the Virgin and Christ to be placed on the altar vary from household to household. A relationship of reciprocal obligation is likewise formed with the saints, by offering them flowers, fruits, cakes and burning candles. During the rites of supplication, the assembled company may also sing and dance. Any event of importance to the household will warrant a ritual to propitiate the saints, in order to ensure their good will.

Although there appears to be no evidence from the ethnographic literature that saints' images are ever cut from paper, other authors mention the incorporation of saints in the ritual framework. Christensen describes Noche Buena in San Pablito. The traditional altars, decorated with papercuts, are set up in the hallway of the municipal offices and a cleansing ceremony is carried out to evict the bad spirits. Later a procession brings the saints from the church, each one carried by four 'mayordomos' and followed by women and children. The floats are decorated with candles and noche buena flowers. At the door of the municipal residence, the shamans responsible for the papercut ritual cleanse the entering congregation with copal and blessed water. They also switch them with rolls of bark paper. The fiesta continues all night with drinks and refreshment being distributed to all the village.

Descriptions of religious ceremony among the Otomi people suggest that, even where Catholicism has been incorporated into the ritual complex, the dominant philosophy has changed very little. Saints are treated as spiritual aspects who can be appealed to for their particular strengths, by a person needing help. Saints have well-defined characters and are considered to have influence in a variety of life's domains. Like other spirits of nature, they must be treated appropriately: venerated and brought offerings. They do not appear to be worshipped in the Christian sense. There is an element of bargaining between humans and saints, who are thought to be the mediators between God and man. Saints are thus additional spiritual forces in the universe. It is this concept of spiritual forces, with which every aspect of nature is imbued, that explains the dynamism of life, growth and movement. It does not contradict the concept of an ultimate power or supreme being. Yet ultimately the origin of the life force must remain a mystery, a mystery which even the sophisticated technologists and scientists of the modern world are unable to solve.

REFERENCES

Benitez, F. (1968). *El mundo de los Otomies en la cuenca de Tula*. Mexico.
— (1972). Los indios de Mexico. *El Libro de la Infamia*. Mexico.
Boiles, C. (1969) Cognitive Processes in Otomi Cult Music. PhD dissertation. Tulane University, New Orleans.
— (1971) Sintesis y sincretismo en el carnaval Otomi. *America Indigena* 31.
Brenner, A (1929). *Idolos tras los Altares*. Editoriales Domes SA.
Carrasco-Pizana, P. (1950). *Los otomies. Cultura e historia prehispanica de los Pueblos Mesoamericanos de habla Otomiana*. Mexico: UNAM.
Cervantes, M. (1980). Secularization and the cult of household shrines among the Otomi Indians of San Pedro Arriba, Temoaya, Mexico. *UOMO* 4, 1.

Chamoux, M. (1981) *Indiens de la Sierra: La communauté paysanne au Mexique*. Paris.

Christensen, B. (1942). Notas sobre la fabricacion de papel indigena y su empleo para bruyerias en la Sierra Norte de Puebla Mexico. *Revista Mexicana de estudios antropologicos* 6, 1–2.

— (1971) Bark Paper and Witchcraft, in Christensen and Martī (eds) *Witchcraft and Pre-Columbian Paper*. Mexico: Ediciones Euroamericanas.

Dow, J. (1975). *The Otomi of the Northern Sierra de Puebla, Mexico. An Ethnographic Outline*. Michigan State University.

— (1982). Las figuras de papel y el concepto del alma entre los Otomis de la Sierra. *Americana Indigena* 42, 4.

— (1984). Symbols, Soul and Magical Healing among the Otomi Indians, Mexico. *Journal of Latin American Lore* 10, 1.

Dyckeroff, U. (1984). La Historia de curacio antigua de San Pablito Pahuatlan, Puebla. *Indiana* 9.

Galinier, J. (1976). Les Frontières Culturelles des Otomis de la Huasteca Meridionale. *Mesa Redonda* 14.

— (1984). L'homme sans pied. Métaphores de la castration et imaginaire en Méso-Amerique. *L'Homme* 24, 2, 41–58.

Huber, B. (1987). The Reinterpretation and Elaboration of Fiestas in the Sierra Norte de Puebla, Mexico. *Anthropology* 4.

Jenkins, J. (1946). San Gregorio. An Otomi Village of the Highlands of Mexico. *America Indigena* 6, 4.

Lens, H. (1984). *Cosas del Papel in Mesoamerica*. Mexico.

León Portilla, M. (1963). *Aztec thought and culture. A study of the ancient Nahuatl mind*. Norman: University of Oklahoma Press.

— (1980). *Native American Spirituality*. London: SPCK.

Lévi-Strauss. C. (1962). *La Pensée Sauvage* Paris: Plon.

Manrique, L. (1969). The Otomi, in *Handbook of Middle American Indians* 6. University of Texas Press.

Martī, S. (1971). Pre-Columbian Bark Paper, in Christensen and Martī (eds), *Witchcraft and Pre-Columbian Paper*. Mexico: Ediciones Euroamericanes.

Munn, N. (1973). Symbolism in a Ritual Context, in J. J. Honigmann (ed.) *Handbook of Social and Cultural Anthropology*. Chicago: Rand McNally and Co., 579–612.

Nicholson, H. (1971). Religion in Prehispanic Central Mexico, in R. Wauchope (ed.), *Handbook of Middle American Indians* 10, 398–446.

Reichel-Dolmatoff, G. (1971). *Amazonian Cosmos. The Sexual and Religious Symbolism of the Tukano Indians*. Chicago and London: University of Chicago Press.

Sahagún, B. de (1950–1969). *Historia General de las Cosas de Nueva Espana.* New Mexico: University of Utah Press.

Sandstrom, A. and P. (1983). Paper Dolls and Symbolic Sequence: An Analysis of a modern Aztec Curing Ritual. *Folk American* 36.

— (1986). *Traditional Paper Making and Paper Cult Figures of Mexico.* Norman: University of Oklahoma Press.

Soustelle, J. (1935). Le Culte des Oratoires chez les Otomies et les Mazahua de la Region d'Ixtlahuaca. *El Mexique Antiguo* 111, 5 and 6.

Starr, F. (1900). Mexican Paper. *American Antiquarian and Occidental Journal* 22.

TEIGO YOSHIDA¹ and ANDREW DUFF-COOPER²

A Comparison of Aspects of Two Polytheistic Forms of Life: Okinawa and Balinese Lombok

I

The Okinawan village (*shima* or *mura*) we are mainly concerned with is Bise,³ one of the constituent villages of the town of Motobu, north Okinawa. This village (see fig. 1) had a population of 816 in 1985. It faces the sea to the west and extends from north to south along the coast of Motobu Peninsula on mainland Okinawa. The village consists of two divisions, a northern side, *shinbāri* (side of the 'back'), and a southern side, *menbāri* (side of the 'front'). The main road called 'middle road' (*nakamichi*) runs north/south through the village. To the north-west of Bise there is ɐ small island called *mīugan*; this island is so sacred that no stones or pebbles should be removed from it. The village graveyard and the place where funerals are held – funerals are considered to be polluting – are situated to the south of the village.

The northern side of the village represents the female, and the southern side, the male. This symbolic association of the two divisions with male and female is clearly evinced in the ritual tug-of-war performed on the 25th of June by the lunar calendar, as part of the all souls' *bon* festival by the inhabitants of the two divisions. Villagers aver that when the northern or female side wins, abundant crops and large catches of fish will result, but that the village will go hungry if the southern, male side wins. They also say that, strangely enough, in the past the northern side has won without any deliberate attempt to make the contest turn out so.

At the boundary between the two 'sides' of the village there is an open space called *asagimō*, where rites are performed. To the north of this space is located the village shrine (*asagi*), which is made of concrete and roofed with tiles. The deity of the fire (*pirukan* or *hinukan*) is enshrined in the eastern part of the shrine, which is opened only by the high priestess (*nuru*) at the times of communal

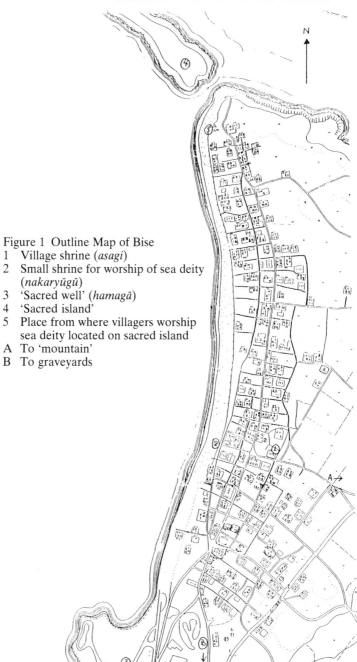

Figure 1 Outline Map of Bise
1   Village shrine (*asagi*)
2   Small shrine for worship of sea deity
     (*nakaryūgū*)
3   'Sacred well' (*hamagā*)
4   'Sacred island'
5   Place from where villagers worship
     sea deity located on sacred island
A   To 'mountain'
B   To graveyards

rituals or on individuals' requests. Located to the north of this shrine are the house where the founder of the shrine and his successors are said to have resided, and the ritual house of the *nuru*. In most communal rituals performed annually, three stones, worshipped as the deity of the fire, are prayed to by fourteen priestesses, some of whom may well not be present at the rites, who, wearing white, burn sticks of incense. A 'sacred mountain' (*gushiku*) is situated at the top of a hill to the east of the village and its shrine. Here there is a concrete shrine in which three stones represent the deity of the 'mountain' who descends from the sky. The direction of the mountain is called 'mountainwards'. Traditionally only priestesses may enter the mountain shrine to worship the deity there, and men were forbidden to enter this place: their presence was considered to pollute the sacred space. There is also a small shrine (*nakaryūgū*) situated near the beach to the west of the village shrine. Here the sea deity is worshipped, particularly by fishermen from the village. While the deity of the 'mountain' is said to be male, the sea deity is considered to be female and to reside at the bottom of the sea. As we have noted, while the 'mountain' is to the east of Bise, the sea is to the west of the village. Thus the west is associated with the sea and with female, the east with inland or mountainwards and with male.

Also, in the ritual called *upuyumi*, performed on the 20th of July by the lunar calendar, priestesses pray seawards or westwards to the overseas deities (*nirai-kanai*), located in the world of ancestors who died more than thirty-three years before. The place of the *nirai-kanai* is believed to be located vaguely far away beyond the sea. With regard to other villages in Okinawa facing the sea on the east, Mabuchi writes (1980: 4): 'in many hamlets that face the sea approximately east, the overseas deities are believed to come from somewhere beyond the horizon or even from the bottom of the sea, far in the direction of sunrise.'

The local term for the east is *agari* (rising or sunrise) and that for west, *iri* (entering or sunset). In villages divided into eastern and western halves on Iheya Island, a ritual tug-of-war is also performed between the inhabitants of the two halves, but in this case the eastern half represents the male side and the western half the female side. According to Mabuchi, 'the female side should ultimately win, otherwise fertility will not be gained' (1980: 4). In Bise, the north is associated with female, and the south with male, but at the same time, as the genders of the deities of the 'mountain' and of the sea indicate, the east is associated with male and the west with female.

In Bise in daily activities men are superior to women: the village head is always a man, and men deal with village and other public matters. In political and secular life men predominate, but in ritual or religious contexts it is women who do so. Although the latter work hard as well in the cultivation of sugar-cane, which is at present the main subsistence crop in Bise, in the communal rites performed every year in every month but October and November, women act as priestesses, and men (barring a few who act as assistants for the ritual activities) are essentially left out of them. In other words, male superiority in political, socio-economic, and other 'ordinary' activities is reversed in ritual activities, which women control.

In the division of the village, north is associated with female, we have seen, and the south with male, but this symbolic association is not clearly related to the relationship of superiority and inferiority just mentioned, though the northern side is more associated with sacredness and the southern side more with the pollution of death (and the former is superior to the latter). In a Bise house, however, the north/south opposition is explicitly associated with this inferiority/superiority polarity. Otherwise, in an Okinawan house, the same relationships obtain between east and west and male and female as are found in the village and in houses in Hateruma (Ouwehand 1986). In a house in Bise (see fig. 2) the 'first room' (*ichibanza*), typically located on the east or superior side, is used for receiving 'formal' visitors. Male guests sit to the most easterly side of the room, women to the west, the inferior side. The 'second room' (*nibanza*), located west of the 'first room', is used for daily activities. In this room sleep the head of the house and his wife and children. The 'back room' (*uraza*), situated on the north side of the house, which is also inferior, but to the south, are used as bedrooms by young couples or marriageable sons and daughters, and for childbirth. The kitchen is located west of the 'second room', and the fire deity represented by three stones in the west wall of the kitchen is here worshipped by the wife of the house-head. The lavatory and the pigsty were traditionally located in the north-west corner of the yard, outside, but in most of the newer houses the lavatory is now located indoors in the north-west corner of the house; pigs are no longer husbanded in Bise.

The basic ground plan of a house in Bise (see fig. 2) and the ways in which the rooms are used are the same as those in Hateruma (Ouwehand 1986). However, in ritual contexts a priestess sits on the most easterly side of the 'first room', occupied by male guests in daily life, while her male and female relatives sit to her west in the 'first' and 'second' rooms of her natal house for the feast held after ritual performances. As elsewhere in Okinawa, those priestesses who married someone from outside Bise and reside away from it

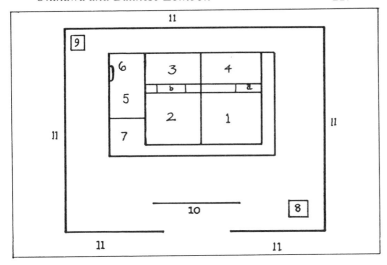

Figure 2 Groundplan of Typical House-Compound and House in Bise

1 'First room'
a 'Alcove' – *tokonoma*
2 'Second room'
b Ancestral tablets – *ihai*
3 'Back rooms'
4 'Back rooms'
5 Kitchen
6 Deity of fire
7 Verandah
8 Guardian of compound
9 Lavatory
10 'Entrance wall' – *himpun*
11 Surrounding wall

because of virilocal rules, as well as those who married inside the village, return to their natal houses to act as priestesses in village rituals. Priestesses are selected from certain village *munchū*, patrilineages.

In the sense that men receive guests coming from outside in the eastern room, east and male are associated with outside, the west and women with inside. While in secular life men are superior to women as east is superior to west, in religious or ritual contexts women are superior to men, and the values ascribed the east/west axis are reversed, and women become associated with east.

Mention should here be made of the right/left opposition. Right is superior to left as east is superior to west. In the village of Noho on

Iheya Island, behind the entrances to most houses is found a wall called *himpun*, as much as three metres long and made of wood. This wall is said to be erected to make it difficult to see into the house from outside, and to prevent evil spirits from entering the house. In Bise, only a few *himpun* are found, because the village was completely destroyed by fire during the Pacific War and in rebuilding their houses villagers thought that a *himpun* would impede their increasing use of cars and trucks. In houses where *himpun* have been erected, one enters the garden by going round the left end, to the west, of the wall in daily life as well as during funerals: houses and compounds always face south. During weddings or other formal occasions and communal rituals, one goes round the right end, the east side, of this wall to reach the house (cf. Ouwehand 1986: 31).

The associations of right and left may be reversed in the case of a graveyard.[4] This is clearly discernible in the communal graveyard of Noho (*supra*), for instance, investigated in 1986 (see n. 1). The graveyard is surrounded by two rock walls with an open entrance. Just inside the entrance there is a *himpun* made of rocks and much larger than those of houses in Bise. The graveyard is divided into three 'compartments' with three closed entrances each. The left compartment has been used, Yoshida was informed, by the high class for their dead, the middle one by the middle class for their dead, and the right one by the lowest class for theirs. Villagers here say that while in daily life the right is superior, after death, the left is superior. This clearly differs from the associations of right and left in Bise and in Hateruma, but the principles that order these social facts are the same.

In Okinawa generally, as in mainland Honshū, warm water that is used to clean a corpse is made by adding hot water to cold; in daily life, cold water is poured into hot water when the latter is to be made cooler. This water used to clean a corpse is called *sakamiji* in Okinawa (*sakamizu* in standard Japanese), 'reversed water' (Nakama 1979: 28). In Bise, the cleaning of a corpse, usually performed in the northern 'back room', involves dressing it in white clothes, the colour of mourning; then the corpse is removed to the 'second room', south of the 'back room', where the corpse is laid out with the head towards the west (in daily life, people sleep with their heads towards the east). In Okinawa, underwear that is used to dress a corpse is often put on inside out (cf. Nakama 1979: 31). A red coffin is carried by four men, and goes round the west side of the *himpun*, to go to the village graveyard. (Corpses used to be buried in Bise but this practice has changed following the opening of a crematorium in Naha City in the post-war period.) Many other reversals may also be observed at the time of a person's death and during the rites held for a deceased person.

As discussed elsewhere (Yoshida forthcoming), while women were traditionally considered to be ritually polluted by such events as menstruation and childbirth in Honshū, Kyūshū, and Shikokū, they are generally considered to be much less so in Okinawa where women act as sacred priestesses. Kiyoko Segawa, an important Japanese folklorist, writes indeed that 'while menstruation is tabooed in mainland festivals, in the southern islands such taboos are lacking and menstruation is even considered to be an expression of divinity in Okinawa' (1984: 103).

This view, that menstruation taboos are wholly lacking in Okinawa, is an over-statement, because such taboos do exist to a certain degree: investigation reveals that menstruation (and childbirth) are considered to cause a certain amount of pollution in northern Okinawa. However, it is true that these notions of pollution are not so strong as in mainland Japan. But if a candidate for priestess is discovered to be menstruating when she is selected for the status, this is often regarded as a mark of the divine in Iejima Island (see n. 3); and while it is said by some priestesses that a priestess can perform rituals during her menstruation period, ordinary women who are not of her status are not permitted to attend rituals during their periods. In Bise, as elsewhere in Okinawa, we have noted that rituals are performed by priestesses, and that when men do participate they do so only as assistants to the women officiants. Other priestesses say that in Bise priestesses refrain from entering the village shrine, the *udun* (*supra*) in particular, during menstruation, though they take part in the performance of rites outside the shrine. The *udun* is the most sacred part of the shrine, located in the eastern part of the shrine complex where four incense burners are set in front of the stones worshipped as the fire deity. At the time of a women's festival called *hashichi*, both priestesses and ordinary women who are menstruating are not allowed to touch or even to approach the iron pot in which ritual foods are cooked. Otherwise the situation regarding menstruation is as described.

As regards childbirth, a Bise fisherman is permitted to go fishing when his wife has just given birth to a child. (This is in marked contrast to the Katsumoto fishermen of northern Kyūshū who are not, because in Katsumotoura childbirth is considerd to be so polluting that even the father of a newly-born child is affected by its birth.) Still, in Bise childbirth is said to be more polluting than death: a proverb says that one should never let one's house to a woman who is giving birth for this is worse than letting the house to a dying person.

All the same, there are strong prescriptions and prohibitions associated with death. Relatives of a recently deceased person, for instance, are not permitted to participate in village rituals for a certain time after the death because of the pollution associated with death. When a priestess's relative dies, she is not allowed to take part in the performance of communal rituals for forty-nine days after the death. The local conception of death is well illustrated in the following case, which occurred in Bise in September 1987: when an old man who had been politically influential in the town of Motobu, of which Bise is an administrative unit, died on the 13th of September, the middle-aged headman of Bise was placed in a great dilemma: he wanted very much to attend the old man's funeral rites on the following day (he owed much to the deceased) but villagers were loath to let him do so because he had a crucial role to play in the series of village rites that began on the same day as the funeral was to be held. Villagers objected to his attendance at the funeral, for they thought that he would pollute (*chigariru; kegareru* in standard Japanese) the series of rites that was scheduled to begin the following day. The headman decided not to attend the funeral, associated of course with death, but to participate in the communal rites (associated with life).

According to villagers' ideas, which are current even today, the corpse of a villager who dies outside the village should not be returned to his or her house there because it is thought that to do so would pollute the village and bring about misfortune. A certain unfortunate incident in the past was attributed to the violation of this prohibition by villagers. Thus the corpse of a Bise man who died in hospital outside the village in September 1987 was not brought back to his house there but was carried directly to a crematorium in Naha City.

Those who have attended funerals have to be purified afterwards by fresh water from a well, called *hamagā*, located on the beach and covered by seawater at high tide.[5] A man dips three leaves of the *susuki* (*Miscanthus sinensis*) into the well and then sprinkles water over the relatives of the deceased to purify them. After this, all present go down to the sea and the same man sprinkles seawater over them with the *susuki* leaves. As noted before, funerals are performed in a place to the south of the village, and near here are sited graveyards and places where the souls of deceased persons are exorcised. As far as Bise is concerned, north is associated with sacred places, south with more polluted areas. North is also associated with female, south with male; while east is associated with good fortune, the west is associated with ill fortune or omens of it: when a bird flies into a house, for instance, it is considered to be a bad omen if it flies out through the west of the house. If this occurs, the household should go to the beach to purify itself. If the bird flies out through the east of the house, no such purification is necessary as it is not considered an omen of ill fortune.

To sum up the present section: in secular, daily life male is superior to female but in ritual contexts female is superior to male; similarly, north is associated with female, south with male. In the sense that the mountain deity, located in the east, is male and the sea deity, located in the west, is female, east is associated with male and west with female. Symbolic inversions (reversals) are evinced in funerals. Menstruation is considered polluting to rites if a woman who is not a priestess attends during her period, and even priestesses may pollute the very sacred *udun*, but it is sacred when women are about to take on the status of priestess. Thus notions associated with menstruation vary according to context. By contrast, death is always polluting, probably because death is essentially opposed to and inferior to social life. This is consonant with the symbolic reversals discernible in matters to do with death, which, as in Balinese ideology, is connected with ideas of rebirth. But these must wait to be expounded on another occasion.

II

The Balinese village (*kaklianan*) we are concerned with here is Baturujung, one of the constituent villages of the residential agglomeration (*désa* or *lurah*) Pagutan, western Lombok (figs. 3, 4). This village is the one furthest mountainwards (*kaler, kaja*) in Pagutan. This is consonant with the people of Baturujung being renowned in Pagutan and in nearby *désa* such as Pagesangan for being excellent Balinese: what is furthest mountainwards, or analogously located (see *post*), is finer than what is seawards (*kelod*) or similarly located.

Baturujung, villagers say, consists of three areas: the temple, *pamaksan*, the residential compounds, and the gardens and rice-fields. The temple consists of three courts, one of which is sited in each of the three blocks of compounds that run east to west (*kangin* to *kauh*) that constitute the residential quarters of the village. The inside (*dalem*) court of this temple is located at the eastern edge of the northern block of compounds. The other two courts – the 'northern outside' (*jaba kaja*) and the 'southern outside' (*jaba kelod*) – are sited respectively in the central and the southern blocks of compounds, in their north-eastern corner. The blocks of compounds, which house the five local descent groups – to one of which all villagers belong by virtue of descent through the male line (and perhaps to others through the female line) – occupy the mid-point

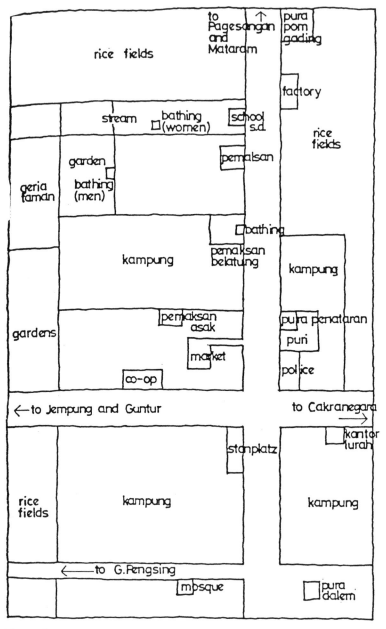

EAST→

Figure 3 Baturujung and Environs

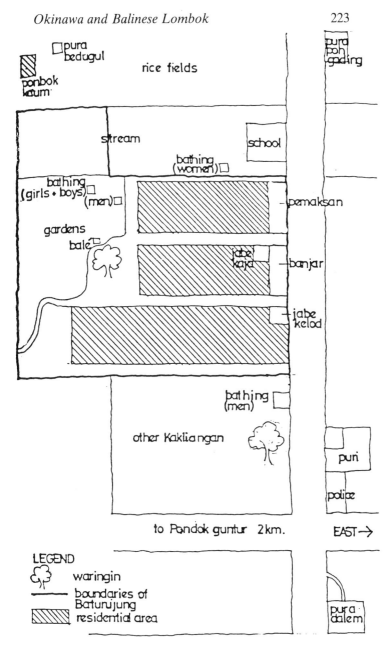

Figure 4 Baturujung: Temple, Compounds, Rice-fields and gardens

moving from east to west between the temple courts and the gardens and rice-fields.

These three areas are organised spatially by reference to the two axes – mountainwards/seawards and east/west – to which we have already referred in passing. Of these points, the highest and purest or finest are the former in each case. Thus the temples are situated in the north-east corners of the blocks. Of the three courts, the finest is that situated in the northern block: this is used for major village festivals, and its 'priest' (*Pemanku*) is male; of the two 'outside' courts, the southern is only very rarely used, the superior court being situated in the central block of compounds. The priest of this court, and of the southern court, is female. The gardens and rice-fields are where such impure activities as the laying-out and subsequent burial or cremation of corpses, sexual intercourse, and defecation take place; in temples one honours pure beings such as village and higher gods; in compounds, consonant with their mid-way position, both pure and impure activities take place: people honour gods and have sex. Here, the areas are organised by reference to the east/west axis.[6]

What cannot be said about these areas, however, is that the temples are 'sacred' and the gardens and rice-fields 'profane', and the compounds a mixture of the two: the sacred/profane dichotomy is not applicable to Balinese ideology. Rather, Balinese life is a (sacred) totality (e.g., Duff-Cooper 1986d, 1986e), in that everything in the Balinese worlds derives from and is pervaded by Ida Sang Hyang Vidhi, the high god of the Balinese. This totality has two aspects, that which is material, generally visible, and in time (*sakala*), and that which is essential, generally invisible, and out of time (*niskala*). Of the two, the latter is pre-eminent. Thus temples, which 'house' pure aspects of Balinese life, are higher physically and by reference to the mountainwards and easterly points of the two axes mentioned, than gardens and rice-fields, where impure activities and beings are located and which are lower physically and ideationally than temples; while compounds are mid-way, again, between the two.

The relations that obtain between the three courts of the village temples may be said to be analogous to the relations between the three temples (*kahyangan tiga*; Duff-Cooper 1985a: 19–21) that a *désa* or *lurah* always contains; but in the present context it is most important to notice that within these three courts, male is to female as inside is to outside, and that in each case the former is pre-eminent or superior.

When we turn to a Balinese house (*umah*) (fig. 5), the same relationships obtain between male and female and inside and outside. Thus it has been suggested (Duff-Cooper 1985b: 40–41) that in the construction of the structure on to which roofing material is fixed, rails which penetrate other rails are male, the penetrated rails, female; and that in the corner bridle or finger joints that collocate the rafters, the tenons that penetrate the stiles are always superior, and hence male, in that they are above or to the front of the stiles. (Front is to back as male is to female; Duff-Cooper 1985e: Tables 1–4.) In sexual activity, also, the male always retains (or should retain) the higher position that he adopts when sleeping with a woman or a junior, and the right hand should not come into contact with the lowest element (waist or navel to feet) of another's physical body (*sthula sarira*), nor indeed of one's own (Duff-Cooper 1985d). In these ways, within a house, male is superior to female. Within a house, too, males have ultimate authority over females, who, through the preparation of food in the kitchen and the small offerings that they make and present after the first daily cooking of rice to the low spirits of the compound, are connected with what is

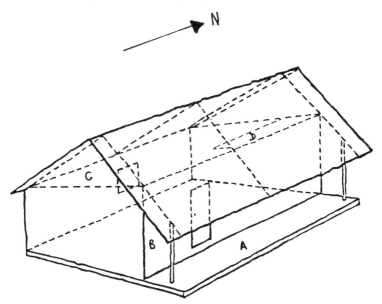

Figure 5 Line Drawing of Balinese House Showing Three
Constitutive Elements

A Stereobate
B Walls, pillars, door, and window
C Roof and rafters areas
D Shelf for offerings and e.g. books

low, an association that is borne out by women generally feeding the pigs which households often husband with *kangkung*, a water-vegetable that the women usually tend in the gardens to the west of the residential parts of the village. Pigs are always sited either to the back or to the south and/or west of the house, and here too people urinate and rubbish is gathered from the daily sweepings of the compound and buried or burnt.

In other contexts connected with the house, however, female is superior to male. The women of a household, for instance, control the production of food for the household, except in exceptional and, to villagers, slightly demeaning circumstances, and men joke, a little fearfully, about the consequences of upsetting the women of the household who might then withdraw this service. Women also control much of the domestic budget, and, moreover, make the offerings that they then present to the gods in the compound temple and in the village temple on behalf of the local descent group to which they belong, all of which is indispensable to the well-being (though not sufficient for it) of the household and descent group. Women also take most care of the children of a household, and this again is a vital contribution to the future well-being of the household and descent group. In these, and in other, spheres, female is superior to male.

A house is also organised by reference to the mountainwards/seawards and the east/west axes already mentioned. Balinese houses, first, are located ideologically speaking mid-way between the temple that always occupies the finest, highest point in the compound, generally the north-east point of it, and the pig-sty and refuse-pit, which are located in the opposite direction, south-west (*kelod-kauh*), generally hard by the compound wall and/or behind the house or other building. Houses may also be ranked within a compound: that of the senior male of the local descent group resident in the compound and his wife and unmarried children should be in the highest or finest position in the compound – that is, furthest to the north-east or the east, but of course to the south or west of the compound temple – and the houses of others should follow in order of seniority, usually determined by birth order of the senior male of each house, 'down' the compound from north-east to south or from east to west. Kitchens are located to the south or west of houses.

Houses are also oriented either so that they run north/south or east/west, or by a combination of both of these axes when the group occupying it is large and of means (see Duff-Cooper 1985b: 35 fig. 2). Within a house, furnishings are arranged so that a household's finest belongings – gold and other jewellery, waist-cloths, and unused sarongs – are stored in the highest direction, in a cupboard placed against a north or east wall, preferably in the north-east corner of the room. Beds are placed south and/or west of this cupboard in such a way that when people recline on them to sleep or rest, they are oriented with their heads (the finest part of the body) to the north to south-easterly quarters of the compass, their feet to the opposite quarters.

A third vertical axis comes into play here too, the one that rises (so to say) perpendicularly from the central point where the two other axes intersect. This axis – from bottom to top associated with Siva, SadaSiva, and ParamaSiva, with SadaSiva in the middle (*ring madya*) – organises the three elements of which a house is constructed and the way in which things are stored in a cupboard. Thus, of the three elements of a house – stereobate, walls, pillars, and door and one or more windows, rafters and roof (*akasa*, sky) – the stereobate is associated with the feet and with menstruating women who sleep here; the middle area, with the ordinary daily round of people who are associated with the middle world (*madyapada*), the world of material living human beings (*mertyapada*); and the top element with such divine beings as the goddess Sarasvati, in the forms of knowledge and writing contained in palm-leaf manuscripts (*lontar* or *rontal*) that are stored here; offerings are also placed in this top part of the house on certain days. In a cupboard, the lowest shelves are where used sarongs, trousers and shorts, and underwear and socks (all used, of course, to cover the third, lowest element of the body) are stored.

What may be called pollution, however, may place a barrier (Ind., *alangan*) between a person and group of people and the physical and ideational structures discussed. When a woman menstruates, for instance, she is barred from cooking and drawing water from a well (always, incidentally, located to the north of the kitchen to which it is attached and sometimes in the compound temple, as Visnu (water) is located mountainwards of Brahma (fire) in the temple and other shrines), and she is not allowed to enter a temple nor to make offerings. Were she to do so, she would be rendered *cemer* and both the temple and the person involved would require rites to return them to a normal state. A menstruating woman, as we have noted, may not sleep at the same height as her husband (nor of other men and non-menstruating women and children in the village, the realm, and the whole island), but must sleep on the floor of her house. She should also avoid addressing or referring to males, and in a Brahmana compound (the senior of the Balinese estates: Brahmana, Ksatrya, Vesia, Sudra in descending order of fineness), she must not address a Pedanda (Brahmana 'priest') (cf. Zurbuchen 1987).

At childbirth, also, a woman and her husband are rendered *kumel*, the former until twelve days after the birth, the latter until the baby's umbilical cord falls. In this state, a person may not engage in many of the activities in which Balinese men and women normally engage, such as working, honouring gods, and enjoying social intercourse. The rite of *nglepas aon*, freeing with ashes, performed by the mother and child at dusk on the twelfth day after the birth, reincorporates the parents and child into normal life (see Duff-Cooper 1986a: 209, 209 n. 15).

Finally, a death[7] in a local descent group renders the deceased's relations – perhaps to father's father's son's son's son's son – *sebel*, and they remain polluted until after the burial of the corpse. Cremation rites render people *sebel* from the day when the day for the cremation is decided upon until the rites of *melaiagin* held three days after the cremation (*ngabén*) or three days after *ngroras* in the case of Sudra Balinese, held twelve days or years after the burning of the corpse or a substitute for it. When one is *sebel*, one may not enter a temple, so that temple festivals (*odalan*) are not held when a group in the village is polluted by death, nor should one take a woman in marriage.

In Pagutan, the periods for which people remain *sebel* is the same for the four estates, which does not entirely accord with the contention that 'the more elevated (a person) . . . the greater the danger of pollution' (Hobart 1979: 448; cf. 1978: 7, 23 n. 5), especially when a Pedanda, for instance, cannot be polluted physically by contact with a corpse (as others are) – though even a Pedanda does not make *palukatan*, a kind of 'holy water' (*tirtha*) when a death has occurred in his or her group. States of *sebel* may be rectified by the passage of time, and by the performance of rites; mortuary rites for the deceased, purificatory rites involving bathing and the use of such waters as *tirtha*, seawater, and the water obtained by straining the charred flesh of an old coconut, as well as giving offerings to the gods at prescribed temples.

Returning now to the relative pre-eminence of male and female in the contexts considered, it seems that we have come across a reversal: in relation to the village temple courts, male is to female as inside is to outside. This short chain of relations is analogous to the situation found when people eat in the course of rites (*magibung*; see Duff-Cooper 1986b): male, here, is to female as east is to west, as older is to younger, and as, for instance, sun is to moon. In all these cases, the first mentioned of each pair of opposites is the pre-eminent aspect of each dyad. However, within a compound and a house, we have noted that in certain contexts male is to female as outside is to inside: while the women deal with matters important within the compound and house, the male represents the compound and the house in their dealings over matters that concern their relationships with other compounds and houses, with the outside. But again in other contexts, we have seen that male is to female as higher is to lower, and as north and east are to south and west, and as front is to back, oppositions that are also evinced in contexts that we have not considered (but see Duff-Cooper 1985f: 156).

These reversals or inversions – these are largely equivalent substantively – are akin to those that are evinced upon a death. For instance, when a person is material and living, it is proper for the head and the feet to be oriented so that the former is in the north and the latter, to south (or to east and to west respectively). (Balinese children, it may be noted, do not turn cartwheels nor play at standing or walking on their hands.) But at death this order is reversed, so that a corpse is buried with its head to the south and its feet to the north (or to west and east respectively), and it is prepared for cremation and cremated in these ways. In life, moreover, people enter and leave a compound through the gate(s) that all compounds have; but a corpse is removed through or over the walls or fences of a compound, places that are usually reserved for such low beings as 'witches' (*léak*), who wish only to harm people, often in the forms of dogs or cockerels.

Clearly, these practices evince reversal or inversion, but the question is: which is a reversal or inversion of which? It has been suggested elsewhere (Duff-Cooper 1986c: 131–3) that it is not possible to answer this question, or rather that it is preferable just to aver that each is a reversal or inversion of the other, and that which is appropriate depends upon the context, like so much else in social life.

What can be said with some surety, however, is that pollution is a state which in its various guises brings with it exclusion from and subsequent reintegration into the aspect of Balinese life that is appropriate to the state in which the polluted person rejoins that life: for a menstruating woman or the parents of a new-born child, one that differs little from the one from which the people in question were removed by their pollution; for a corpse buried in the gardens or cemetery and waiting for cremation (and all, *pace* Huntington and Metcalf's implication (1979: 85), may be cremated), that of *pirata* who may trouble their relatives if they are left too long waiting for the freedom that cremation brings; for a cremated person, that of *pitara*, a state of purity and location in temples and, hopefully, heaven (*sorga*) where one is honoured by others.

These states are marked by reversals or by disruption, both of which are common enough ways of ascribing to an event or to a status, as well as to other things, in a pragmatic sense, some special, abnormal, or perturbing significance (e.g. Needham 1979: 39–42). Moreover, these ideas and practices employ the series of odd and of even numbers, among very many other things such as colours, sounds, and smells, associated with life and death respectively, to mark the statuses as one of temporary, social death or as one that marks a return to social and mystical life.

Pollution, then, may be seen as a symbolic complex, and one in which the notions of the 'low' and the 'dark', as opposed to 'high', 'fine', and 'light' are implicated. Menstruation, for instance, involves the woman sleeping on the floor (and previously, at least in the Brahmana Gria Taman, seclusion alone in the gardens); it involves the flow of blood, an offering in the cockfight to spirits of the low regions (*bhuta*), and the colour red, that of Brahma, the god of fire, associated with the south (*kelod*) and with the temple of death (*Pura Dalem*) to the south of every Balinese *désa*. Red and Brahma are, of course, also associated with the funeral pyre, from which one later requires purification, and with the very low status, as Hobart puts it (1978: 16), of the dead. (People of low status are associated with such unclean tasks as agriculture and animal husbandry and are opposed to people of such high status (i.e. purity) as Pedanda and kings, whose lives are entirely geared to protecting them from such pollution.) Childbirth involves the lowest part of the physical body (from navel to feet) and the association of childbirth with what is low is made explicit in, for instance, the burial of the placenta to the right (for a boy) or to the left (for a girl) of his or her parents' house, the places where rubbish is usually disposed of from the verandah of the house, and later swept off to the impurest part of the compound near the pig-sty.

Death, finally, is associated with the 'low' parts of the village: with the temple of death and with the gardens and cemetery, and with the coast where one also encounters harmful, ugly beings and perhaps Caucasians (*turis*), who are in many ways akin to demons. The ashes of a cremated person are, also, cast out to sea after the rites of burning. Furthermore, these forms of pollution are associated with what is 'hot', which is opposed to and less valued than what is 'cool' (Duff-Cooper 1984: 495): water (Visnu) cools, fire (Brahma) is hot, and are opposed as north is opposed to south, as white is opposed to red, as day is opposed to night, as right is opposed to left, and in various other ways, most importantly perhaps as life is opposed to death.

III

In comparing aspects of different forms of life, Barnes writes (1987: 120), we are concerned with ' "likenesses *and* differences" . . . not just with lists of likenesses and differences, but with particular configurations between them . . .'. Unfortunately, he does not provide any examples of such configurations, but we will try to fall in with his suggestion: although it is not exemplified, it is cogent.

In the contexts of Okinawan shrines and Balinese temples, east is to west as mountainwards is to seawards and as male is to female. Here east is superior to west and mountainwards and seawards are similarly asymmetrically related. In the context of daily activities, also, the relations that obtain between male and female are asymmetrical such that male is pre-eminent; while in daily life, right is to left as east is to west such that right and east are superior or asymmetrically related to left and south respectively.

When we come to consider Okinawan and Balinese graveyards, we encounter a reversal of what obtains in daily life: here right is inferior to left. The same operation is evinced in the social facts of Okinawan and Balinese ideas and practices connected with death: in daily life, cold is superior to hot, right is superior to left, east to west, and inside to outside; where death is concerned, these values are reversed or inverted, so that hot, left, west, and outside are superior to cold, right, east, and inside respectively. In both islands, death is always polluting and is inferior to life.

The mention of pollution brings us to the differences between our two forms of life, for while in Okinawa menstruation may be polluting, it may also be a mark of what is called in section IV the sacred; but among the Balinese it is always polluting. The same goes for childbirth: in Balinese ideology this event always results in the exclusion of a mother and father and their newly-born child from normal daily intercourse for a period; in Okinawa, a father may or may not be polluted by the birth of a child to his wife, though the mother is always polluted.

Other differences are discernible in the aspects of the forms of life examined. Take the house, for instance: while in connection with secular activities in Okinawa and similar occasions among the Balinese east is to west as formal is to informal[8] as male is to female and as outside is to inside, such that the first terms are superior to the second, in matters connected with sacred activities (what 'we' generally term rituals), in Balinese ideology east is to west as male is to female, as before, but in Okinawa east is to west as female is to male, where female is superior to male. This latter dyad is a reversal of the relative values that attach to male and female in secular affairs connected with the house.

A similar difference is evinced by the way in which the Okinawan and Balinese villages discussed above are divided ideologically by the people who reside in them. It might be thought that here comparison is being pushed too far. After all, the Okinawan village is divided into two halves, a north and a south half, while the Balinese village is divided into three areas that run from east to west. But we had no compunction in comparing matters based upon Okinawan and Balinese houses, and they are as different phenomenally as these areas. What justified us comparing the houses was that they are ordered by the same principles: duality, asymmetry, and reversal. This applies here too.

Another ground justifies the comparison. In Bise, for instance, the two halves stand in opposition one to another. In Baturujung, the three areas may under one aspect also be considered as an instance of opposition, one that is not dyadic, however, but one that admits an intermediate term (cf. Needham 1987: 197). As such they are comparable.

The north/south division of Bise is matched by the east/west division of Baturujung. In both cases, the divisions create two areas that are opposed asymmetrically one to another. In the former case, this asymmetrical relationship is associated with good and misfortune; in Baturujung it may well be that villagers consider that the eastern area (temple) is associated with a sub-species of good fortune, safety, and the western area (gardens and rice-fields) with a sub-species of misfortune, danger, and the intermediate area, perhaps, with a mixture of the two: on Bali east is to west as safety is to danger (Hobart 1978: 6). As in Balinese ideology north is to south as east is to west in many contexts, such that these pairs are analogues one of another, in these regards the aspects compared are alike.

Where these aspects differ is in the associations among the terms of the dyads: in Balinese Lombok, as before, in the division of the village east is to west as male is to female such that east and male are pre-eminent. In Bise, however, while these associations obtain in other regards, in the present context they are reversed. Here, north is to south as female is to male such that north and female are superior. This association was expectable on the basis of what we have already seen: the divisions of the village are connected with the ritual tug-of-war held on all souls' day, and in such contexts female is superior to male. Then in shrines and temples (*supra*) while east is to west as mountainwards is to seawards in each case such that east and mountainwards are pre-eminent, in Balinese ideology male is associated with these superior directions, but in Okinawa female is associated with them.

These lists of likenesses and differences reveal what Barnes might concede is a configuration of likenesses and differences. Where the sacred or ritual is concerned in Okinawa, female predominates over male; in daily (profane) affairs, male predominates over female. In Lombok, although there are contexts in which the female is superior – connected with domestic affairs or with left-handed magic – male is ultimately so in all contexts.

One way to proceed here is to establish correlations between these likenesses and differences and sociological aspects of the two modes of life concerned, showing, for instance, that notions about descent and other matters relating to, say, naming, inheritance, residence, give more room, as it were, to the female in Okinawa than is allowed in Balinese Lombok. Such correlations could, in our view, probably be established – though what value and interest would attach to and derive from them is another matter. In any case we take another tack, concerned more directly with the ideologies from which these aspects derive.

The similarities among the social facts examined may be said, first, to derive from the aspects all being constituted by the same 'steady components' (Needham 1985: 138). These components are: duality, asymmetry, opposition; cardinal points, lateral values; reversal. Second, these similarities may be put down to the recourse of both ideologies, and in similar contexts, to the same things (in a pragmatic sense) as symbolic vehicles: among these are elevation, water, scent, fire, and colour.

These features are patent enough. But what about the differences we have noted? An answer to this question involves the dyad sacred/profane. We have seen that in Balinese ideology these distinctions are not made or employed, so naturally it could not be that what is superior in one of these spheres is inferior in the other, and *vice versa*, as in Okinawa. Where spheres such as inside and outside are discriminated one from another, however, as aspects of a whole (in this case of what is *sakala*, material, generally visible, and in time) then we have seen that whereas male is superior to female in one sphere, the outside, female is superior in the other.

In Okinawa, by contrast, life may be divided into those aspects that are daily and those that are ritual. Given the premiss of two sexes, which is far from global (see Needham 1987: 211; Duff-Cooper forthcoming–a), it makes sense that one should be associated with one sphere in some contexts and one with the other sphere in other, contrasted contexts. In Okinawa, as in many parts of Indonesia but not among the Balinese (see Duff-Cooper 1985f:

156), female is associated with the ritual (sacred, mystical) sphere, male with the daily (profane, jural) sphere.

In Balinese ideology, one of the most basic oppositions is that between *sakala* (*supra*, sections II, III) and what is *niskala*, essential generally invisible, and timeless. We have noted that as regards what is *sakala*, male is to female as outside is to inside. As regards what is *niskala*, male is to female as high is to low. In both cases, male is ultimately pre-eminent of male and female, though the latter may be superior in some contexts.

The data presented in section I show that in the Okinawa context, either ideological or physical, or both, is of great importance. Thus menstruation and childbirth are sometimes polluting, sometimes not. Different evaluations are placed upon these events, and the reversals that may be associated with them mark them as more or less special, abnormal, or perturbing in some way, or not, as the case may be.

Menstruation, of course, may occur in priestesses as in 'ordinary' women. If it occurs to the former in a ritual context, it is not polluting and may even be considered a sign of the divine (sacred); but in ordinary women in such contexts it is polluting, as it is in priestesses who are not acting in a ritual context (in such daily contexts it is also polluting in ordinary women). Childbirth is said by villagers in Okinawa to be 'more polluting than death' and may place a barrier between a woman and daily life as well as ritual life, be she a priestess or not, and it may affect the mother's husband. Death affects men and women, and although one must respect and take serious account of the views of one's instructors in the field (see Needham 1973: xxxi-xxxii; De Josselin de Jong 1983b), the numerous reversals and prohibitions and prescriptions associated with death, and that it is always polluting, suggest that it is more polluting – or at any rate considered more special, abnormal, or perturbing – than childbirth.

Among the Balinese, however, not all these distinctions are evinced. All social action, we have seen, is ritual and 'sacred'. This sacred whole has various aspects, two of which are the *niskala/sakala* dyad already discussed. We saw that inside and outside are aspects of the latter; they are also aspects of the former, but they are more appropriately expressed as high and low in this context, such that male is to female as high is to low. Women who menstruate, the parents of a newly-born child, and the relatives of a recently deceased or cremated person are barred from ordinary Balinese life, which takes place, in Hobart's phrase (1986: 136), on 'the high ground', rather as other aspects of the mystical – gods on Mount

Rinjani and in temples, 'priests' who should not go out to have fun (*macanda-canda*) as other Balinese may and often do, witches (*léak*) who do not attend temple festivals but do their worst in the temple of death and in the graveyard, which people do not generally visit, and which they avoid at night – are kept apart from many important aspects of Balinese daily life.

Section II shows that among the Balinese, menstruation, childbirth, and death are all associated with 'low' and are correlatively impure; women are too, relative to men. A combination of menstruation with femininity is enough to bar her from ordinary life for the period of a woman menstruating; childbirth pollutes both parents longer; death pollutes all relatives of the deceased for a longer period still. Reversals of increasing complexity, numerically and ideologically speaking, mark these events as respectively less and more special, abnormal, or perturbing than the others. The evaluation of these events in Okinawan life seems to follow a similar line: menstruation possibly pollutes; childbirth also does so as far as the child's father is concerned, but is always polluting for its mother – and although this is said to be more polluting than death, the prohibitions and prescriptions associated with death mark it as perhaps more special, abnormal, or perturbing than childbirth. Fewer and more reversals mark the differential evaluations of these events.

IV

The findings of section III are of some interest in that they suggest that different basic concepts play a major role in establishing differences among two ideologies that are otherwise very similar, at least by reference to the steady components and the symbolic vehicles that constitute them. That findings of interest can be derived from the comparison of such apparently unrelated forms of life as those compared above conduces to the conclusions that the consensus of the contributors to *Comparative Anthropology* (Holy 1987), that it is useful and desirable to restrict comparisons to modes of life that are closely related linguistically and/or historically or to those within specific regions, has more to do with matters of temperament than with anything else (cf. Duff-Cooper forthcoming – b); and that Needham's contention that 'comparison stands a better and quite different chance of success if it is conducted in formal terms' (1983: 62), which is again borne out by a consideration of empirical cases, is most cogent.

We would be less than frank, though, if we did not apprise the reader of a number of reservations we have about the study and its findings. First, the comparison is limited: it does not consider the opposition life/death in any depth; nor many aspects of Okinawan and Balinese life; nor does it examine some of the substantive concordances between our two modes of life, not related historically or linguistically, that nonetheless emerge from the material reported in sections I and II: for instance, that reversals often implicate the same things pragmatically speaking – entrances and boundaries, dress, and orientation of the body – in Lombok and Japan (as indeed in many other parts of the world). But no study can be complete, and the present one is at least a start. Another study will take up these matters; more fundamentally, it will consider the reversals pinpointed in sections I and II, which we realise do not constitute a monothetic class (see n.5), more rigorously than is attempted in section III under a polythetic aspect (cf. Needham 1983: 117).

Then, the comparison takes very little account of local usage. This might be taken as a drawback by some; but the present essay aimed to avoid such comparison because it can have 'only limited objective value if proper account is to be taken of the meanings that are intrinsic to each mode of life' (Needham 1971: cviii). There is now, though, a renewed interest in the comparison of such usages that goes under the rubric of the comparison of 'metaphors for living' (see Fox 1981: 483; Duff-Cooper forthcoming–a). This approach has proved amenable to the comparison of Balinese life on Lombok with eastern Indonesian cultures, but whether it would be feasible to compare, say, Okinawan and Balinese life via these metaphors must remain a question. The possibility is there, at least for those who find the approach adopted above perhaps a little dry for their taste.

The approach adopted was seen as a way of avoiding these problems. The concepts employed have been discussed at length elsewhere, especially by Needham, and we cannot go further into them here. We should say something about 'superior' and 'asymmetry', however, before we close. 'Superior' – and of course 'inferior': what we say about the one goes for the other – has been employed regularly in earlier sections, but only as a matter of expository convenience. The term has little if any analytical value, its meaning depending upon the very social facts that allow an analyst to suggest that in a particular context male is superior to female and that in another context female is superior to male. The term implies asymmetry, of course, but this latter term is not unproblematical.

Stimulated by an adventurous study about the transformation of prescriptive systems in eastern Indonesia (Needham 1984), it was suggested (Duff-Cooper 1985a) that in Balinese ideology degrees of asymmetry were evinced or discernible. Apart from the ways that these degrees led to further studies (listed in the References below) by the same writer, one of their main uses turned out to be that their employment could integrate what might be termed the 'economic' aspects of Balinese life into the whole in a way that had apparently not been achieved before (cf. De Josselin de Jong 1983a: 26). If the establishment of degrees of asymmetry was not wrong-headed,[9] the employment of 'asymmetry' *tout court* to compare social facts from Balinese life with such facts from Okinawa is inexact: in Balinese life, as matters stand analytically, there do not obtain such asymmetrical relations between two or more entities but relations that are asymmetrical to one of four increasing degrees. It has been suggested, on the basis of Hendry's study (1981) of Japanese marriage on the mainland, mainly Kyūshū, that such degrees of asymmetry may be discernible in or evinced by aspects of Japanese ideology also (Duff-Cooper: forthcoming–b), but for lack of sufficiently detailed data the suggestion could not be taken very far.

In as much as investigation of such matters in Okinawa has not even been begun, it should be said that the comparisons of instances of asymmetry in its cultural guises in Okinawa and in Balinese Lombok carried out above may be premature, though they can also be considered akin to the instances of reversal pinpointed above – as a start. In any case we have composed this piece because, as Leach somewhere writes, we should be cautious and sceptical in our work but never timorous.

NOTES

1. Yoshida did field research in Bise and other villages in north Okinawa with Sakumi Itabashi, Takuma Shirakawa, Hideo Kimura, Shoichi Nakanishi, and several undergraduates majoring in social anthropology at Keio University, Tokyo, during the spring and summer vacations from 1982 to 1987. From 1986, fieldwork was supported financially by the Scientific Research Fund of the Japanese Ministry of Education. Thanks are due to these collaborators and to the Ministry for supporting this work. Duff-Cooper did fieldwork on Tokunoshima, Amami Islands, Nansei Shotō (Southwestern Archipelago), Japan, in 1986.

2. Duff-Cooper carried out field research in Pagutan, Western Lombok, in 1979–81 with the financial support of the Emslie Horniman Anthropological Scholarship Fund, the

(now defunct and much lamented) Social Science Research Council of Great Britain, and the Philip Bagby Fund, University of Oxford, and with the sponsorship of the Indonesian Academy of Sciences. He is much indebted to these bodies for their support. Yoshida did fieldwork in southern Bali in 1974–75.

3. For the material collected in Bise and Iejima we owe 'much to Ryoko Shiotsuki, a student of Yoshida at Keio University, who has kindly allowed us to use her field data.

4. We leave aside here and in other places in the text the question whether these reversals are covered by one of the five modes that Needham distinguishes (1983: 115–16), or whether they are 'new' modes, which is not only possible but also to be expected on Needham's account of the operation (1983: chap. 5), which is not meant to be formal and hence exhaustive but merely to reflect the empirical variety of cases that he happens to have treated.

5. Several graveyards have been removed elsewhere because of the construction of a Marine Exhibition Park in the area south of Bise. Although plans for the Park included the destruction of the sacred well (*hamagā*) this did not go ahead, and the well is now located in the Park: villagers petitioned the local authorities that the well be preserved.

6. Hobart suggests (1978: 6) that the mountainwards/seawards axis is 'primary', the east/west axis 'secondary', though later in the same study (p. 20) he writes that these 'two principal axes form equal parts of a more elaborate construct, the Panca Dewa (the five gods at north, south, east, west and centre) system'. An argument has been made, however, for the pre-eminence in some contexts of the east/west axis (Duff-Cooper forthcoming–c). In the present context, the two axes are equally implicated if not 'equal'.

7. On ideas and practices connected with death in Baturujung, see Duff-Cooper (1983: chap. IX; 1985c: 80–81; 1987: 53). On Balinese 'death' more generally, see for example Wirz (1928), C. Hooykaas (1976a; 1976b), and J. Hooykaas (1956).

8. This dyad emerges from the comparison of the two forms of life: it had not previously been isolated as a significant contrast in Balinese life that formal meetings generally take place towards the east (or north), informal gatherings towards the west (or south), usually near the kitchen.

9. This proviso is included at this point in the text because one authority, a very senior British social anthropologist, has intimated that on the score of degrees of asymmetry he remains more than dubious: degrees of difference or similarity are one matter, but it seems to this authority that a

relation is either asymmetric or it is not, without the possibility of further qualification, like perhaps + and − which
are as it were closed relations, entire and complete. Clearly
the matter of degrees of asymmetry requires further consideration, but as matters stand they have not been shown
to be erroneous in print.

REFERENCES

Barnes, R. H. (1987). Anthropological Comparison. In *Com-
parative Anthropology*, ed. Ladislav Holy, Oxford: Basil
Blackwell, 119–34.
Duff-Cooper, Andrew (1983). A Study of the Collective Ideas
of a Community of Balinese on Lombok. Unpublished
D.Phil. thesis, University of Oxford.
— (1984). Principles in the Classification, the Marriages, and
Some Other Relations of a Community of Balinese on
Lombok. *Anthropos* 79, 485–503.
— (1985a). Duality in Aspects of a Balinese Form of Life in
Western Lombok. *Cosmos* 1, 15–36.
— (1985b). Analytical Notes about some Balinese Residences
and Related Physical Structures in Western Lombok. *Sociologus* 35, 21–52.
— (1985c). An Account of the Balinese 'Person' from Western
Lombok. *Bijdragen tot de Taal-, Land- en Volkenkunde*
141/1, 67–85.
— (1985d). Notes about some Balinese Ideas and Practices
Connected with Sex from Western Lombok. *Anthropos*
80, 403–19.
— (1985e). The Family as an Aspect of the Totality of a
Balinese Form of Life in Western Lombok. *Bijdragen tot
de Taal-, Land- en Volkenkunde* 141/2&3, 230–52.
— (1985f). Hierarchy, Purity, and Equality among a Community of Balinese on Lombok. In *Contexts and Levels;
Anthropological Essays on Hierarchy*, eds. R. H. Barnes,
Daniel de Coppet, and R. J. Parkin, Oxford: JASO,
153–66.
— (1986a). Twins and Transvestites: Two Aspects of the
Totality of the Balinese Form of Life in Western Lombok.
Zeitschrift fuer Ethnologie 111/2, 205–29.
— (1986b). Ethnographic Notes on Two Operations of the
Body among a Community of Balinese on Lombok. *Journal of the Anthropological Society of Oxford* 16/2, 121–42.
— (1986c). Aspects of the Symbolic Classification of a Balinese
Form of Life in Western Lombok. *Sociologus* 36, 121–37.

— (1986d). A Balinese Form of Life in Western Lombok as a Totality. *Journal of the Anthropological Society of Oxford* 17, 207–30.

— (1986e). Some Ways of Delineating the Structure of the Form of Balinese Life in Western Lombok. *Philosophy* 83, 225–49.

— (1987). Incorporation and Alliance among a Community of Balinese in Western Lombok. *Zeitschrift fuer Ethnologie* 112/1, 45–69.

— (1988). The Formation of Balinese Ideology in Western Lombok. *Philosophy* 86, 151–98.

— (forthcoming–a). 'Metaphors for Living' and a Balinese Form of Life in Western Lombok, in idem, *Shapes and Images: Aspects of the Aesthetics of Balinese Rice-Growing, and Other Studies*. Yogyakarta: Gajah Mada University Press.

— (forthcoming–b). An Ethnographer of the Balinese Looks at Japan. *Occasional Paper*. Berlin: Free University, East Asian Institute.

— (forthcoming–c). Mediated Relationships in Aspects of Balinese Ideology on Lombok, in idem, *Shapes and Images: Aspects of the Aesthetics of Balinese Rice-Growing, and Other Studies*. Yogyakarta: Gajah Mada University Press.

Fox, James J. (1981). Review of Cecile Barraud, *Tanebar-Evav: Une société de maisons tournée vers le large* (Cambridge and Paris: Cambridge University Press and Editions de la Maison des Sciences de L'Homme, 1979). *Man* (n.s.) 16/3, 483–4.

Hendry, Joy (1981). *Marriage in Changing Japan*. London: Croom Helm.

Hobart, Mark (1978). The Path of the Soul: The Legitimacy of Nature in Balinese Conceptions of Space. In *Natural Symbols in South East Asia*, ed. G. B. Milner, London: SOAS, 5–28.

— (1979). A Balinese Village and its Field of Social Relations. Unpublished Ph.D. thesis, University of London (SOAS).

— (1986). Thinker, Thespian, Soldier, Slave? Assumptions about Human Nature in the Study of Balinese Society. In *Contexts, Meaning, and Power in Southeast Asia*, eds. Mark Hobart and Robert H. Taylor, Ithaca, N.Y.: Cornell University, South East Asia Program, 131–56.

Holy, Ladislav, ed. (1987). *Comparative Anthropology*. Oxford: Basil Blackwell.

Hooykaas, C. (1976a). Counsel and Advice to the Soul of the Dead. *Review of Indonesian and Malayan Affairs* 10/1, 39–50.

— (1976b). Balinese Death Ritual – As Described and Explained from the Inside. *Review of Indonesian and Malayan Affairs* 10/2, 35–49.

Hooykaas, Jacoba (1956). The Balinese Realm of Death. *Bijdragen tot de Taal-, Land- en Volkenkunde* 112, 74–93.

Huntington, R. and P. Metcalf (1979). *Celebrations of Death; The Anthropology of Mortuary Ritual.* Cambridge: Cambridge University Press.

De Josselin de Jong, P. E. (1983a). Introduction. *Structural Anthropology in the Netherlands; A Reader*, ed. P. E. de Josselin de Jong, 2nd edition, Dordrecht & Cinnaminson, N.J.: Foris Publications, 1–29:

— (1983b). The Participants' View of their Culture. In *Structural Anthropology in the Netherlands; A Reader*, ed. P. E. de Josselin de Jong, 2nd edition, Dordrecht & Cinnaminson, N.J.: Foris Publications, 231–52.

Mabuchi, Toichi (1980). Space and Time in Ryukyuan Cosmology. *Asian Folklore Studies* 39, 1–19.

Nakama, Gishō. (1979). Okinawa no Sōsō, Bosei (Okinawan Funerals and Graveyards). In *Okinawa Amami no Sōsō, Bosei*, eds. G. Nakama and Y. Ebara, Tokyo: Meigenshobo, 9–167.

Needham, Rodney (1971). Introduction. *Rethinking Kinship and Marriage*, ed. R. Needham, London: Tavistock Publications, xiii-cxvii.

— (1973). Introduction. *Right & Left. Essays on Dual Symbolic Classification*, ed. R. Needham, Chicago and London: University of Chicago Press, xi-xxxix.

— (1979). *Symbolic Classification*. Santa Monica, CA.: Goodyear.

— (1983). *Against the Tranquility of Axioms.* Berkeley, Los Angeles, and London: University of California Press.

— (1984). The Transformation of Prescriptive Systems in Eastern Indonesia. In *Unity in Diversity; Indonesia as a Field of Anthropological Study*, ed. P. E. De Josselin de Jong, Dordrecht and Cinnaminson, N.J.: Foris Publications, 221–33.

— (1985). *Exemplars.* Berkeley, Los Angeles, and London: University of California Press.

— (1987). *Counterpoints.* Berkeley, Los Angeles, and London: University of California Press.

Ouwehand, C. (1986). *Hateruma; Socioreligious Aspects of a South-Ryukyuan Island Culture.* Leiden: E. J. Brill.

Segawa, Kiyoko (1984). *Onna no Minzokushi (The Ethnography of Women).* Tokyo: Tokyo Shoseki.

Wirz, Paul (1928). *Der Totenkult auf Bali.* Stuttgart: Enke.

Yoshida, Teigo (forthcoming). The Feminine in Japanese Folk Religion: Polluted or Divine? in *Unwrapping Japan. The*

Contribution of Japanese Studies to Anthropology, eds. Brian Moeran, Eyal Ben-Ari, and James Valentine, Manchester: Manchester University Press.

Zurbuchen, Mary S. (1987). *The Language of Balinese Shadow Theater*. Princeton: Princeton University Press.

Notes on Contributors

ELIZABETH BAQUEDANO took her BA in Art History in Mexico City, and an MA at the Institute of Latin American Studies, University of London. She took an M.Phil. qualifying examination at the Institute of Archaeology, University of London, where she is now completing a Ph.D. on Aztec Sculpture. She teaches in the Department of Extra-Mural Studies, University of London, and at the City University.

ALAN BRUFORD has been Archivist of the School of Scottish Studies (University of Edinburgh) since 1965, mainly concerned with recent Scottish and Irish folktales, songs and beliefs. However, he originally trained as a medieval historian, and keeps up an interest in the early Irish roots of the more recent material.

HILDA R. ELLIS DAVIDSON was formerly President of the Folklore Society and Fellow and Vice-President of Lucy Cavendish College, Cambridge. She is the author of *Gods and Myths of Northern Europe* and a number of other books and articles on Norse mythology and early religion in western Europe.

GLENYS DAVIES is a lecturer in Classical Archaeology in the Department of Classics, University of Edinburgh. Her main research interests are in the field of Roman funerary imagery, and she is currently Treasurer of the Traditional Cosmology Society.

ANDREW DUFF-COOPER is a visiting lecturer at the Institute of Cultural and Linguistic Studies, Keio University, Tokyo, and an assistant professor at Seitoku Gakien College, Matsudo, Chiba. Since completing his doctoral thesis in Social Anthropology at the University of Oxford in 1983, he has worked on the description and analysis of Balinese life in Pagutan, Western Lombok, and has also been engaged in the study of aspects of Japanese life.

GAVIN FLOOD teaches Religious Studies at Bath College of Higher Education. His main interests are in Indian Religions (his doctoral thesis was on Kashmir Śaivism) and Phenomenology.

JOHN GIBSON was minister of a parish in rural Aberdeenshire before coming in 1962 to teach in the department of Hebrew and Old Testament Studies, University of Edinburgh. He was elected to his Chair in 1987. He has published several editions of Semitic inscriptions and mythological texts and is specially interested in the mythological background to the Old Testament Scriptures.

DEIRDRE GREEN is a Lecturer in Religious Studies at St David's University College, Lampeter (University of Wales). Her research specialism is in comparative mysticism and she has published several articles in this and related areas. She is also the author of *Gold in the Crucible: Teresa of Avila and the Western Mystical Tradition* (1989). She is secretary of the Traditional Cosmology Society.

GORDON HOWIE is a lecturer (on the Greek side) in the Department of Classics, University of Edinburgh. He specialises in early Greek poetry and prose, with a particular interest in Pindar.

CAROLINE KARSLAKE is just starting fieldwork among the Otomi. She is studying for a Ph.D. at the London School of Economics, and has a place at the Colegio de Mexico for her following year abroad.

GLENYS LLOYD-MORGAN developed an interest in the Roman and Classical world during her first archaeological excavation in 1962. A graduate of Birmingham University, she has specialised in the study of ancient mirrors and other items of daily life, and has published and lectured extensively on various aspects of the subject at home and abroad.

EMILY LYLE is an honorary fellow at the School of Scottish Studies, University of Edinburgh. She has been visiting lecturer at the University of Stirling and visiting professor at UCLA, and has held fellowships at Harvard University and The Australian National University. Her publications include editions of folksong collections and articles on literature and on oral tradition. Her book *Archaic Cosmos* is due to be published shortly by Polygon Press.

ANTHONY SHELTON is a Smithsonian Fellow and Curator of American Collections at the British Museum (Ethnography Dept.): he has previously been an Institute Assistant in the Institute of Social Anthropology, University of Oxford, and a lecturer in Pre-Columbian Art at the University of East Anglia. He has carried out fieldwork among the Huichol of Northwest Mexico and Nahuatl and Tlapanec communities in Guerrero, Mexico.

L. BOUKE VAN DER MEER is assistant professor in Classical Archaeology at the Leiden University (universitair hoofddocent: 'univ. headteacher', directly under ordinarius). He researches and publishes on Etruscan religion and myths.

KAREL WERNER is the Spalding Lecturer in Indian Philosophy and Religion in the School of Oriental Studies, University of Durham.

TEIGO YOSHIDA is professor of Social Anthropology at the University of the Sacred Heart, Tokyo, visiting professor of Cultural Anthropology at Keio University, and Emeritus Professor of the University of Tokyo. He has held visiting professorships at Tulane, Northwestern, and Pittsburgh, and has been visiting fellow at the Nissan Institute for Modern Japanese Studies, University of Oxford. He has done field research in Bali, Indonesia, Chamula, Mexico, and extensively in Japanese villages, and is currently engaged in fieldwork in Okinawa. He is President of the Japanese Society for Ethnology.

COSMOS is the yearbook of the Traditional Cosmology Society

The Traditional Cosmology Society exists for the international study of myth, religion, and cosmology. It aims to provide a forum for discussion and to provide interdisciplinary exchange. Members receive annually two issues of the Journal, *Shadow*, and the Yearbook, *Cosmos*.

For further details of the Society's activities and current subscription rates, please write to:

The Membership Secretary,
Traditional Cosmology Society,
School of Scottish Studies,
University of Edinburgh,
27 George Square,
Edinburgh EH8 9LD,
Scotland.

Past and future issues of *Cosmos* are on the following themes:

1. 1985 Duality.
2. 1986 Kingship.
3. 1987 Analogy.
4. 1988 Amerindian Cosmology.
5. 1989 Polytheistic Systems.
6. 1990 Contests.
7. 1991 Women and Sovereignty.